GANGSTERS, KILLERS AND ME
A Detective's Story

GANGSTERS, KILLERS AND ME

A DETECTIVE'S STORY

GERARD GALLACHER

BLACK & WHITE PUBLISHING

First published 2011
by Black & White Publishing Ltd
29 Ocean Drive, Edinburgh EH6 6JL

1 3 5 7 9 10 8 6 4 2   11 12 13 14

ISBN: 978 1 84502 362 1

A CIP catalogue record for this book is available from the British Library.

Typeset by Ellipsis Digital Limited, Glasgow
Printed and bound by MPG Books Ltd, Bodmin, Cornwall

To the memory of my parents.
If I possess a single redeeming quality as a human being,
it is the result of their example and tutelage. RIP.
And . . . to Marjorie, who has endured so much,
often, without my support. Unstinting in turn in her support
and encouragement for this project, 'Thank you' is inadequate.

ACKNOWLEDGEMENTS

I am indebted to the following, for their varying levels of assistance during the writing of the book.

First and foremost, my cousin, George Gallacher, who proofread the original manuscript and offered such sage and perceptive advice. A founding member of the iconic Scottish band, The Poets, he is nonpareil the best rock, pop and soul vocalist we've produced.

George Thomson, Geographics, Glasgow, for sourcing the 'in' to my publisher Black & White, and also for printing the original manuscript.

'Macca' for his IT advice, when I feared I'd lost half of the original manuscript.

Kenny Macleod, for advising me to completely redraft a chapter (and being right).

AUTHOR'S NOTE

This book has not been ghostwritten. These are my words and, consequently, interpretations of situations and opinions of people are mine alone. Dealings with informants happened as I have described, but in order to ensure their continued safety, I have disguised their identities.

CONTENTS

INTRODUCTION

This book covers my time as a police officer (primarily as a detective) in Glasgow during the 1980s, 1990s and the start of the new millennium, when drugs took hold of the city (and never relinquished their grip). Many of the robberies, murders and deaths in this book stem from the drugs trade, but many don't and owe their origins to the culture of violence that is endemic to Glasgow. You can't live any time in the city without becoming either a passive or active victim of that violence.

I had experience of the violence well before I joined the police. I'd witnessed it as an innocent fifteen-year-old coming home from football training in Govan. I was on the top deck of a bus and it stopped outside a pub and below me on the street, I could see a man and woman arguing. The man, with no warning, headbutted the woman full in the face and she fell prostrate to the pavement, blood pouring from nose and eyebrow.

It both horrified and shocked me. I'd been in plenty of fights of my own, typical young boy scrapes, but I'd never seen a woman struck before. I got home and relayed the story to my parents. Both had been brought up in the rough Garngad district of the city and no doubt had seen all that and more. Their response was, 'That's drink and life in Glasgow, son.'

About a year later, I narrowly avoided becoming another victim of the youth gang violence that was rampant in Glasgow during my formative years. That I escaped was due solely to being fleet of foot. Walking home from public swimming baths in Springburn, I was asked by a group gathered in a close where I was from. When I stupidly gave the name of my scheme and it wasn't Springburn, I heard the words 'chib him'; Glasgow parlance for 'slash'. I didn't hesitate before taking to my heels. I can vouch for the phrase 'fear lends wings'.

A lad who played casual football with a group of us every night of the week didn't have my blessed fortune. A quieter, more decent lad you couldn't find, but he was savagely and randomly murdered. One

Friday night, returning from a Partick Thistle supporters meeting, he stepped off a bus in Barmulloch, 100 yards from his house. Near the bus stop was a gang from a nearby area on the rampage. He was the first boy they encountered and they bludgeoned him to death.

'Dear green place' is how Mungo, the Christian saint credited with discovering Glasgow, allegedly described it, but somehow, through the centuries following its founding, the 'dear green' on the traffic lights jumped to blood red and skipped the amber.

Glasgow has achieved worldwide prominence for shipbuilding, contributions to medicine, science and architecture, but also football rivalry and savage violence – often intertwined.

The innovation and beauty of the architecture can leave you breathless but there is no beauty attached to the violence, only stark ugliness that so often takes the breath away from the victim . . . permanently. Glasgow didn't invent violence but many of the citizens seem determined to prove they've perfected the art.

The violence requires little or nothing to set it off: territory; religion; football rivalry; drugs; a misplaced look at a wife or girlfriend; or simply a misplaced look. You could be a victim purely because you had facial features someone disliked.

Tempers as unstable as gelignite combined with unquenchable alcohol consumption produces a volatile cocktail. The weapons are whatever is readily available, which tends to be anything bladed: knives; razors; swords; meat cleavers; axes – weapons hardly different from those wielded in 1314 at Bannockburn, and every bit as deadly.

In the 1980s, the use of firearms in Glasgow violence increased owing to the availability of stockpiled Eastern Bloc guns, but they tended to be the remit of gangsters. For the most part, the city's victims are stabbed, slashed, chopped and diced. The forces of law and order, the police (or in Glasgow 'the polis'), have been tasked with, at best, combatting the tide of violence or, at worst, trying to stem the (blood) flow.

Glasgow back in the 1930s had the razor gangs, so-called because of their use of open or cut-throat razors to slash the faces of their victims. With no plastic surgery specialists available, the legacy of the facial wound was a raised, jagged and ugly scar. Doctors stitching the wound sometimes asked the victim if they knew their assailant and were told, 'Yeah and I'll send him in for you to do the same job next week.' And invariably, they did.

Sir Percy Sillitoe, who would eventually head MI5, was Chief Constable of Glasgow at the time and was credited with smashing those rampaging gangs. His officers were instructed to meet violence with violence and through split heads and long jail sentences, leave gang members in no doubt that their time was over.

The 1960s and '70s brought a resurgence in gangs and similar police tactics. Membership and territory were everything. Battles raged nightly in the various housing estates, pubs and dance halls in Glasgow city centre. Pubs like the Lunar Seven, which sat at the junction of Buchanan Street and Bath Street, were the scenes of murder and mayhem every second weekend.

The police response? The formation of a group nicknamed 'The Untouchables', simply because they appeared to operate outwith the confines of natural justice. They were hard-nosed men, who drove around – team-handed – in vans, with blacked-out windows and a similar remit to their 1930s predecessors.

It was iron-fisted policing in an iron glove, although its success owed much to a sympathetic judicial system. Sentences of ten and fifteen years for serious assault, attempted murder and mobbing and rioting quickly concentrated the minds of the sixteen- to twenty-year-olds responsible for the violence.

From the 1980s onwards, the focus of the violence was often created by those earning vast illegal profits, who dictated what was sold in the city and where. I joined the police in 1981 and was to witness the city at its worst over the next few decades.

Brothers trying to murder brothers; a drug courier double-crossed and murdered for his consignment; a newborn baby thrown into a canal and left for dead; prison riots; a father trying to murder his children before attempting suicide; mafia-style revenge killings; the slaughter of a Procurator Fiscal; the rape of a foreign national; and among all that, I would find myself falsely accused of being respon-sible for a murder and distributing drugs.

What a birthplace. What a profession to choose.

No mean city? Too damn right!

1

POSSIL (NOT GORKY) PARK

September 1995, late afternoon, and I was standing in a bin-shed area in a lane that ran behind a pharmacist's shop in Saracen Street, Possilpark.

'It's like Gorky Park,' said the young Detective Constable who was with me.

'It's an utter mess, real life and it's Possilpark,' was my response, but I knew where the analogy came from. In the novel he was referring to, three bodies are found dead under the frozen skating rink in Moscow's Gorky Park.

Our scene may have been nowhere near as dramatic, but we were still looking at three males being worked on frantically by ambulance and paramedic staff. The drug paraphernalia in and around the bodies told us all we needed to know (for now). At that time, Possilpark was the heroin capital of Scotland and the itinerant traffic was so great it was well-nigh unstoppable.

I had a professional reason for being there, but still felt vaguely like a voyeur as I stood watching dedicated human beings attempting to save the lives of three complete strangers. Incongruously, a television advert flashed into my mind, for a chocolate bar called 'Bounty'. In the advert, a lean, tanned, impossibly handsome and beautiful group of boys and girls are on a white sand beach and the voiceover declares 'they came in search of paradise'.

The three lying in a dirty bin shelter had been among the dozens who came daily into our policing area looking for their own particular taste of paradise. Unfortunately, the rush these three had hoped for when they depressed the plunger into whatever vein(s) still functioned never happened. Whatever the dealer had used to cut the filth he sold proved fatal and near-fatal. All three had collapsed almost simultaneously.

1

The preservation of life was obviously the prime consideration, but I had to try and ensure that the potential crime scene retained as much sterility as possible. I wasn't best pleased, then, to turn around and see a uniform sergeant marching towards the lane at the head of a Sky News camera crew.

'Where the hell do you think you're going?' I shouted.

'They've been given permission by the Chief Constable to attend and film incidents of note for their documentary series on the police,' was the sergeant's reply.

Commonplace now, but reality programmes featuring UK cops at work were then in their infancy.

'I couldn't care less if they've been given permission by the Prime Minister. This is a potential crime scene so get them out of here.' I was abrasive and very task-intense in those days.

Things didn't look too good for our three. They were unconscious when the paramedics removed one to Stobhill hospital and the other two to the Royal Infirmary for treatment. Two survived, although it was touch and go for a long time, but one died and I found myself later that evening at doors to deliver bad news.

I knocked and thought how much cops are like grief butterflies. They float into strangers' lives delivering news that shatters and impose on private grief, then just as quickly move on to the next horror show.

I happened to catch sight of a mat outside a neighbour's door, one of those camel-coloured mats made of horsehair with the word 'welcome' woven in black lettering. I knew what I had to impart wouldn't be welcome at all, but as I waited on the door being answered, the word caused me to reflect on the first day I had reported for police duty nearly fifteen years previously. I hadn't felt welcome then either.

WELCOME MAT

'When we heard we were getting someone from Balornock on the shift, we were a bit apprehensive, but you seem to have done okay at Tulliallan [Police Training College] and they've been fairly happy. So we'll see how you get on.'

I was sitting opposite William Turnbull, my shift Inspector. I was vainly attempting eye contact through the fog of pipe smoke he was generating. He wore spectacles and had a full head of hair, which he wore in the old-fashioned style of 1940s and 1950s footballers; brushed straight back with a centre parting. He had a serious demeanour and his words were hardly the most inspiring or welcoming address to a new start, but that was my formal introduction to policing.

A similar greeting would await me some five years later when I transferred to the Serious Crime Squad. Sociologists refer to it as 'labelling'. A person's character is categorised solely by the area or environment they're from. It is 'guilty until proven innocent' by any other name. I'd been born and raised in one of the numerous housing schemes in the Glasgow area and so, in this senior officer's eyes, that made my character suspect.

My first day of official duty at Kirkintilloch Police Office had begun earlier when I'd taken my place in the muster room and been introduced to the various shift members. The muster room was and still is basically a gathering place. There, officers are detailed their tasks and areas of patrol for that day and, hopefully, brought up to speed with the various crimes and incidents of note that have taken place locally and Force-wide since their last period of duty.

My pep talk from the Inspector extended to those few sentences and that was the extent of the interview; no further advice or words of wisdom. Talk about KISS (Keep it simple, Stupid!); it seemed more like a kiss off. With the talk over, it was now time for me to supplement the bones of the previous twelve weeks' training I'd undergone with practical flesh.

I'd hardly been expecting ticker tape and cavalcades, but felt that having won the Endeavour Trophy, the Sports prize and been pretty highly assessed while at Police Training College, a slightly warmer greeting may have been extended.

Perhaps it is illusionary, but I've found that pipe smokers tend to choose their words carefully. Perhaps the ritual of igniting the tobacco in the pipe bowl affords them time to ponder. It may well have been that the inspector, having looked at my Police College appraisal, decided the best tack was to adopt a low-key approach, or it may have been reverse psychology. Whatever the reason, I walked out of the room absolutely determined that he would have no complaints about my abilities as a police officer.

3

My official commencement date with the police had begun several months earlier on 5 January 1981, when along with almost thirty others, I'd been 'sworn in' at Force Headquarters in Pitt Street, which is located in Glasgow city centre. There, we spent the first day being measured and supplied with our uniforms.

A wooden baton and handcuffs formed part of the issue. The baton was supposed to be an item of defence and to be used to fend off an aggressive attacker, but the vast majority issued had the density of a piece of balsa wood and were so lightweight that it would have required several strikes to damage a light bulb, far less an aggressive human.

Most cops tried to charm an officer who was retiring, or who had been allocated a desk job, and who had batons made of *lignum vitae* or teak. They'd then look to trade them and the retiring officer would return the lighter baton along with their items of uniform. Batons made of these materials were far more effective.

The inadequacy of those poorer quality batons was rammed home to me almost ten months later when attempting to smash the window of a house where a father had barricaded himself inside with his children and begun to stab them.

After the issue of the uniforms, our next stage in the induction process was a trip to the Identification Bureau. This was, by and large, staffed by civilians whose job consisted mainly of attending crime scenes where they'd carry out fingerprint examinations, photograph the scene and assist in gathering trace evidence. They could also be utilised to photograph crime victims' injuries.

Over the years, the members of that unit were to become good and valued colleagues to me and I was to be grateful to them and the chemists and biologists who staffed the Forensic Science laboratory for their assistance on times too numerous to mention.

The purpose of this first visit, however, was to capture our fingerprints and photographs. The photos would be used on warrant cards – laminated plastic, which were the means whereby someone could identify themselves as a police officer to members of the public if they weren't in uniform.

The fingerprinting would ensure that if a police officer was careless in what he handled or touched at a crime scene, then, in theory, any prints inadvertently left could be compared and eliminated from 'marks' or prints obtained at the crime scene.

After uniform issue, photographing and fingerprinting, we were instructed to report the following day to the Force Training Centre, which in those days was in Oxford Street on the south side of the River Clyde, where we'd commence formal training.

At the end of that first day, I had time to wonder what the next thirty years would hold, if I'd get through those years, and whether I'd come up to scratch in my chosen profession. I also reflected on the journey that had brought me to this particular stage in my life.

GETTING THERE

I was born to my parents Mary and George, the second youngest of eight children: five boys and three girls. My parents provided a loving, stable environment and I couldn't have been given better role models. They were both very strong in their Catholic faith, but never lacked humour or a sense of fun. The way they lived their lives ensured I knew right from wrong and they instilled in me a set of values that assisted me greatly in adapting to the discipline expected of a police officer.

In addition to recognising right from wrong, my parents also tried to instil manners in me, such as giving up a seat on the bus to older people, looking people in the eye when speaking to them and respect for the property of others. Strangely, they taught me so well in relation to the latter that I underwent some awkward times in the police initially when it came to searching a house.

Although totally focused on the requirement to perform professionally and conduct a thorough search, I have to confess that it took me some time to become comfortable rummaging through and displacing someone's personal property. That discomfort was assuaged fairly rapidly, when it transpired that the personal property in question had been obtained by stealing it from someone else.

My recollections of childhood are of never being inside unless I'd been dragged in by my mother to eat (or as punishment for fighting, which was pretty regularly). Like all kids of that age, I played football morning, noon and night. If there were three of us, the game played was 'crossing in' with one in goal and one crossing the ball for the third to try and score a goal. If there were four, we played 'headies' or head tennis. Anymore and it was sides for a football match. In the summer, we would play until after 10 p.m. when you couldn't see the ball for the lack of light.

We played on a grassy area, with an unstructured path running through it, which connected the Balornock 'scheme', or housing area, to the Barmulloch area. In the past ten years, the Council have erected lighting along that path. Just as well it wasn't lit in our day or we'd have been there until three in the morning playing under the 'flood-lights'. In the summer, we'd go up to the local public park at Springburn and pretend we could play tennis, or we'd go swimming at the public baths.

On leaving primary school, I made a decision, possibly with a gentle push from my mother, to attend a seminary at Langbank. I don't think my father was in 100% agreement, probably feeling that at that age, I was too young to make such a commitment, but he would not have forbidden it.

It was only in later years that I realised my parents must have had to make sacrifices to enable me to attend seminary. Uniforms and sports clothing were required, and my dad was a manual worker all his days – predominantly with British Rail – so he never earned huge money. He was also a football talent scout and was Everton's Chief Scottish Representative, which supplemented his income.

I'm not sure what most people's idea of life at a seminary would be, but it was fun. Obviously, religion played a large part in college life, but not to the detriment of formal education and sport. The boys who were pupils at the college came from all over Scotland and weren't 'Pious Peters'.

The majority were from housing schemes in Glasgow, Edinburgh and Fife and I wasn't installed twenty-four hours before I was involved in a fight with an older boy. That was to prove the first of about eight scraps I was to have while in seminary, invariably with older guys, and my record probably worked out at: lost four, won two, drew two.

I was cocky, mouthy and didn't back down so, no pun intended, I 'copped it' from older students. I suppose I was cursed with one of those natures that if placed in the 'fire or fall back' scenario, I invariably fired. That was to be a trait that I carried with me into my subsequent police career.

As well as plenty of time for playing football, I also learned how to play basketball and volleyball and loved both.

I spent a year at Langbank and another year at Blairs College in Aberdeen before realising that whatever my vocation in life, it wasn't in the priesthood. When I left, however, I'd received two years of first-class education.

On returning home from the seminary, I was enrolled in St Mungo's Academy, Parson Street, in the Townhead area of Glasgow. St Mungo's had a large catchment area encompassing the north, east and west sides of the city.

It was a highly regarded educational establishment and its former pupils range from captains of industry, eminent surgeons, scientists, lawyers, radio station founders, disc jockeys, pop stars, footballers to some of the best bank robbers and fraudsters this city has seen.

I encountered many former pupils in the course of my police duties. Many of them had entered the legal profession, while others funded those in the legal profession through fees paid to ensure they remained out of jail.

On leaving school, I worked at a variety of jobs, most of which were to supplement playing semi-professional football. At eighteen, I began clerical work with British Rail in their Glasgow headquarters at Buchanan House. I was also playing youth football with Campsie Black Watch and was 'spotted' there and signed by my first professional club, East Fife.

Over the next ten years, I was to play for several of the lower league clubs such as East Stirling, Morton, Stranraer and Albion Rovers, as well as playing for a year in the USA and two years in Sweden. I also worked variously in a factory, supermarket and slaughterhouse, on a building site and I even co-owned a menswear shop at one point. A rather eclectic pre-police career granted, but it provided me with extensive 'life experience' and a solid foundation when I began policing.

Having worked with people from all parts of the socio-economic spectrum, both in this country and abroad, prior to the police, I under-stood that situations weren't simply black or white, but were often tinged with grey. Similarly, everyone not wearing a police uniform wasn't automatically a criminal. That was something that colleagues with narrower life experience failed to grasp on occasion.

I felt that I'd led a fairly interesting life up to that point, but what was to follow as a police officer over the next twenty-odd years wasn't exactly going to leave me yawning with boredom.

2

BEGINNINGS

It may seem strange, given my varied life experience, but my first tour of duty as a police officer was also my first time in a police office. In those days, when a shift grouped in muster, the sergeant designated duties for that day. Officers would be allocated a patrol car, a foot beat or plain clothes duties. The sergeant had the option of rotating the allocated roles, allowing everyone an opportunity to diversify and combat potential staleness.

A two-year probationary period allows the police to assess whether someone is suitable to continue as a police officer. Working in a practical policing environment, a probationer is paired with a more experienced officer and that officer is tasked with guiding and supervising. It is a well-tried and effective method of affording a probationer experience, and hopefully, the end return at the conclusion of the probationary period is a grounded officer who has a basic platform on which they can continue to build.

Having been used to a dressing-room environment, I settled easily into working as part of a team and enjoyed the humour and *esprit de corps* that a close unit generated.

Traditionally, a probationary officer caught the less enjoyable tasks, which could range from waiting at a road accident for a tow truck to remove the damaged vehicle, to school crossing patrols, or guarding the scene of a serious crime. These duties often involved long periods of boredom in all weathers.

Thankfully, I managed to steer clear of one I heard about where the probationer, on assisting the Mounted Branch, found himself tasked with washing underneath the horse's foreskin. Not quite sure how you would phrase that task to enhance any future CV.

At the time I joined, all British Police Forces were on high alert following the death of the Northern Ireland MP Bobby Sands, who had died in prison following a hunger strike protest. There were fears that the death could result in reprisal action on the UK mainland, with police offices being viewed as potential targets.

As a result, someone came up with the bright idea of stationing an officer outside every police office twenty-four hours a day. Quite how some unarmed police officer with a balsa wood baton and handcuffs could have deterred a determined terrorist attack is up for debate, but being a probationer, I was nominated for the task.

The detail was supposed to be rotated, but the then sergeant had other ideas. He was from one of the Scottish islands and whether he wasn't too fond of me or just thought it might be funny, I don't know. Either way, I found myself, for seven nights in a row, standing outside the office, from 10 p.m. until 7 a.m. the following morning, without so much as a five-minute break or relief. I didn't complain or try and make an issue, as I thought it might well be a tester or an attempt to sicken me.

Not long afterwards, I found myself summoned down to Springburn to assist in guarding a murder scene. The number of officers required to protect the integrity of a crime scene is fluid and dependent on various factors, such as whether there are primary and secondary scenes, the area required to be covered and where the crime took place.

On this particular occasion, the victim had died as a result of being stabbed through the heart. A death in suspicious circumstances requires a casualty surgeon to certify death and that is their sole involvement at the scene, as cause of death and interpretation of the crime scene is the remit of forensic pathologists.

However, being fresh out of the box and totally unfamiliar with death and dead bodies, I believed that if someone had been stabbed through the heart, they would have haemorrhaged pints of blood, rendering the scene like a slaughterhouse.

Being brand new, though, I wasn't going to be allowed anywhere near a crime scene, so when the casualty surgeon (a doctor of Indian origin) emerged, I thought I'd ask – what I thought would be – some smart questions.

'Was it bad, Doctor?'

'Not good for him. He is dead.'

'Was there a lot of blood?'

'No, no.'

'Was he not stabbed in the heart?'

'Yes, stabbed in heart.'

'I thought there would have been a lot of blood.'

'Sometime, little blood,' came the laconic reply before he drove off to file his claim for payment and leave me bemused.

Over the subsequent years, I was to learn, sadly, the accuracy of his parting words. Several times, I was involved in murder scenes where the victim had died from a stab wound to the heart.

The first was when I was in the Serious Crime Squad. One night shift, we were called to a murder outside a pub in Drumchapel. The victim was only nineteen and after being stabbed, had collapsed barely twenty yards from the attack. You would have struggled to locate the wound and the blood shed would have hardly filled a thimble.

The other occurred in the Glenavon flats at Maryhill when a woman, who claimed to have been the victim of prolonged domestic abuse, stabbed her husband as he lay sleeping in bed. As in the previous case, the almost indiscernible wound and bloodshed merely reinforced what, by that time, I knew only too well – the fragility of the human body.

I was to become well versed in the many and varied ways human beings can inflict damage on themselves and their fellow man.

I attended my first violent death a few weeks later. It was Saturday morning and I was early shift and had been partnered in a car with Eric Young, an officer who was to have a strong influence on my desire to pursue a role as an investigative officer in the police.

Eric had been a Detective Sergeant, but at a time when the police were poorly paid, and having a wife and family to feed, he thought he could earn more money taxiing and had left to do just that. After a year or so, however, he found that he missed the police. As chance would have it, he met the then Chief Constable Sir Patrick Hammill while shopping.

Sir Patrick knew Eric from a time when Eric was a Detective Constable and Sir Patrick had been a Chief Inspector and he rated Eric's work highly. He told Eric to apply to rejoin and although it would be initially as a Constable, he gave Eric strong indication that when the first suitable vacancy arose for a detective sergeant, he would get the position.

Barely a month back in the police, Eric had a domestic argument which resulted in the police being called to his home. The incident was 'flagged up' for the attention of senior management and Eric was summoned to the Divisional Commander's office; a man he knew well and had worked with previously.

In Eric's words, he found John Blincow, the Chief Superintendent, with his head in his hands. The man proceeded to tell him, 'Eric, what a total arse you've made of yourself.' He didn't sugar-coat the pill, but instead told Eric that it would block him from any move to his previous rank. Eric accepted his punishment.

Even though he knew the incident had finished any chance of regaining his former rank, when he returned to the shift, he continued to share his extensive experience with those less knowledgeable shift members (me especially). I suppose, in many ways, I benefited from Eric's misfortune because it was actually the equivalent of having a detective sergeant as a tutor, and one of the foremost reasons for my wanting to specialise in crime investigations.

That morning, we were marked to a call just North of Lenzie railway station where a young man had accessed the railway line and laid his head on the track in front of an Edinburgh to Glasgow train. The train had decapitated him with the rear skull sustaining the major damage. The face itself was almost intact and recognisable. Collecting the remains of such a violent end was a sobering experience.

From property we found on the body, we were able to establish that he was only twenty-one and from Moodiesburn. He had spent the previous evening in police custody. On being released, he'd made his way to the railway line, which lay on his route home.

It was the first, but certainly not the last, violent death I'd attend. The many and varied forms of death I was to encounter over the coming decades would render me, like most cops, a level of detachment when it came to viewing corpses. So much so that now the only one I couldn't look at is the one I'll never have to.

I mention this death for another reason. Nowadays, should a death occur in similar circumstances, it would merit greater enquiry. Currently, such an incident would require the contacting of the Duty Assistant Chief Constable. There would then follow a full review by a high-ranking officer of procedures with regard to police involvement with the deceased, and a copy of the subsequent report would be forwarded to the Complaints and Discipline Department.

But at that time, Eric guided me through the completion of the Sudden

Death Report, which I submitted, and that was basically that. There was no real enquiry into what had prompted him to take that action; a young man with no apparent or evidenced problems. The offence that he'd been charged with wasn't of a serious nature and he hadn't displayed any obvious self-harm tendencies. It was an early lesson that all the questions don't always have answers.

3

IN EARLY TROUBLE AND ON PATROL

I worked in a satellite office or Subdivision. The policing area covered by the Subdivision was geographically large and encapsulated pretty much the whole socio-economic spectrum: huge houses in exclusive estates, housing schemes that incorporated pockets of social deprivation, sprawling farm properties, hotels, nightclubs, social clubs, as well as welcoming and not-so-welcoming public houses.

Consequently, this led to officers experiencing all aspects of policing, from crimes of violence, to various facets of acquisitive crime, anti-social behaviour, drug and road-traffic offences, and all points in between.

Policing such a diverse area also ensured there was a freshness to each tour of duty. It allowed me to experience the feelings of fun, enjoyment, excitement and satisfaction that carrying out good police work can bring.

I may have been too enamoured with a desire to do good police work, or perhaps the 'thrill of the chase' overtook me, because six months in, I found myself carpeted at a high divisional level, for trying to progress some raw criminal intelligence.

There was a pub-cum-club near Kirkintilloch Cross with ambitions to present itself as upmarket. I'd received some information that a male from an area of Garthamlock (a housing scheme on the north side of the city) was frequenting the club and may be involved in the drug trade. He certainly had the superficial trappings: flash sports car, designer clothes and no discernible or tangible means of income.

I found out that he had left the country several days previously and travelled to the Far East, which, in 1981, was not the regular tourist destination it has since become. I didn't, however, know which airline he had used or when he was scheduled to return. I did, though, know what could be acquired in the Far East, so decided to see if I could find details of his return date.

It was my absolute intention that if I could ascertain his return date, I would then contact the Criminal Intelligence Department and afford them the opportunity to carry out an intelligence evaluation on the information gleaned.

I started with taking a note of the likely travel agents who would deal with a trip of that nature – and believe me, there were not many at that time. Those that existed were situated in and around Glasgow city centre.

I finished my night shift on the Monday morning having worked a block of seven nights, and was scheduled to next start work on Wednesday for a late shift. So, following a few hours' sleep on the Monday, I made my way into town and started wearing out my shoe leather.

With some luck, I managed to locate the travel agent responsible for making the booking, which was located in a large department store on Argyle Street, and the girl in question was quite willing to assist. This was long before the Data Protection Act engulfed police work in bureaucracy. She did, however, ask if I objected to her clearing the matter with the store's head of security, who was an ex-police officer.

I had already identified myself as a police officer and shown my warrant card, so of course I had no objections. When he attended, I went through the same procedure, but when pressed by him as to why I was looking for the information, I declined to enlighten him. My view was that he was no longer a police officer and even if I had no reason to doubt his integrity, it would have been indiscreet of me to share my reasons with him.

Invariably, the people occupying these types of security positions had been high-ranking police officers and would not have been accustomed to being told 'no'. Consequently, he decided I wouldn't be given access to the information I sought.

What he didn't realise was that I'd already charmed the information from the travel agent girl while awaiting his arrival. With a disguised conspiratorial wink to her, I left things at that.

The following day, late morning, there was a knock on the door. On opening it, I found myself confronted by a uniform police sergeant who informed me that he was from Baird Street Police Office, which was my Divisional HQ.

He told me that I'd been summoned to see the Deputy Divisional Commander and I was to be driven by him. With that and no other word on the twenty-minute journey, he deposited me at the Commander's office, where I found myself being verbally lashed like a recalcitrant schoolboy.

Who did I think I was carrying out work while off duty, outwith my area, and even outwith my Division? Blundering about in areas I knew nothing about!

I politely laid out the scenario for him and how I intended to progress any information gleaned, but I think he had difficulty grasping the concept that someone would actually, in their own time and for no recompense, carry out police work.

For one of the only few times while in the police, I kept my counsel and let his verbal hurricane blow itself out. I was still in my probationary period and could have been dismissed for almost anything, and I got the distinct impression he would have loved an excuse to do just that.

Eventually, he finished his rant and I was told to leave. After the conclusion of the not-so-convivial chat, I toyed mentally with the idea of asking him (since it was my rest day) whether I could claim for overtime. Perhaps I should have. The resulting surge in his blood pressure may have caused the old bastard to have had a stroke and would have been worth the sacking.

Had this lashing been based on a desire to ensure an inexperienced officer did not involve himself in something outwith his ken or experience, I could have understood, but it lay in the bruised ego of the ex-senior officer.

It transpired that he and the Deputy Divisional Commander were golfing buddies and both had climbed the promotion ladder in the police through social networks rather than by doing good police work. When I declined to enlighten him as to why I was seeking information, he got on the phone to his friend. It was my worse luck that his friend also happened to be the Deputy of my working Division.

I later made discreet enquiries to establish whether the information gleaned had been forwarded to Criminal Intelligence, but nothing had.

It was only ten years later, when I was being interviewed by my Divisional Commander at London Road in the East End of Glasgow, prior to being promoted, that I realised how close I'd come to being dismissed. Rather than the tongue-lashing having been the end of the matter, he'd caused a report – poisonously slanted – to be placed in my personnel file . . . and it was still there.

I'm glad things didn't come to a shudderingly early halt, as I would have been deprived of some incredible adrenalin rushes, moments of exhilaration, excitement, hilarity, poignancy and abhorrence. September and October were to deliver bursts of those emotions in equal measure.

The poignancy arrived on 10 September, when I was on early shift and partnered with Robert (Bob) Harvey. We hadn't long cleared the morning briefing and had been allocated mobile duties. Bob was great to work with. He was only in his mid-twenties but had been a cop for seven years and was a competent guy who loved to have a laugh. He had a good line of chat and was good at sizing up a situation. He would also back you to the hilt.

We were dispatched to a call at the Crow Road car park. Crow Road is a narrow circuitous route that runs through the very scenic Campsie Hills. It is often referred to as 'the big car park in the sky'; a term coined by CB radio users. It affords the most wonderful views, but we weren't driving there to enjoy the scenery.

A passing motorist had noticed a car sitting in the car park. The engine was running and there was a length of hose leading from the exhaust into the front of the car via the driver's window, which had been opened just enough to allow the exhaust fumes inside the car. It wasn't a 'cry for help' attempt. Whoever was inside had been intent on taking their life.

The motorist had turned the engine off, but was too late to revive the single occupant. In pre-mobile phone days, he'd then had to drive down the hillside to ask a nearby householder to contact the police.

Robert and I arrived at the car and although we knew it was hopeless, carried out checks for any vital signs. The driver displayed what I was to learn subsequently were the classic signs of carbon monoxide poisoning, mainly a cherry-pink complexion. It is a rather perverse anomaly that victims of carbon monoxide poisoning, because of that 'cherry pink', have an almost healthy complexion as opposed to the fish-belly bluish-grey tinge of other corpses.

On looking around the car, I was jolted as surely as if I'd stuck my finger in an electrical socket. Laid out neatly on the rear parcel shelf were a set of police numerals, of the kind that officers would attach through the loops of their police dress shirts, and a police hat.

The numerals bore a 'D' prefix mark, which meant that not only was the deceased in all probability a police officer, but he had been an officer in our Division. We radioed this information to the Control Room and awaited the update.

I wondered later whether his having been a police officer, and well aware of how offhand cops can sometimes be at death scenes, he'd hoped the numerals and hat would ensure he was afforded an extra degree of respect. Maybe, having been at numerous death scenes himself, he'd simply wanted to assist us in quickening his identification. Who knows what occupies the last thoughts of suicidal individuals.

A little while later, Jimmy McKillop, who at that time was the Detective Inspector at our office, arrived at the scene, together with the Detective Superintendent for the Division. Some enquiry had been carried out and the dead officer had been identified as Albert Raybould, who had been an officer working from Easterhouse.

Albert, it seemed, was a witness in an upcoming trial and whatever his evidence, it was worrying him greatly and he also may have been suffering domestic problems. It seemed he had damaged the inside of one of the rooms of his house; he'd broken a dressing table mirror and thrown things around the room. A nail polish bottle had been among the broken items and when it had smashed, it appeared that the contents had splashed across his back and left a stain.

I had no experience of the investigation of deaths or the interpretation of scenes, but the stain looked to me to be what it was – nail polish – but the cigar-smoking Detective Superintendent declared that it looked like blood.

I raised my eyebrows and caught McKillop's eye and it was obvious he was clear in his own mind what the staining was, and he wasn't for exacerbating a sadness with a full-blown circus. Albert's wife had been located, was safe and well, and had been informed of the tragedy.

McKillop spoke exactly like Mark McManus in *Taggart*; the same tone and gruff to the point of being brusque. He was, however, approachable and knew how to dispense praise with a few well-chosen industrial phrases.

He wanted a quiet word with the Detective Superintendent, so, to facilitate this, he sent Bob and me to check the gully adjacent to the car park. The gully bottomed out at a mini waterfall but had about a 1:10 gradient and would have challenged a Tibetan Sherpa. We ensured that we conducted as comprehensive a search of the area as possible before puffing, struggling and cursing our way back to the top.

When we got back, they had satisfied themselves that Albert had sadly, for whatever reasons, taken his own life and there was nothing suspicious in his death.

It was a sobering thought that as a cop, just because you pull on that uniform, it doesn't make you a superhero. It doesn't imbue the wearer with superhuman powers; police officers in their private lives are every bit as susceptible to human emotions and frailties.

It was September and the following weekend was a bank holiday weekend in Scotland, which was to afford me a bit of fun and excitement. It was a Sunday and I was working night shift and had been allocated the main thoroughfare of the town as a walking beat. I was partnered with an officer from another shift who was working overtime and although he had barely completed his probation, he was, like me, a mature officer. We'd probably been walking the beat for an hour or so when my partner asked casually if I fancied getting a drink at a certain social club that lay on our beat.

At that time in the police there existed a culture which when viewed retrospectively appears surreal. Cops drank on duty. I'm not talking about the having a nip of spirits after having jumped into an ice-cold river to save someone from drowning kind of drinking. I'm talking night shift briefing; into vehicles or out on walking beats; then straight to licensed premises for two, three or more pints of beer, courtesy of mine host the licence holder.

It wasn't restricted to a singular Division, Subdivision or even particular shifts either. It appeared endemic throughout Strathclyde and, I would venture, every other Force in Scotland. My shift was no different and that included the sergeant. Even though I'd come from a 1970s football culture where players' alcohol consumption probably accounted for 80% of the brewer's profits, it still came as a shock to me.

I was then and still am teetotal. I'm also a strong-willed character, so when shift members I was partnered with headed to a pub or social club, I remained in the car and told them I'd monitor the radio for calls.

It caused initial friction, but when the shift realised that I wasn't running to bosses or trying to score brownie points, and would be first into a rough situation, the friction rescinded.

I wasn't being judgemental or some kind of Pious Pete, but I loved what I was doing and didn't want to miss anything by malingering in licensed premises, or have my ability to do my job compromised by being in the debt of a license holder. I was also being paid damn well to do the job and really didn't like the idea of money under false pretences.

Consequently, on that night, I told my partner that I didn't drink on duty and having no problem with my stance, he continued with me on the foot patrol. We came to a part of the main thoroughfare that housed a thriving butcher's shop and which is now, ironically, a lawyer's office.

We then heard the faintest of noises, almost like a scratching, coming from inside the butcher's shop. If there had been passing vehicular traffic or any noisy partygoers, we'd have missed it. If the shop had been located at either end of the main thoroughfare, where the main pubs and clubs were located, we wouldn't have heard it. There were no houses nearby, so it made for a good target.

The front shop door and display window were protected by padlocked metal shutters, no one could get out that way, so we very quietly made our way to the rear of the shop premises to check for insecurity. The rear of the shop was elevated with a flat, toughened, corrugated plastic roof.

My partner boosted me up onto the roof and I crawled along it, almost missing the hole that had been made because it was so dark and I didn't want to alert anyone inside by shining a torch, but it was there and I could hear voices.

Despite what anyone thinks or attempts to tell you, apprehending housebreakers 'in flagrante' is a rarity. In all the years, it's happened to me maybe three times. Cops may have caught perpetrators near to a scene, as a result of broadcast descriptions, or them being in possession of the stolen property, but actually catching them in the act is uncommon.

Police officers are sometimes called on to display physical courage but they also have to use common sense. There is a difference between taking a chance and stupidity. Using a football analogy, there is a difference between a player who will whole-heartedly challenge for a ball they have a less than 40% chance of winning and one who will stupidly contest a challenge that will result in him breaking his leg. There is a big difference.

We were faced with an unknown number of persons in a shop where all sorts of razor-sharp knives were used daily and we would be dropping down into the dark. It wasn't even a decision. We called for the assistance of a dog. Some of the German Shepherds used as police dogs are larger than Shetland ponies, move like ninjas and love to tattoo arms, legs and backsides with their teeth.

Once the dog arrived, we delivered the good news to whoever was inside and afforded them the option of emerging one at a time where we could control the situation, or book an appointment with the canine tattoo parlour. Probably to the dog's frustration, they decided handing themselves over to police officers was a better option.

It transpired there were two of them – both males. They'd forced open the safe, which, because of the holiday weekend, contained several thousand pounds. My partner that night eventually rose to the rank of Inspector but periodically I used to goad him about how he'd have missed that arrest if he'd been propping up a bar.

It was October 1981. I had been with the police for almost ten months and one of the most intense situations I would encounter in my time as a police officer was about to manifest itself.

As with the break-in at the butcher's shop, it was luck – good or bad – which involved me in the incident.

I was on late shift with Eric Young and it was evening. We were en route to a nothing enquiry, a follow-up to a minor road traffic accident. It's strange how even trivial details from some incidents remain clear.

We were on the Glasgow Road approaching a roundabout that affords drivers three options: straight ahead towards Glasgow; left to a rural area which housed HMP Low Moss; or right to Torrance, a small village that consisted of middle-class housing estates and council-rented properties.

A controller or dispatcher passed an urgent call over the radio requesting a free unit to attend a report of a man who had allegedly barricaded himself into his house in Hawthorn Street, Torrance, and was threatening to harm his children.

We were two or three minutes away from the scene. I wasn't a driver at that time, so Eric was driving, which meant I responded to radio broadcasts. I looked at Eric, who shrugged and nodded. I radioed the control room and asked them to mark us as attending and gave them our estimated arrival time.

We arrived outside a semi-detached house that had front and rear door entrances. A male was at an upper-floor window that was ajar and situated over the front door entrance.

Eric told me: 'Get him talking. I'll speak to neighbours. See who's in there normally.'

With that, he was away to chap doors.

Get him talking? About what? Films? Sport? The weather?

I was going to have to wing it and hope that a supervisor arrived soon.

I had his first name. Let's call him 'Stephen'. I started things off with something like, 'Stephen, what's the problem here?'

'Don't try and come in. I've got my kids in here with me.'

'I'm not looking to come in. I'm only here to try and help you.'

'Then get my wife up here.'

'Where is she?'

'You know.'

'I don't. Tell me.'

'Youse moved her the other night.'

'Stephen, I don't know what you're talking about. I've only just met you. I hadn't anything to do with that. Look, my name's Gerry. Why don't you come down and open the door, and we'll see if we can resolve things face-to-face.'

'Naw. You get her up here first and then we'll talk.'

I hadn't the first clue about negotiating tactics. It wasn't in the Probationer Training Manual at the Scottish Police College and I don't think the Force even had trained negotiators at that time, so call it utter fluke or call it divine inspiration, but something told me not to promise anything I couldn't deliver.

'Stephen, I'm just the message boy here; a normal cop. It would take someone higher than me, and it would take time to arrange something like that. Why don't you just open the door and you and me can talk.'

I was winging it for all my worth, trying to keep the dialogue going in the hope that he'd see sense. I'd made sure I'd kept my tone even and hadn't raised my voice.

'Stephen, we can sort this out. We can fix this, but you need to open the door and talk to me.'

I caught sight of Eric coming back to the police van and signalling he wanted a word.

'Stephen, I've got to speak to my colleague. Don't move from the window and I'll stay in your sight. No one is going to try and come in.'

Eric: 'How's it going?'

I answered with one word: 'Fuck.'

'He had an argument with the wife and she was moved by Women's Aid. His kids are three and seven and are in there with him, as far as I can find out. I'll update the control and see if a supervisor's en route. Keep him talking.'

I went back and called up to him.

'Stephen, if you don't want to come out, why don't you let the kids out? Would you think about that?'

'My kids are with me and staying that way. Get my wife up here.'

'Stephen, I can't make that happen right away. I'm trying.'

I persisted in using his name as much as I could, hoping that he'd see some kind of empathy between us.

I can't recall if he'd waved a knife at me or produced a knife at some point during the dialogue, which I find really strange, as I can recall the rest of the incident so clearly.

His voice had been raised and stressed and his manner aggressive throughout, and he gave every indication of someone on the edge. His next line chilled me.

'Then you'd better get your fucking gun crew up here because I intend to die with my kids tonight.'

I had absolutely no reason to doubt him.

I was so locked into the dialogue, I was oblivious to the fact that other uniform officers had arrived at the scene. In my peripheral vision I caught sight of two of them making their way down the pathway of a house two doors away. They were looking to access the rear of the target house and – I take it – test the security of the rear door. Being in an elevated position, however, he was obviously better-placed to view the whole scene and saw them before I did.

I started to shout to them to stop, but whether he perceived their movement as threatening, whether he thought I had lied, whether he was so mentally unbalanced and was going to carry out the threat regardless, I don't know.

What I do know is that he disappeared from sight and I knew what was about to happen.

Decades later, I watched a film called *Hostage* in which Bruce Willis played a negotiator. In the opening scene, a father has barricaded himself in his house with his child, and Willis at some point realises that the father intends to carry out his threat of harming his son. At that point, he is desperate and abandons all standard rules of negotiation and begs, pleads and even offers to get down on his knees and pray with the guy.

I could relate to that scenario because as soon as he moved away, I started to shout up to him. I shouted that his wife was on the way, that no one was going to try and approach the house . . . anything that came in to my head. With no flippancy intended, I can say that if he'd asked me to stand on my head, I would have done that or anything else that would have appeased him.

The scream was blood-chilling.

I charged the door and launched a kick at the lock where it was most likely to splinter. I'd kicked open several doors in my short time as a cop, so I fully expected movement. I bounced off it. I started to kick at it frantically but it wouldn't budge. You see actors in films putting their shoulders to doors and they magically spring open. Believe me, you try that in real life, you'll break your shoulder. It later transpired that his forward planning was such that he had barricaded the door and wedged knives into the jambs.

I ran the short distance to the lounge window and began to try to smash it with my baton. Using one of those balsa wood batons I mentioned earlier, I could just as well have been striking it with a piece of soggy linguine. One of the cops, however, had a baton of some substance and managed to smash the window.

Even though the opening he'd created was jagged and the windowsill elevated, I got up and through the window. I think I may even have been boosted up to the window by the same cop who had smashed it. The adrenalin coursing through me at that point would have fuelled the Space Shuttle.

A girl who looked about seven came running through the door crying and shouted, 'My daddy's stabbed me.' I don't know whether the adrenalin was allowing me to process information more rapidly, but I made the snap decision that because she was moving, walking and talking I'd let the cops climbing in behind me care for her.

I thought, 'He's in an elevated position, armed with fuck knows what,' but I desperately wanted to reach the second child I believed was in the house, so I still took the stairs four at a time to the landing. The other wee girl was up there with a penetrating wound to the abdomen.

I now had to find him and neutralise his threat, although how I intended to do that, I hadn't a clue. I was fortunate because he'd taken care of that himself. He was propped up against the side of the bed with self-inflicted chest wounds. I kicked the knife away, rolled him over and handcuffed him behind his back.

I carried the little girl out to the ambulance while he was taken down the stairs supported by two officers. I travelled in the ambulance with the girls to the hospital, where both were initially wrapped in aluminium blankets to combat shock. I was so wired from the adrenalin that any jangle emitted by the ambulance siren en route to the hospital resonated like the Hammer of Thor. They were admitted, treated and, thankfully, both eventually made a full physical recovery, as did their father.

The week after the incident, the Detective Inspector, Jimmy McKillop, saw me passing in the corridor and with a, 'Hey you,' summoned me into his room. In that gruff voice of his, he said, 'That was good work at Torrance. You've been doing well recently. Don't get fuckin' swollen-headed. Now away and get me some more fuckin' criminal bodies.'

Probably thirty seconds in total. Nowadays, if he spoke like that to someone, they'd probably raise a complaint of oppressive conduct. Me? When I walked out of his room, you'd have needed a dozen lemons to wipe the grin off my face.

McKillop had instructed the Detective tasked with preparing the case to submit a separate report recommending me for a commendation for my actions, but he neglected to do it. It didn't overly concern me. No lives had been lost and I'd take that result any day of the week.

Around this time, we also had a change of supervisor and his arrival coincided with the end of the drinking culture – certainly on our shift. Our shift sergeant retired and was replaced by a sergeant who was a product of the Force's Accelerated Promotion (AP) System. This was a system designed to identify and fast-track potential future senior management.

The shift was wary of his arrival, given that products of the AP system were generally regarded as promotion-driven, self-serving and lacking in police experience. As it transpired, he improved the shift immeasurably as a unit and individually as officers.

He was lean with jet-black hair and a moustache and had been raised in the tough Roystonhill housing scheme in Glasgow, so he knew how many beans made six. He had been a police officer for eight years, but those had been spent in the East End of Glasgow, where you learned and gained police experience quickly. He'd also completed a six-month secondment with the Criminal Investigation Department. Once on the shift, he began to arrange things like five-a-side football as a means of team-bonding and was very adept, not at self-promotion, but at highlighting to senior staff good work carried out by the shift, and ensured the troops received proper recognition. He was responsible for making certain that the drinking culture on our shift ended, which was fine by me. It was, however, the way he dealt with the matter that impressed me.

One of the most senior shift members was having personal problems, which were impacting on his work. Nightshift saw him drinking what one would expect of someone socially, and this was placing shift members in an awkward position, especially Tommy Loan.

Tommy was, like me, still a probationary officer, albeit a few years younger and with about nine months more service. Tommy was and still is a fitness fanatic and had been a police cadet. He came from exemplary parents, was really keen to learn and do good police work and wanted to do a decent day's work for his pay. But he was basically having to support the senior cop with whom he was working and wasn't getting the opportunity to do the work he wanted. However, he was loyal to team members, so didn't complain.

One night, the senior cop was, there's no other way to phrase it, drunk, and was in the canteen for his break along with several of the shift, including me. He was worsening the situation by drinking crème de menthe liqueur neat from the bottle, in the belief that the peppermint from the liqueur would disguise the smell of the other alcohol he had consumed.

He asked me if the alcohol could still be detected and if it hadn't been so tragic, it would have been comedic.

I asked him outright: 'Are you stupid as well as pissed? Of course you can smell it. You're howling.'

He responded with: 'You're nothing but a fucking arse.'

I owed him a lot because he was probably one of the reasons I had aspirations to specialise in investigative work. He taught me the varying interview techniques and how to obtain information and recruit inform-ants. I understood the problems he was having outwith the police and had tried to speak to him, but he was destroying the respect the shift had for him, as well as his standing within it.

The sergeant happened to come walking through to the canteen and it didn't take a Sherlock Holmes to assess the cop's condition. The sergeant did something then that could have cost him his career and what no other sergeant involved in the accelerated promotion system would have done. He had the cop taken home and had one of the shift drive the cop's personal car. It was a compassionate act by a decent human being. He should have suspended him. He should have reported him. He did neither.

The following night, after muster, he asked the cop for a quiet word. No shouting or screaming. He told him simply and firmly that he was highly regarded by shift members, who looked to him for advice and guidance, and that he was letting himself and the shift down. The cop knew that he owed him big time and cleaned up his act for the remainder of his time on the shift.

The shift, for their part, never mistook the sergeant's actions for weakness or as an excuse to take liberties (quite apart from the fact that he certainly wasn't the type you'd try it on with). On the contrary, they realised that he could easily have handled things other than compassionately, just to get himself noticed. We knew then that we had a decent guy as a sergeant and, more importantly, the drinking stopped and the public, for their part, gained a more focused, produc-tive group.

The sergeant progressed through the police to the rank of Chief Superintendent before retiring. He currently lectures on police subjects, is a published author and has the prefix of 'Doctor' to his name.

I had returned from my second period at the police college and was, by now, some fourteen months in. Tommy had just about completed his probation. The sergeant, knowing we were both as keen as mustard and had garnered decent experience from our tutors, partnered us together and gave us the town centre as a walking beat.

That suited us both and we enjoyed having responsibility for an area. Ask most officers and they will, I would imagine, tell you that an area was never as well known to them as when they walked it as a beat. If you worked it properly, you knew those who should be on it and those who shouldn't. You knew your shopkeepers, publicans, and people in general. You spoke to the public and were highly visible and, in turn, available to be approached. You built contacts and gleaned intelligence. If a pattern of crime occurred or a repeat problem arose, you took it as a personal sleight and were determined to resolve the issue.

Walking a beat and learning how to police appears to be a fast-disappearing skill. Nowadays, even Community Officers don't appear to want to patrol an area on foot. They want to be mobile. If an officer were to be designated to walk for their period of duty, they would feel they were being punished, and yet, walking a beat affords cops an opportunity to develop the decision-making and communication skills that ownership of an area brings. With ownership comes responsibility.

Someone has even had the great idea that community officers should patrol on pedal cycles, which affords another opportunity to whizz past the public. It seems anything is preferable to being physically present and interacting daily with the public they're asked to protect and whose cooperation they seek.

It may be partly because officers recruited within the last five or six years are of a generation versed in remote communication. They text, e-mail, converse through Facebook and Twitter, and play each other on Xbox and Playstation . . . all in isolation.

Consequently, in an organisation designed to function by means of communication, these new cops, when placed in situations where they're required to take control, provide direction and actually interact with human beings face-to-face, are often palpably ill at ease. Even holding eye contact requires great effort. Walking a beat (or 'ward', to give it the fashionable police term) would greatly assist them in acquiring those basic social skills.

Additionally, with a high profile presence on a beat, you wouldn't require facts and figures to gauge the level of public satisfaction, and I'm sure the level of recurring complaints and crimes would drop.

Officers allocated their own area of responsibility quickly address complaints or crime patterns, and they'll do it for one of two reasons – either through pride in policing their allocated area or, rather less praiseworthy, because they're sick of having their day taken up listening to the same grievances. Either way, the public win. The intelligence system would also benefit greatly as, believe it or not, most people enjoy speaking to an officer they know and with whom they are comfortable. As a consequence of that familiarity, they're far more likely to alert the officer to something untoward or of concern.

Tommy and I began our partnership with a suicide call. We were in Lenzie to follow up on a warrant enquiry when the radio message announced that a woman had received a call from her brother. He'd informed her that he intended to take his life. He was apparently in a depressed state as a result of various life issues.

The dispatcher was trying to ascertain if any unit was nearby and could attend. The house in question was in an affluent area. As with Torrance, we were nearby and although on foot, we were quick enough to reach the location before the patrol car.

Nowadays, whether through a reticence to make a decision or because they haven't been afforded the same opportunities to develop decision-making skills, cops constantly contact their supervisors for permission to force a door. Perhaps they're worried that they may face censure within the police if they act incorrectly and the Force is sued for damages, or receives a bill for compensation.

Me? I always viewed crashing doors as being covered by my basic commitment as a police officer – to protect life and property. Also nowadays, due to Health and Safety rules, officers are invariably required to use a 'Ramit' to force entry. A 'Ramit' is a short, solid piece of reinforced steel with a flat head and handles and is more effective than a foot in forcing open a door. Accessing that equipment can, however, cause delay as it is stored at the police office and, additionally, the equipment requires an officer to be trained in the use of it.

Things were far simpler then. We splintered the door. Truth be told? I always derived a guilty pleasure from kicking in a door. When we got inside, we were greeted by a male who had tied a rope around his neck and secured the other end to the spars of his upstairs banister and in his despair leapt. The resultant jerking when the rope reached its tether should have broken his neck and/or resulted in asphyxiation.

Our victim, however, was writhing on the floor in agony with broken ankles. He'd totally miscalculated the length of rope he was using and when he leapt off, he didn't stop until he crashed onto the tiled flooring. I can't recall his profession but I'm sure he hadn't majored in mathematics.

While waiting on the ambulance, I think we drew lip blood trying to stop ourselves laughing out loud. The last I checked, he was still in pretty robust health, so perhaps the shock cured him of any further thoughts of self-harm. He can, however, probably tell from the rheumatics in his ankles when it's scheduled to rain.

I was virulently anti-drugs and became even more entrenched in that view when I eventually began working in Possilpark, Saracen and Maryhill; inner city areas blighted by the drug trade. The situation I mentioned earlier, with the three collapsed drug-users, wasn't uncommon. Working those areas, you often found yourself looking at the lifeless corpse of some nineteen- or twenty-year-old sprawled across a filthy toilet bowl with a syringe plunged deep into their arm. It was such an ignominious end.

When you traced the parents and broke the news to them, most bore a look of resignation. It was news they'd probably been expecting and dreading for some time. It was no doubt my imagination, but I sometimes wondered if I also caught a fleeting hint of relief cross their face. They'd no doubt watched children they'd borne and raised descend into a cesspool of a lifestyle, and had had to endure the numerous thefts of sentimental items, broken promises and lies in their thousands. Those rock stars who attempt to glamorise drug usage should have attended some of those bathroom scenes.

Early in my uniform service, I witnessed the devastating effects addiction can have on a family and what a rapid downward spiral it induces. From patrolling our area, Tommy and I got to know a local girl from seeing her at the clubs and pubs on our beat. She had a lot going for her. She was in a good job (nursing), from a nice home and a very attractive girl. She took what is tragically the classic drug-descent route.

She began with cannabis, whether through peer pressure or not, got in with a 'jack the lad' crew and progressed to amphetamine, heroin, loss of job and, thereafter, shoplifting to earn money. She had been adopted as a baby by a lovely local couple whose hearts had been broken by her behaviour.

As well as the local clubs, she frequented Glasgow city centre. Tommy and I had both tried to speak to her because her parents were such nice people, but unless someone truly wants to give up drugs, alcohol, cigarettes – or whatever their personal addiction – then all the reasoning in the world isn't going to have an impact.

She took up with a long-term target of the Scottish Crime Squad who revelled in the nick name 'Wide Boy', believing he was too clever for the police. He was more than happy to use her reliance on substances as a control mechanism. That way, she was more likely to accompany him when it came to his shoplifting sprees. Not surprisingly, I didn't like him.

The Crime Squad personnel were having a difficult time 'housing' him, as he moved around frequently and was constantly changing hire cars. Both he and the girl used the cars to travel throughout Britain committing large-scale shopliftings. At some point, a journey to London in a hire car resulted in her collecting a Fixed Penalty Notice (FPN). Obviously, when a check was carried out with the hire company, they ascertained who had hired the car and forwarded the Fixed Penalty Notice to our office for serving.

Along with Tommy, I contacted a Detective Inspector at the Scottish Crime Squad and told them we had an opportunity to have her attend at the police office. I was sure she would be in a hire car and if they took up positions around the office, they could commence surveillance and see where that led. He was keen to try and apprehend both and asked that he be contacted with the time and date she was attending.

I left word at her house to contact me at the office, leaving the impression that a warrant had been issued and that I was trying to avoid any potential arrest. Obviously, wanting to know how there could be a warrant in existence, she phoned me at the office. I told her that there had been a misunderstanding with the phone message and explained that what I had was a Fixed Penalty Notice from the Met and that if collected and dealt with quickly, that would be the end of the matter. If not, however, the Met would in all likelihood issue a warrant for her arrest.

We fixed a time and date for her to attend and after serving the FPN, I walked her out to the front door of the office so the surveillance officers would be in no doubt as to the identity of their target. They followed both her and her boyfriend through to Dunfermline, where they were apprehended after stealing jewellery from three separate jewellers totalling over £5,000.

He'd been the target and we (naively?) hoped that if we could separate her from him for a period, we may have persuaded her to try rehab, but ultimately, a year or so later, she died of a drugs overdose – like every other drugs death, an utter waste of life.

Tommy and I continued to police our beat and were always highly visible; we both enjoyed being responsible for and having control over how we policed an area for the duration of our shift. We perhaps didn't always administer the law equitably, but in our eyes, we administered it justly and a couple of minor examples perhaps illustrate that.

We had a fruit and vegetable shop on our beat, operated by three men, two of whom were brothers. They were from the East End of Glasgow and were in our opinion 'fly by nights'. One of the three – David Santini – would eventually receive a thirteen-year prison sentence when apprehended in his West End flat, in 1997, with almost £1 million worth of heroin. When on duty, we used to charge them with any minor infraction, including when they placed their wooden produce boxes too far onto the footpath. We afforded the other shopkeepers much more leeway.

One day, the charity shop box in their shop went missing. We were certain that they had taken it themselves once it had been filled with change. We gave them two choices. They could either lead us to the box or we would close the shop, take them to the office and carry out 'further enquiries', which would take quite some time and have an impact on their revenue. We got the box and contents back and charged one of the three.

The Community Sergeant who liaised with the local newspaper made sure the incident was picked up and publicised. The article may well have affected trade as they literally shut up shop and moved not long afterwards.

The other incident resulted in me being mentioned on the front page of the local newspaper. It was a hot Saturday afternoon and we were given a call that a child had been left locked in a car in the town centre and had grown very distressed. We ran along and found a crowd gathered around the car trying without success to entice the child, who was about four, to lift the door lock.

He was red-faced and crying. Tommy used his tact to move the well-meaning people away from the car. I signalled to the child to pull up the lock switch but got no joy. I then tried a different tact and I took my police hat off and offered him that if he would pull the door lock, but still nothing.

I then shouted to the control room on my radio – the communications system carried by officers then comprised a separate receiver/transmitter. I explained to them what I wanted and arranged for them to broadcast any old gibberish over the radio, which I held up to the side of the car window and dangled the receiver towards him, indicating it would be his if he pulled up the switch. I didn't think it was going to work and was thinking we may have to force the window, when he popped the lock switch.

I lifted him out of the car and got him some juice and crisps and, of course, I had to let him hold the radio. His mother showed up just after. She had gone to do some shopping; the child had been sleeping and she hadn't anticipated being long. The child had woken, it was hot within the car and his mum wasn't there, so he became stressed and the queue in the supermarket was longer than expected.

Technically, we should have libelled a charge against the mother under Section 12 of the Children and Young Persons Act for neglect of the child, but we made the decision to let matters rest there. It was obvious the child was well cared for. He was thriving bodily, well-dressed and his mother was distraught and her contrition genuine.

If one of us had taken himself off street duties to submit a crime report and a subsequent case to the Procurator Fiscal, what would the outcome have been of any judicial proceedings? Realistically, who would have benefited from prosecution? In my judgement, her self-recrimination was greater punishment than anything a court could have imposed.

However, the local newspaper had received a letter from a passer-by and placed it on the front of their next edition. His letter had described the child as being 'overcome with heat and on the point of collapse' and if not for the officer who had 'personality plus' and who succeeded in enticing the child to spring the door lock, a more serious scenario may have developed. I'm sure it was just a touch of melodramatic, journalistic licence but for the next couple of weeks I had to endure Bob Harvey breaking into the song 'Mr Wonderful' any time I reported for duty or came into the office for refreshment.

Not long afterwards, our sergeant, who by this time had had an opportunity to review the area we policed, decided that the former mining village of Waterside deserved to see a uniformed police officer for their taxes. It lay off the main track and typical of its former status as a mining village, the houses were row clustered and could be walked around in thirty to forty-five minutes. The sergeant decided that when we were early and late shift, I would be dropped off at the village and walk around once before refreshment and once after.

I wasn't jumping for joy at the instruction because I loved being involved and in the thick of things, and thought there was nothing to be gained from wandering aimlessly about a small former mining community. Now, that may appear a contradiction of my earlier point concerning the absolute necessity for visible, approachable beat officers, but it was the final outcome, achieved as a result of following my sergeant's instruction, that convinced me of the benefit of localised policing.

Wullie Nicol was to be one of my initial tutors and later my partner for a period in the CID. His mother then lived in Waterside, a small former mining village near Kirkintilloch and within an hour of my first walk around the area, had phoned him to say that she had seen a policeman walking the village and that it was the first time she'd seen that in a decade. I enjoyed it and was pleasantly surprised at the number of adults and kids who wanted to stop and have a word. In addition to creating a 'feel good' factor for those residents, it was to reap the additional benefit of solving a fire-raising (arson).

On 31 October 1982, the pulp mill that was situated adjacent to the village was set alight and sustained £250,000 of damage. The enquiry was allocated to the CID, but no initial headway was made and there were no obvious suspects. About a week later, with the crime still unsolved, I was on my walk around the village and was stopped by about four or five kids of about eight or nine years old. They wanted to see the radio, baton and handcuffs, and asked if I had ever used the baton . . . just the usual things kids ask cops.

After we'd been joking around for about ten minutes, one of the kids mentioned the fire at the pulp works and there followed almost a fight amongst them to tell me who had caused it and how. Without so much as a pause, they named three youths who they said had started the fire and could even name the shop where they had bought the matches. I spoke to the kids' parents as a courtesy and relayed what they'd told me. Then I took a note of the names they'd given me and passed them on to the investigating officers.

I think they were rather sceptical initially, as they had considered various possible reasons why the mill might be the subject of a fire-raising, but I don't think any of the reasons had included fourteen- and fifteen-year-old kids buying matches and torching the place.

Shortly after, the sergeant was attending a morning briefing for supervisors chaired by the Subdivisional Officer who was a Chief Inspector. The Chief Inspector was waxing lyrical on how 'his' CID had solved the fire crime and locked up three boys, two aged fourteen and one fifteen-year-old – no mention of me, or my input. My sergeant waited and then enlightened him as to how exactly the crime had come to be cleared.

Later, the same Chief Inspector asked me how I had managed to get information from people, as by this time I had recruited some informants who were providing me with both criminal intelligence and crime-solving information. He asked whether I got information and then gave them money, or gave them money first which resulted in information. I joked that given the age of the kids who had supplied the information regarding the fire, I may have been arrested myself if I'd been caught giving them money.

I think that much earlier in life he'd undergone that complex surgical procedure that removed his sense of humour because his countenance resembled those of the sombre-faced statues on Easter Island, and gave off the resonance of concrete. Given his length of service and rank, he was strangely ignorant of how information was gleaned and crimes resolved.

In fairness, he wasn't a member of an exclusive club. Many senior officers rose through ranks with little or no experience or involvement in the investigation of anything other than the most basic crimes. It was highly unlikely that they would have had involvement with informants, possibly viewing those skills as some sort of 'black art'.

John Sharkey had replaced McKillop as Detective Inspector and had been impressed by my work rate, which included well above average criminal apprehensions and drug-dealing cases. After the information concerning the fire, I investigated and resolved several crimes that, in those days, should have been the sole remit of CID. He was more than happy with the manner in which I dealt with those enquiries and with my work generally, and he informed the Chief Inspector that he wished me to be the next Aide to the CID.

An Aide or Trainee was a six-month secondment to the Detective Department and afforded the CID senior management an opportunity to gauge the suitability of prospective candidates for a full-time position as a Detective Constable.

The Chief Inspector, however, refused flat out, citing the fact that I was still a probationary police officer and it was unheard of for an officer of that service to be seconded as an Aide or Trainee Detective Constable. I often wondered if my early carpeting by the then Deputy Divisional Commander had coloured his view, as he would have had access to my personnel file. Maybe it was my flippant remark concerning the money and the kids, or perhaps he felt that it was not a position suitable for someone with so little service. Whatever the reasons, I missed out on the post that time around.

I thoroughly enjoyed my work, as well as the people I worked with on my shift, but from very early in my service, I had a strong desire to specialise in investigative work and most of my apprehensions were of a criminal nature. I was hopeful that having been denied the previous opportunity of a six-month attachment to the CID, I would be successful on the next occasion the opportunity arose. An incident in April 1983 compounded John Sharkey's determination that I would be seconded at the next available opportunity.

It was about 6.30 a.m. and I had been on night duty, partnered with Andy McDonald. Andy was a lad who was tall, looked good in uniform and was popular with the public, and eventually rose to Chief Inspector rank. His forte and preference veered more towards traffic-related enquiries, which may have stemmed from his absolute love of cars. For my part, it was a great partnership, as Andrew was happy to leave the crime-related side to me, while I was more than pleased to have him take on traffic work. We split anything else.

Andrew had a fixed routine for the last half hour of the night shift – exigencies of duty allowing. He would head to an early morning bakers shop to buy fresh rolls and to the adjacent newsagent to buy a morning paper. That way, when he went home at the conclusion of his shift, he was set for breakfast and a read before his bed.

As we drove towards the bakers through an area known as Harestanes, we saw a Ford Escort that was accident-damaged to the front passenger side. There were three males in the car and we decided to have a word with them. Andy stopped our car to turn it around and as he did so, the damaged car increased speed. We drove after it but the pursuit ended very quickly when the car slowed but didn't stop and the three 'bailed out', leaving the car's progress to be halted by a garden hedge.

I got out of the car and began a foot chase. I was pretty quick in those days and, after about thirty yards, managed to trip up the one who had exited the rear of the vehicle. I handcuffed his hands behind his back and threw him on the ground for Andy, who wasn't far behind, to deal with and continued after the other two, managing to grab hold of one of them. We took our two prisoners back to the car and when we searched them, one had a loaded air pistol and makeshift mask on his person. It also transpired the car they were in had been stolen.

En route back to the police office, we saw a male walking head down about a mile or so from where our foot chase had begun. As I turned to see if Andy recognised him as possibly the third suspect, one of the two we had in the back of the car blurted out that it was, in fact, their other accomplice. I suppose misery loves company.

When we interviewed them at the office, they told us that they'd intended to rob a newsagent's shop near to where we'd first spotted them. They also led us to where two more replica pistols and masks had been discarded. It was a decent piece of crime prevention. I requested and was permitted to retain the enquiry and compile the report, although technically, given the severity of the charges, it should have been allocated to a Detective Officer.

The three who were aged twenty-one, nineteen and sixteen were to face fifteen charges, including conspiracy to rob, possession of firearms with intent to rob, and two charges of car theft, and were subsequently prosecuted on indictment at the High Court.

Only a few years later, one of those three boys, Martin Gorrian, was found guilty, along with another male, of the horrific and premeditated murder of two men in the scenic Campsie Hills. He and his co-accused in the murders also managed to waste weeks of police time by persuading investigating officers that they'd murdered numerous others and buried their bodies in the same hills.

If you'd suggested to me when I was seated in that police car with those three hapless, would-be robbers that one of them would, a short time later, callously murder two men, I'd have laughed in your face. At that time though, I probably didn't realise that in the majority of cases, people responsible for carrying out the most horrible of deeds look exactly like any normal person and rarely exude some kind of aura that marks them out as monstrous.

Although cited to appear as witnesses and attend the High Court, neither Andy nor I were required to give evidence, as pleas were submitted and accepted.

A few months later, I was seated at the night shift briefing when the shift sergeant announced that I'd been seconded to the CID. The shift members were happy for me and knew that was what I'd been working towards, although not everyone was jumping for joy. One member who had been performing plain-clothes duties when I first arrived on the shift felt that he should have been awarded the secondment well before me. If truth be told, however, my investigative work and criminal apprehensions at that time had been superior to his. At the conclusion of the briefing, he stormed from the room in a rage, almost taking the door off the hinges. Andy McDonald, with absolute comic timing, announced, 'I think he's in a rush to buy you a "Congratulations" card.'

4

(STEEP) LEARNING CURVE

A few weeks later, some two and a half years after joining the police, I found myself seconded to the CID I was assigned to work with two experienced Detective Constables, Wullie Nicol and John Stobo.

Wullie was smallish with unruly hair, and never concerned himself with style. He could be curt and nippy with colleagues who tried to use the CID as a means to offload work that they were too lazy to continue with. He was, however, very good at his job and a good tutor in Divisional CID work. He knew how to short-circuit an inquiry and get to the heart of things, but not to the detriment of professionalism. He knew what was 'fat' and needed to be excised while retaining the 'meat'.

John was bearded every other day, being one of those guys who could finish at 5 p.m. in the evening and by 9 a.m. the following morning have the makings of a good growth. He had a dry sense of humour and could handle a car pretty well in a vehicle pursuit.

They were extremely different personalities for sure, but both very good detectives in their own right. They were also patient and supportive. I provided both of them with a laugh at my expense on my very first day.

Ironically, after he'd tried to recruit me to the CID, John Sharkey had transferred to Easterhouse as Detective Inspector, so I didn't work with him. He had been replaced by Iain Mackay, who had arrived from the Serious Crime Squad. Iain was an absolute gentleman; calm demeanour, very approachable and always smart in appearance.

On my first day, all the Detective Officers, including Iain, had been cited to attend court, which left me holding the fort but knowing next to nothing. There were four males in custody at the office who were to be released after they had been fingerprinted and photographed.

Before everyone left for court, Iain asked me to undertake that task and with that, they were gone.

Nowadays, civilian assistants fingerprint prisoners and the prints are captured electronically. In those days, however, the fingerprinting of prisoners was the sphere of the CID and prints were obtained by taking an inked roller over the fingers and palms and then applying the inked hands to paper forms.

I hadn't fingerprinted anyone in my life but I had been left to do it, so decided to try, thinking, 'How hard can it be?' When Wullie and John returned from court, I showed them the four forms and asked where I should forward them to now. They took one look at my efforts, burst out laughing and told me to confine them to the rubbish bin.

'Who were you printing? Four fucking yeti?'

The quality did leave a great deal to be desired, so my first lesson was on the capturing of fingerprints.

For some reason or another, just about every first day of any new post I undertook brought with it a strange situation, and my first as an Aide proved no different. Our number had been supplemented by a CID supervisor from another office. He was very softly spoken and dressed in a fastidious fashion with a silk hand-kerchief in his breast pocket. He had a moustache and protruding front teeth.

Lunchtime arrived and I said I was going to buy something to eat from a local bakery, which was located only about 100 yards from the office. Our new arrival decided he would join me on the walk to the shop.

While living in Sweden, I had bought a black leather coat, which had been an expensive purchase. It was a sharp coat and I had worn it that first day.

We were perhaps fifty yards from the office when my tag-along colleague casually asked me what the colour of my coat lining was. I opened the coat and showed him the grey silk lining.

'Strange question,' I said. 'You don't have some kind of lining fetish do you?'

'No, someone who worked with me had a leather coat stolen and it had distinctive green lining so I always check leather coats.'

I looked at him to try and catch the punchline of the joke, but he was absolutely serious. Here he was, basically trying to ascertain if I had reset* a stolen leather coat. He'll never have come closer to having free cosmetic dentistry on his protruding teeth and I think it is fair to say that I never saw eye to eye with him on anything thereafter.

Not long before I'd begun my secondment, a man from the Moodiesburn area had been reported as a missing person to the police, but information emerged a short time later that he may, in fact, have been murdered and his body dumped in a local rubbish tip. The information resulted in the police mounting an operation to section off and excavate areas of the rubbish tip, in a search for human remains. A Detective Officer was required to be there at all times to check anything that may have emerged as potential evidence.

None of the officers from the Detective Department were exactly clambering over each other to take on that role so I was nominated. I had basic instructions to TFA (touch fuck all) should anything suspicious emerge, which for inexperienced officers was actually a very good tenet in basic crime scene management.

Every morning I was dropped off at the rubbish tip to await the utter stench that assailed the nostrils when the driver of the mechanical digger broke the crust of the rubbish tip surface. It really was an assault on the olfactory senses. I've attended countless post-mortems and scenes of all manner of body decomposition but the stench from that initial crust breakage took a lot to beat. The dig carried on for about a month but produced nothing of a tangible nature and was eventually called off and the enquiry petered out.

It brought home to me how difficult it was to conduct a murder enquiry without the presence of a body. So much physical and forensic evidence can be gleaned from a corpse and, additionally, the absence of a corpse compounds the difficulty in establishing that the missing person has been the victim of foul play. A few short years later, I was to be involved in just such an enquiry which led me to stints working in London and Bristol to establish that a man, that Avon and Somerset Police had listed as missing, had in fact been murdered.

The remaining six-month period I spent as a Trainee really amounted to a learning curve without my being involved in anything spectacular. I was involved in an Interpol enquiry but Nicol managed

*A term in Scots law meaning to handle stolen goods. Also known as 'fencing'.

to shatter my illusions on that particular organisation. Prior to joining the police and in my short time as a police officer, I'd had a romantic notion that Interpol was some sort of global, high-tech, multi-faceted gang-busting unit. Consequently, when I was allocated an early inquiry which emanated from Interpol I was like a dog with two tails.

Maltese police had intercepted a container of whisky which had been destined for the Eastern Bloc via Rotterdam in Holland, but which had turned up suspected as stolen in Malta. Having obtained a batch of numbers from the crated container they were looking for an enquiry to be carried out at a local distillery which produced its own brand of whisky (Buchanans).

Armed with the numbers, a director of the firm was able to interpret them and pinpoint the official intended destination of the whisky. I telexed* this information to Interpol expecting there to be some exciting follow-up, but Nicol punctured my balloon.

'Interpol's just a clearing house. They don't arrest anybody. It's basically some lazy bastard, in an office in London, that doesn't want to work for a living getting telexes and phone calls and passing it on. Like a conduit. That's it. You're far quicker phoning your opposite number yourself. The guy you speak to will be like yourself, trying to clear an enquiry. The guy at Interpol will take forever. It's just another one of dozens he's got to work through.'

Nowadays, Interpol has morphed into Europol, has moved to a huge office in The Hague and will be armed with modern technology and an impressive budget not to mention, I'm sure, a vast library of intelligence, but whenever I've heard Interpol mentioned Nicol's words have always caused me to smile. I picture some little guy in a trilby and raincoat seated in a room with a single light bulb with no lampshade, redirecting requests.

For my own part, over the years, I did indeed find friendly and fast assistance abroad by phoning officers directly, probably in direct contravention of Strathclyde Force Policy. Whenever I utilised Interpol, which is a bureaucracy, it took an age for the enquiry to be progressed. I'm certain modern-day technology has, however, increased response times immeasurably.

* * *

*An electronic system of communication superseded by fax and later by e-mail.

I dealt with a variety of crimes from serious assault to attempted murder, and various forms of acquisitive crime. We policed an area which encompassed a great many public houses and social clubs, where the gaming machines and spirits were targets often for travelling criminals. Thanks to Eric Young's tuition, as well as guidance from Nicol and Stobo, I was developing into a reasonable interrogator. I enjoyed the interaction and challenge of trying to obtain admissions of criminal involvement from people who obviously would rather not admit to committing crime.

My clearance rate was good thanks to several 'roll-ups', police jargon for multiple clearances for a succession of crimes. In my case, they were for thefts of cars, thefts from cars and breaking into houses. Bosses liked multiple clearances because it increased their overall detection rates and helped stave off criticism from the hierarchy. These clearances were hard-earned and didn't appear just by spinning on the spot three times and saying the magic words. It took time, patience and persistence to manoeuvre someone towards committing themselves to multiple crime admissions.

My learning curve continued. I received notification from the Scottish Fingerprint Office that they had identified a male for a housebreaking enquiry I had. He had left his fingerprints at both the Point of Entry and a touch grab surface within the house. I brought him to the office and, as I was preparing to interview him, asked Nicol what would be the best point in the interview to confront the suspect with the fingerprint evidence.

Nicol gave out a large sigh followed by, 'What do you want to do that for?' using his best teacher explaining an arithmetic sum to a dim pupil voice.

'Because it'll be difficult for him to deny being responsible for doing the housebreaking.'

'So you tell him about the prints and he admits it, what then?'

'Well, charge him and then a case to the [Procurator] Fiscal.'

'What do you think the time gap will be between you reporting the case; proceedings by the Fiscal and a subsequent trial?'

'Could be up to a year.'

'You think there might be a chance that he'll commit any crimes between now and then?'

'Absolutely.'

'You think there's a hope in hell of him leaving his prints again if you let the cat out of the bag and tell him he's been identified by prints for the job you're going to speak to him about tonight?

'Walk him round the houses. Close off every avenue he might have for leaving his prints at the house legitimately, and when he can't come up with one you charge him, but don't mention the prints. He'll be none the wiser and I'll lay you money he keeps leaving them.'

He was 100% correct and it was another lesson learned.

My six-month secondment flew by all too quickly and I found myself undertaking both uniformed and plain-clothes duties for a few months until a permanent vacancy arose within the CID. Ironically, the vacancy I filled was as a replacement for John Stobo who had been promoted to Sergeant. I was once again to be working with Nicol.

5

KEEPING IN TOUCH

While I had been on my six-month secondment as a Trainee Detective Constable an informant had offered up a man, from the Hillhead area of Kirkintilloch, who was involved in dealing quantities of drugs and making a decent living from it. The informant had been reliable previously and I obtained a warrant for the target house, which I raided together with other officers. The informant had, as usual, been accurate and we recovered a variety of drugs, including cocaine, amphetamine and cannabis. He also kept a 'tick list'.

A 'tick list' was then good evidence when establishing that someone was concerned in the supply of drugs, and was basically a means whereby not-so-smart drug dealers listed their clients and their orders. Some were even kind enough to include what prices they had sold the various drugs at. Given modern technological advances such as the Internet, mobile phones and texting, paper 'tick lists' have been rendered obsolete. Many drug dealers continue making the same mistakes, although nowadays they're caught through electronic examination of their dealings. The guy I charged received four years at the High Court as a consequence, but that didn't conclude my contact with him.

One evening while working the backshift with Wullie Nicol, I was contacted by the wife of the dealer, who informed me that her husband would like me to make arrangements to see him in prison. Although pressed she wouldn't elaborate further, except to indicate that he wanted a long talk with me.

Intrigued, I spoke to Iain Mackay the following day, and made him aware of the approach. As luck would have it, while in the Serious Crime Squad, Iain had dealt with the governor of the prison in question. He called the governor and explained the situation. The prison governor indicated that he would be happy to have the prisoner brought

to his office on a bogus routine matter which would afford us the opportunity of a meeting. It was unusual and irregular, but he trusted Iain.

We met the male in question and it turned out a good deal for both
the police and the prison authorities. It transpired that our man had
been keeping his ears open while a prisoner and had some valuable
information on a robbery and drug-dealing in the city. We knew it
would be a one-off deal.

Any further visits would arouse suspicion or increase the possibility
of some inmate working on the Governor's corridor becoming suspicious, which could, potentially, place our man's life in jeopardy, so we
had to obtain everything we possibly could at that meeting.

The governor of the prison was, for his part, equally happy because
he now had someone within the prison who could, through circuitous
means, alert him to potential trouble or incidents within his prison.

I learned from that incident and later, while a Detective Sergeant at
Saracen and Maryhill, utilised variations which, I'll elaborate on later,
to maintain contact with informants who were serving prison sentences.

6

RESPECT FOR THE DEAD

In June 1985, there was a murder in Moodiesburn. I had no real involvement in the actual enquiry which wasn't any kind of 'whodunit'. A thirty-five-year-old male had murdered another man with whom he'd had a relationship. Both were locals and like so many murders involving former intimates, one of whom was consumed by rage, the violence perpetrated was savage in the extreme. The wounds totalled over forty in number.

Until that point I hadn't attended a post-mortem examination of a body; the English term is 'autopsy'. The various crime dramas shown on TV have made the procedure very familiar to laymen. However, at that time, the mysteries of dissection were largely the territory of pathologists and police officers. Iain Mackay decided that it was time for me to broaden my knowledge of exactly how a pathologist's examination was crucial to the structure of a murder enquiry.

At that time, the Detective Chief Inspector was George Dunwoodie. George was bespectacled, had receding hair and was softly spoken. He had an avuncular demeanour except when angry. There was always, however, an elegiac quality about him and I could understand why. His young son had been knocked down and killed as a result of a road accident, which George himself had come across not knowing his son was the victim. I couldn't even begin to imagine the devastation that such a tragedy would invoke.

George had been the Senior Investigating Officer on this particular murder and Iain his Deputy. As was standard procedure at that time the Senior Detective and his Deputy attended the post-mortem examination. Indeed, in those days the detective in charge ran all aspects of the enquiry: from attending the crime scene to viewing the corpse, allocating enquiries to be carried out by junior officers, harvesting of productions or exhibits, arresting the suspect and charging him. He would also be cited to attend court and give evidence. Basically, it was an autocracy.

Nowadays, the Senior Investigating Officer has overall control, but may not even enter the crime scene or see the corpse. Nor will he arrest, interview or charge the suspect and will very rarely, if ever, attend court for evidential purposes.

Major enquiries have undergone a massive change and currently have evolved to a more corporate approach. Technically, if a senior officer with limited investigative experience was appointed as a Senior Investigating Officer, the theory is that they could oversee the incident successfully if they just follow *The Major Incident Enquiry Booklet.*

There are now specialist roles allocated to numerous officers. You have Interview Strategists whose job it is advise the officers nominated to interview the suspect. You have Production Officers whose task is to gather and log items seized from a crime scene, and ensure the integrity of these items when presented at future judicial proceedings.

You have Crime Scene Managers who will be one of the first Detective Officers on the scene and who, in conjunction with photographers, fingerprint officers and forensic scientists, will decide how the scene is to be administered.

There will be an Intelligence Cell staffed by officers who will research the background of the victim, associates and suspects, and will be responsible for the gathering of technical evidence such as CCTV footage or the examination of mobile phone records.

Family Liaison Officers maintain close contact with the family of the victim, and provide them, in a limited fashion, with information on the progress of the enquiry.

Junior Detective Officers will also be tasked with charging the suspect and preparing the case for submission to the Procurator Fiscal.

Then was a far cry from now and, consequently, I found myself standing next to my Detective Inspector and Detective Chief Inspector at the mortuary adjacent to the High Court at the Saltmarket.

Iain Mackay gave me a useful tip prior to the commencement of the dissection. He handed me a Victory V lozenge to counteract any smell emanating from the decaying flesh. I was to keep a packet of those lozenges squirrelled away in my drawer throughout the years, for times when I would be required to attend a post-mortem examination.

Again with the onset of Health and Safety Regulations, officers attending a post-mortem examination today will, in all probability, be stationed behind a thick Plexiglas screen, which affords them a view of proceedings. Then, however, officers stood only a few feet from the working pathologist.

Prior to the post-mortem's commencement, I was utterly astounded to discover that that one of the pathologists scheduled to conduct the post-mortem examination was a petite, blonde, attractive woman who, prior to pulling on her gown, gloves and white Wellington boots, had been attired in an expensive business suit. I'd presumed she was a lawyer and, at the risk of being labelled 'sexist', hadn't even considered that one of the pathologists would be female.

Her name was Marie Cassidy and, currently, she is the State Pathologist for the Republic of Ireland. She was very professional but also had a sunny disposition for such a gruesome job. I was to find her – along with others such as Mike Curtis (now her Deputy in Eire), Jeanette McFarlane and Marjory Black – very professional, helpful and patient over the years.

In fact, I once phoned Marie at the Forensic Medicine Department at Glasgow University, following the admission of a baby to Yorkhill Hospital for Sick Children. There was doubt over whether the baby's injuries were accidental or deliberate. I thought that, although more used to bodies where life is extinct, who better to interpret wounds and injuries than a pathologist.

Even though her department always carried a busy workload and was not technically within her remit, she attended at the hospital and provided me with her analysis of the injuries' origin. That assistance typified the professionalism of her and the other pathologists.

When the post-mortem began, I felt strangely detached as the victim was not someone I knew or was related to, but given that it was utterly foreign to any experience I'd had previously, I found the procedure morbidly fascinating.

I was aware of George at my side saying in his soft voice, 'You okay, Ger?' As it was, I was perfectly okay. There was certainly no danger of my fainting. I accepted it as part of the job I'd signed up to do and it was an experience I would be party to often in the future. Consequently, my reply to George probably sounded too flippant to him and maybe there was a touch of bravado when I responded, 'Just a piece of meat, Boss.'

George then made a comment which was to colour my approach to so many deaths subsequently. He said almost in reprimand, 'No, it's the Temple of the Holy Spirit, Gerard.' George was Catholic and had suffered horrible personal tragedy, but he shouldn't have had to remind me of a basic tenet of the Catholic Faith. Albeit, in my case, 'RC' would have stood more accurately for 'Rotten Catholic', I had had a seminary education and the sanctity of a human body is a basic teaching for Catholics.

Thereafter, I tried to ensure that, although I was there to cast an impersonal eye over the scene and operate professionally at any deaths I attended, I afforded the deceased a degree of respect and even uttered a silent prayer for their repose. My view was that whatever I thought of them personally they were facing a far harsher judgement or sentence than any that could be imposed in this life. I have to confess, however, that there were some death scenes I attended when I couldn't bring myself to extend that Christian charity, owing to the manner they'd lived their lives and the lives they in turn had taken. *Mea culpa.*

7

CARLOS (NOT 'THE JACKAL' ONE)

There'd been a robbery on the Southside of Glasgow and one of the vehicles involved had been stolen from our area, and belonged to a local fish and chip owner called Guido. We received a request to go and speak to Guido to see if he could add anything to the initial statement he'd given to uniform officers, and which might help the robbery enquiry. It was to turn into a *Fawlty Towers* farce.

I was with an officer who was a local lad and, having been born and brought up in the same area as he worked, knew just about everyone and could be a goldmine of information.

I tagged along for the interview with Guido, who spoke English with a heavy Italian accent. It was explained to Guido that his car had been recovered, but had been used in a robbery and we were just trying to establish if there was anything he'd missed in his original statement. There was absolutely no question that the theft was anything other than genuine.

After speaking to Guido for a period and gleaning what he could, the cop I was with finished by saying,

'That'll be you carless then.'

Guido in a puzzled voice, 'No, Guido.'

My colleague continued 'Yeah, yeah, but you're carless.'

'No, no. I Guido.'

'No, no. You're C-A-R-L-E-S-S,' said my colleague, carefully enunciating every letter.

'I G- U- I- D-O,' came the same carefully worded response.

'Guido, I know, but you're CARLESS.'

'You know me. Why are you saying I Carlos?'

'I'm not saying you're Carlos. I'm saying you're Car-less.'

'There! You just say I Carlos.'

51

By this time Guido is looking at the cop like he's on weekend leave from a mental institution. The cop is looking like he's ready to morph into the Hulk out of frustration. The tears are streaming down my face, and the only thing missing was John Cleese emerging from the back shop shouting, 'Don't mention the War'.

The cop in total exasperation said, 'Guido you've no fucking car. You are without a car. You're carless!'

'Ah, sì, sì. No fucking car.'

8

NEW POSSIBILITIES

Around midsummer 1986, I saw an advert in an internal bulletin for vacancies in the Serious Crime Squad. At this point I'd had five and a half years in the police, half of which were in the CID. Looking back it was cheek, but I was keen to become involved in the investigation of serious crime and enquiries, unrestricted by Divisional boundaries.

Although I didn't think I would have any chance of being accepted at that stage in my service. I submitted an application, thinking that it would at least register my interest should any future opportunities arise. To my utter surprise I was invited for interview.

It is in my nature to approach things with a positive attitude but I tempered that with realism, especially when, pre-interview, George Dunwoodie told me that although he had endorsed my application he had qualified his endorsement. He had indicated that he believed me to be a first-class detective with great potential, but felt that I required more Divisional experience before transferring to the Serious Crime Squad.

I was interviewed by a panel of three people consisting of Joe Jackson who was the Detective Superintendent at the Squad, Ronnie Tennant who was his Detective Chief Inspector, and a uniformed female Inspector from the Personnel Department.

Joe later told me I looked keen and hungry and he believed that hunger, allied to the qualities George Dunwoodie had outlined, would outweigh any inexperience, and I got the position.

Joe was a humorous, charismatic, strong personality, and a snappy dresser. Most detective officers purchased their suits from Ralph Slater (a huge menswear outlet in Glasgow city centre). This meant that on any given day at court there were half a dozen officers attired identically. Joe, however, purchased his suits from Robert Dick, a tailor in the East End of Glasgow, who made suits for Sean Connery and Jock Stein.

I found it very interesting that Joe used a football term to describe me as 'lean and hungry'. I'd played football professionally and felt he would have made a very good football manager in the Alex Ferguson mould, if he'd chosen that route. I discovered subsequently that he was very keen on the game.

Joe was a wonderful motivator and would make officers, who had carried out even the smallest role in a major enquiry, feel as if they had been a major contributor to it. He was decisive, confrontational and led from the front. Like Alex Ferguson, however, he was someone you crossed at your peril because he wouldn't forget. Joe was firmly of the view that you were either on his train or under the wheels of the train.

I was given a starting date for joining the Squad and was genuinely thrilled at the thought. Before I left the Division, however, I was to become involved in a murder enquiry; one which I ultimately solved only to find myself the subject of an investigation by Tayside Police for allegedly being complicit in the murder and for dealing drugs.

I was to learn how the taste of a successful result can quickly turn to ashes in the mouth. Although the allegation against me was bizarre and utterly absurd, other subsequent insinuations emerged which were to cast a shadow of doubt in my mind concerning the personal and professional integrity of fellow officers.

The discovery of a dead body set the chain of events in motion.

9

OUTSIDE FORCES

Hudson Cairns was a thirty-three-year-old who came from the Moodiesburn area on the outskirts of Glasgow. About 6'2", with reddish untidy hair and a moustache, he was a heroin user with convictions for possessing controlled drugs, theft and theft by shoplifting.

As with the vast majority of intravenous drug-users, the crimes of dishonesty were, for the large part, a means to facilitate drug usage. Once drug-users have developed a dependency they resort to stealing anything which can be resold, and any money obtained is used to buy more drugs.

Cairns had an elder brother who had also been a drug addict, and who had been the victim of an attempted murder when masked men forced their way into a house in the Easterhouse district of Glasgow and stabbed him repeatedly. He survived that attack but died about a year later, and although the death was not attributed directly to the assault it would probably be fair to say that the incident was a facilitator. That allied to his drug usage would certainly have weakened his immune system severely.

His family believed that the motive for the attack was in revenge for his having been a police informant and, understandably, bore a resentment towards the police and specifically Easterhouse-based officers, since that was where he had allegedly supplied information.

I had never worked Easterhouse and never had dealings with him, nor for that fact with any of his family.

Hudson Cairns was discovered under a piece of broken boarding in July 1986, near a ruined property called Woodhead House, Burnbrae Road, which is a lonely country road several miles from Moodiesburn. He was discovered by a man out walking his dog who noticed a foot protruding from underneath the boarding.

I was at the scene early. The body had evidently been dumped there and covered by the boarding to prevent discovery. Police investigations fortunately benefit from mistakes. Possibly through fear of discovery the body hadn't been completely disguised. Had it been completely covered by the boarding it may have lain undiscovered for months, or longer.

The site of the body dump wasn't too far from the rubbish tip where we'd searched for another alleged murder victim when I'd been a Trainee Detective Constable. Those dumping a human body are never going to do so with any degree of reverence, but I couldn't help reflect on how ignominious it was to discard the body like an empty fish and chip wrapping.

I was seconded to the enquiry team, which was headed by George Dunwoodie. George was assisted by Detective Inspector Wullie McCafferty; a very erudite man and solid investigator. The logical first task for the police when a body is discovered is to establish the identity of the deceased. Once you have identified the person you look to 'timeline'; i.e. establish their known movements prior to the body's discovery, and find out whose company they last kept.

In most cases, the body discovery area is also where officers would begin to knock on doors, or in police parlance, 'commence door-to-door enquiries'. This is a vital part of an enquiry because of the potential goldmine of information it can provide. Given, however, that the body in this case had been dumped in a remote area, with no dwellings nearby, there wasn't a lot that could be done in that respect. The pattern of post-mortem lividity told us that he hadn't died at that location but had been transported there.

Post-mortem lividity, or hypostasis, occurs immediately following death, and causes a purple staining of the skin as a result of gravity drawing the blood to the veins in the more dependent areas of the body. It is defined by how the body is positioned at the moment of death, and so is an indicator in determining whether a body has been moved following death. In this case, there was no great degree of body decomposition so we knew that he hadn't been there too long.

His family having not seen nor heard from him for several days had become concerned, contacted the police and, consequently, we identified our deceased. We established that the clothing he had been wearing at the time of discovery was the same as that he had worn on the last occasion they had seen him; namely, blue jeans, checked shirt and training shoes.

In any major enquiry many people are interviewed and while there are decent people prepared to assist the police, there are also people who don't wish any involvement. In addition, there are people who will lie to the police, either through a desire to cover their own involvement in the crime or, rather strangely, because lying to the police comes naturally, whether the interviewee had any involvement or not.

Often then it becomes a task for the police to establish, 'Who's lying?' 'Who's lying more?' 'Who's lying most?' Family members may also, through familial loyalty, attempt to conceal less savoury aspects of the deceased's life, so it can be like peeling an onion, layer by layer.

In Hudson Cairn's case we had conflicting times of last-known sightings. His family maintained that they had last seen him two days before the body's discovery. Some neighbours, however, were adamant that they had seen him leaving the family home a day later than the date listed by family members. George Dunwoodie wanted to clarify whether the family was attempting to conceal an involvement in, or knowledge of, his death. I was tasked with re-interviewing the family.

As I suggested previously, the family wasn't fond of the police and blamed them for the death of their other son. I was aware that it was an especially sensitive time for the family, but it is also an established fact that the vast majority of murders are committed by intimates. I was in the situation of having to probe and pose awkward questions and it didn't matter how innocuously or otherwise I framed the questions . . . they had to be asked. So I asked.

I didn't shout, threaten or pressure, but I did lay out hypothetical situations and alluded to the possibility that someone within the family might have had a reason for being economical with the true facts. I was happy at the conclusion of the re-interviewing process that, in my opinion, the neighbours were genuinely mistaken and that the timeline for last sighting was as given by the family.

For their part, however, the family had my name, as naturally I'd introduced myself when interviewing them. On their return and when speaking to other family members I wasn't the most popular, given that I'd asked those questions. My name then was uppermost in their minds.

We continued with enquiries and on the Saturday after the discovery of the body we brought in several persons from the Cumbernauld area for interview. We believed Hudson Cairns had gone to their house but didn't know why. It could have been to obtain drugs, to use their house as a place to use drugs, or for a social visit. The post-mortem examination had revealed no sign of body trauma, but it bore fresh injection marks, so cause of death appeared to have been the result of drugs.

Our enquiry was being run from Muirhead Police Office which was a small satellite office. It was convenient, as it was the nearest to the site of the body discovery and to Cairns' family home where our main enquiries were centred. Muirhead office had a wooden-type annexe which the local officers used for their meal breaks, which had a snooker table, dart board and kitchen facilities.

I had been in the office with Kenny Simpson, another Detective Constable, interviewing a potential witness. It wasn't an interview that was advancing the enquiry a great deal. Kenny was a very articulate, methodical investigator with good interview techniques, and it was his turn to take the statement. That left me at a bit of a loose end, so I told Kenny and the witness that I would go out to the annexe and get them both a coffee.

As fate would have it another two Detective Constables, Keith Harrower and Davie Russell, were using the annexe to interview John Ruddy, whose home we knew Cairns had visited. The annexe didn't stretch to individual rooms and certainly not an interview room, so I was listening, while setting up the coffees. They were doing a pretty good job and it seemed that Ruddy had a story to tell, but they had reached a sort of impasse.

It can happen in an interview that the interviewing officers reach a point where something other than the tactics they've agreed on are needed to pry the truth from the interviewee, and that may even involve a third party. I was out of Ruddy's peripheral vision and signalled to Keith and Davie whether they'd mind if I stuck my nose into the inter- view. They gave a subtle nod of approval and I began to question Ruddy.

Now I'm sure I didn't ask anything Keith or Davie hadn't asked, or wouldn't have asked, but sometimes you can strike a rhythm with an interviewee or suspect, and that was what happened. Ruddy began to implicate himself in Hudson Cairns' death.

Up to that point he'd been interviewed as having possible knowledge of Cairns' last known movements, but when he began to place himself at the scene I had to caution him. A caution is required under Law to be given to anyone suspected of a crime. It basically informs them that they can choose to remain silent, but if they decide not to exercise their right to silence then what they say may be used at any future judicial proceedings.

Ruddy was more than happy to speak, even after being informed of his right to silence. He had been friendly with Cairns so probably wanted the mess off his conscience.

Cairns had gone to Ruddy's house in Cumbernauld having obtained or 'scored' heroin. Cairns had a phobia in respect of needles and always enlisted someone to inject or 'jag' him once the solution had been cooked. Ruddy had done exactly that on the night in question and gone to bed leaving Cairns on the couch. Cairns had overdosed and no one had been there to either try and resuscitate him, or to summon medical assistance, and he'd died where he lay. In a panic, Ruddy had placed the body in a car and dumped it where it had been discovered.

I took the information to George Dunwoodie who arrested Ruddy and charged him with murder.

I was delighted, as I felt I'd done a decent job of work and apologised to Kenny Simpson and the witness for never having got those coffees to them.

Things, however, were to sour soon after.

Out of courtesy, and to ensure that they didn't hear the news from either the television or radio first, George and Wullie went to the Cairns' family home to let them know that someone had been arrested for their son's death.

Mr Cairns senior, however, was having none of it. He told George that it was the police who were responsible for his son's death and that whoever we'd charged was innocent.

George and Wullie sat for quite some time and attempted to reason with him, but couldn't make any headway and were basically thrown out of the house. They put it down to Mr Cairns being unable to reconcile having lost another son.

A case was submitted to the Procurator Fiscal's office for the following Monday and Ruddy appeared at the court from custody.

Arrangements were made for trial and I put the incident to the back of my mind and looked forward to taking up my post in the Serious Crime Squad and, hopefully, further challenging enquiries.

In Scots Law serious cases are prosecuted under Solemn Procedure; i.e. the trial is heard in front of a jury, either at the Sheriff or the High Court. To prepare for such cases the Procurator Fiscal Service holds precognitions.

This is a procedure where witnesses scheduled to give evidence are interviewed pre-trial by a Procurator Fiscal Depute, who will examine the statement provided by the witness, to ensure there are no discrepancies or deviations from that obtained by the police. The legal representative of the accused person is afforded the same opportunity.

Precognitions are still conducted nowadays, although their importance has perhaps lessened as, following Article 6 of the European Convention of Human Rights, all and every piece of information, either paper or electronic, is now available to the defence simply by asking.

The Indictment or charge against Ruddy stated that:

On 16 or 17 July 1986, you did insert into the person of Hudson Cairns a syringe containing diamorphine, being a noxious substance, and you did recklessly inject into the person of Hudson Cairns said noxious substance in a quantity dangerous to his health and life whereby he became unconscious, and you did fail to summon medical assistance for him and he died there shortly thereafter, and you did kill him and did thereafter transport his body to Muckcroft Road, Kirkintilloch, place it under a hoarding board and abandon it there.

Given the severity and the unusual nature of the charge, the Procurator Fiscal began interviewing witnesses and one of these was the deceased's father. His statement was progressing extremely well until the very last sentence when Mr Cairns dropped his bombshell, and said: 'I'll never forgive that DC Gallacher from Easterhouse CID, who sold my boy drugs.'

Not surprisingly, the Procurator Fiscal Depute conducting the precognition almost took a convulsive fit, and asked him what he was talking about. Cairns then alleged that it wasn't John Ruddy who had killed his boy but me as I had been supplying him with drugs, and it was those drugs which had killed him.

Naturally, the Procurator Fiscal's office decided that the allegation should be referred to the Deputy Chief Constable for Strathclyde Police, who oversaw all matters involving the conduct and discipline of officers.

The Deputy Chief Constable at that time had, in my opinion, a face which gave the impression that he lacked compassion and lifeless brown eyes, but appearances can be deceptive. I didn't know him well enough to pass any kind of judgement on his nature. He may have been the kindest, most generous man who walked the earth.

To ensure impartiality of investigation the Deputy Chief Constable referred the allegations made by Cairns senior to an outside force (Tayside Police) and, in fairness to him, given the severity of the allegation, he had no other option and I would, in his position, have adopted the same tactic.

I was blissfully unaware all of this was taking place and remained so until sitting at home one afternoon I received a phone call from two colleagues who didn't wish to speak on the phone, but asked me to meet them at an agreed location. I'd worked with both in the CID at Kirkintilloch and two straighter arrows you couldn't meet. Both were polite and quiet, and dressed so soberly they looked like a couple of accountants or bank managers.

I met them and listened open-mouthed and dumbstruck as they told me that they had been interviewed by senior officers from Tayside and each had been obliged to complete a questionnaire, of which I was the subject.

Officers were asked whether they had worked with me previously; in what capacity; whether they had ever known me to have offered drugs for information, or for any other reason; and whether I'd had any kind of dealings with the Cairns family. It was apparently quite a comprehensive questionnaire, and every officer who had worked with me in any capacity in the CID was obliged to complete one.

I sat in the car waiting for one of them to spring the punchline but they were absolutely serious. I remember saying, 'The only thing I'm guilty of is solving a murder.' Here I was, accused of being complicit in a murder through supplying drugs. They were horrific allegations and, other than child molestation, probably the worst type that could be libelled against a police officer.

Once I'd calmed down sufficiently I welcomed a thorough investigation, secure in the knowledge that the allegations were spurious and had neither truth nor substance. What did worry me was whether it would impact on my transfer to the Serious Crime Squad, which fortunately it didn't.

Nicol was interviewed and in his inimitable manner said to the senior officers, 'If you're intending locking him up, you'll end up having to arrest me too.' He was questioned as to why that would be and told them:

Because he's a pest. In fact, that's my nickname for him, 'The Pest'. He isn't a police driver so I had to chauffeur him anywhere he went. Any enquiry he had, I had to be there with him too, and neither of us had any dealings with any Cairns, and he's never been over at Easterhouse.

I was eventually interviewed without forewarning by the investigating officers at Force Headquarters in Pitt Street. It was lunchtime and I was in the squad general office when I took a phone call from Joe Jackson, Head of the Serious Crime Squad who was out dining. He told me that I had an appointment with senior officers from Tayside at 2 p.m. that day, regarding an allegation that I'd handed out drugs for information. Joe said:

'Interesting MO [*modus operandi*], son, and if I thought there was even a smidgen of truth to the allegation you would already have been in the Bar [HMP Barlinnie]. They'll speak to you at 2 p.m.'

The Detective Superintendent and Detective Chief Inspector who spoke to me were thorough and professional, but courteous. They double-checked that I wasn't a police driver. They'd gone over all my previous enquiries and confirmed that I had never worked Easterhouse, nor had any dealings with Cairns or any member of his family. At one point, one of them asked, with a ghost of a smile, whether I had a nickname, and I told him what Nicol called me.

They compiled their report for both the Deputy Chief Constable and the Procurator's Fiscal Office, which exonerated me completely and ensured there were no nasty surprises that would have tainted the judicial proceedings. I attributed the allegation to overwhelming grief on the part of Mr Cairns, and thought that perhaps losing loved ones may have unhinged him slightly. Although it wasn't pleasant being under investigation it hadn't impacted on my family life or sleep patterns. I'd been secure in my innocence.

At the eventual court case, Ruddy was found guilty of the culpable homicide (by injecting him with heroin) of Hudson Cairns; the first such conviction in Scotland, I believe ... and that, I thought, was that.

There was, however, to be a sinister addendum some years later.

While seconded to the Serious Crime Squad, I was at a social evening to celebrate the successful conclusion of a high-profile enquiry I'd been part of. I seldom attended these types of evenings as I found much of the back-slapping hypocritical, but this had been a particularly difficult and extremely well-run enquiry. The enquiry had been overseen by a Detective Chief Superintendent, but he hadn't been the main senior investigator.

The Chief Superintendent had been drinking. He wasn't drunk, but drunk enough to be slightly indiscreet. We were in a corner of the bar which was adjacent to the Sheriff Court in Carlton Place, just across the River Clyde on the south side of Glasgow. He thanked me for the contribution I'd made to the enquiry we were celebrating and then, out of the blue, said words to the effect, and I'm paraphrasing because it knocked me sideways: 'That Hudson Cairns thing wasn't fair on you. The father had the wrong guy, but wasn't far wrong.'

My brain, I think, convinced me initially that I'd misheard, but I don't drink so my senses were crystal clear. I chose the next words carefully.

'There's no way somebody was dishing out kit (heroin), Boss, surely?'

'Sadly, some people doing the wrong thing with the right intentions.'

If I could have kept a cooler head I may have been able to elicit something further, but was so enraged and said, 'How the fuck can supplying kit to junkies be the right intentions, Boss?'

He was a very educated man and, I think, had a Law degree. He obviously realised from my reaction that he'd said too much. Conversation over, he moved to another area of the room. Try as I might, I couldn't subsequently firm up on the conversation.

There were rumours, nothing concrete, that some officers had been providing heroin to drug-users in return for information; never any names and not a shred of proof. If there had been, I would have been happy to put the steel bracelets on them myself. There is no way, irrespective of how you slice that cake, that you could justify dealing heroin. If you've obtained heroin as a result of locking up some dealer, and you then decide to hive some off and use that to elicit information, that's wrong on any level you view it.

I've since asked myself if there was a difference between that and the times I've followed the correct police procedure and dispensed money to drug-users. They provided information and I knew that, in all likelihood, they intended to use the informant money to purchase drugs, but I had always offered them the chance of rehab or assistance, so to my way of thinking there was most definitely a discernible difference.

Realistically, it's not even a question. There was a system in place for handling informants and in the main I followed those procedures. Yes, I did deviate on occasion, and I'll highlight those instances later, and people can judge for themselves whether I was right to do so. What I didn't do was exercise my police powers to take drugs off the street, charge someone with drug offences, then turn around and hand out drugs like sweets from an ice cream van.

If the allegations had substance I wonder at what point any officer involved had their moral compass corrupted. Did they deem it pious corruption? How did the system operate? Was there a sliding scale of drug-supply, based on the value of the information?

'Sorry, that's only worth a ten bag.'

'Yeah, that'll get you a quarter ounce.'

'Listen, we're a bit short, but if you can wait an hour or so we've a raid planned, so we'll be able to re-up.'

Was there a health warning issued?

'Listen, we have to tell you that the Surgeon General has indicated that injecting heroin is bad for your health.' Or, 'Listen, careful how you go because we don't know if the drug dealer we got this from, when we raided his place, practised good quality control on his product. He may be using rat poison as a cutting agent.'

Me? I preferred an uninterrupted sleep.

* * *

My first day in the Serious Crime Squad followed the same pattern as when I began a new position in the police and was accompanied by a supposedly smart comment, this time delivered by a Detective Sergeant and for the amusement of the general throng.

He spoke from the side of his mouth, which was a trait I was to see applied mostly in the Squad, and seemed to be unique to those who regarded themselves as 'big city type detectives'. I found it hilarious, as it made them look as if they'd stepped off the set of a bad 1930s spy movie.

Then, the Serious Crime Squad operated from the fourth floor of Police HQ at Pitt Street. There was a large general office where everyone tended to gather in the morning. At any given time the various subdivided 'teams' could be involved in assisting Divisions in the investigation of murders, or series crimes (crimes that display a repeat pattern), or one of a dozen duties.

Officers would first report to the Squad office, sign the duty book, collect car keys, grab a quick tea or coffee and then head out to their respective enquiries. Consequently, there were always sizeable numbers.

The Detective Sergeant asked loudly where I was from and on my answering 'Balornock' responded, 'And you've no criminal Record? You must be some runner or some liar.' It was a good line and got a good laugh, and I could appreciate it. Having a football dressing-room background, where any sign of weakness was pounced on by players, I was used to the jokes, testers and wind-ups.

I let the laughter subside and casually threw back, 'No, just fortunate that any cops I had dealings with were "cocks" like you'. Deathly initial silence, like the westerns when the stranger walks into the saloon, but it was followed by as good a laugh as his original comment.

I loved the time that followed in the Serious Crime Squad, also known as 'The Serious', 'The Squad' and, to villains, 'The Mob'. I had perhaps rather naively believed that the Squad would be populated by the cream of Strathclyde detectives, and in some instances that was absolutely the case.

However, as with every group of workers, or professionals, be they police officers, lawyers, doctors, joiners, plumbers or whatever, they encapsulated the varying degrees of skills, dedication and incompetence. There were, as I've indicated some first-rate detectives working there and I managed to broaden my experience greatly, owing to the nature of the enquiries I became involved in. I use the line 'became involved in' specifically, because I always tried to get my nose into the enquiry trough, but the same charge could not always be libelled against some fellow 'Squaddies'. In conjunction with the excellent officers, there were also the chancers and the poseurs.

There was a group known collectively as 'The Nolan Sisters' (although they were all male), after that pop group's hit record, 'I'm in the Mood for Dancing'. Whenever they were scheduled on late or night duty, the latter part of the late or the first part of the night found them at one of the city's dance halls. No doubt they were acquiring criminal intelligence.

The 'side of the mouth' group viewed themselves as being the 'seen it, done it' group. They generally stood in small groups in the corner, with their mouths twisted to one side in conversation, ensuring no one outside of their inner sanctum overheard their nuggets of information.

There were the poseurs who loved to appear at Divisions armed with their clipboard and declaring 'Serious Crime Squad' for effect. They were content to float on the periphery or 'dinner jacket' bounds of an enquiry, as opposed to the 'donkey jacket' or hand-dirtying areas. They did just enough to ensure they were part of the overtime gravy train without actually contributing practically.

There were also the downright incompetents who had been identified by their Divisional CID as such, and then quickly dumped onto the Squad.

Where I fitted into this particular jigsaw was indeed a puzzle for my new colleagues. I was a total anomaly to them. I didn't drink, smoke or gamble, wasn't yet qualified to drive police vehicles, and had only five and a half years' police service. To be a member of a Divisional CID with that service was quick, but to be seconded to the Serious Crime Squad with no service to speak of was unique.

I think if they hadn't known that Joe Jackson had approved my recruitment they would have figured me as working undercover for the 'rubber heels', or more accurately the department of the police dealing with Complaints and Discipline.

The following three years found me, among the various murders and robberies that are sadly so much a part of Glasgow life, investigating the abduction and rape of a four-year-old girl; the search for a missing child at a holiday camp; a terrorist incident that led me to Mull and later Perth High Court; the shooting of members of the McGovern family; a murder which was almost dismissed as natural causes; an abandoned newborn baby, left to die in an idyllic tourist spot; a murder enquiry with no body; and a siege at HMP Barlinnie.

10

IS THAT SMOKE I SMELL?

Having begun my secondment in September 1986, most of the remainder of that year was spent on either driving or detective training courses, although I did have an opportunity to interact with one of the most powerful Triad members in Glasgow.

Before I began in the Squad there had been the murder of a Chinese male, Philip Wong, which bore all the hallmarks of a Triad execution. It had taken place in the Garnethill area of Glasgow, and Mr Wong had suffered horrific injuries inflicted by sharp-edged weapons.

In enquiries, police like to retain items of 'specialist knowledge' from the public; pieces of information which would only be known to someone who was involved in, or had intimate knowledge of, the enquiry under investigation. This helps to ensure that someone is not making a false confession.

For example, if an item had been stolen from a victim during a murder, or an unusual means had been used to commit the murder, then the police would expect the suspect to know these details. Consequently, this would strengthen the veracity of any admissions.

In Philip Wong's case, the assassins used a very simple but ingenious method to delay Wong as he attempted to enter his car, which allowed them the opportunity to approach him from cover and carry out the murder. They were a four-man assassination team and members of the Soi Fong Triad: one from Liverpool; one from Dublin; and two from Hong Kong.

Wullie Williamson was one of the Detective Sergeants in my unit when I joined the Squad, and had worked the Philip Wong enquiry prior to his transfer to the Squad. Like most detectives involved in unsolved enquiries, it rankled. So it was that on my first night shift, I found myself with him in a Chinese restaurant, in the centre of the city.

We were speaking to a tall, immaculately dressed Chinese male who, Wullie had told me beforehand, was known in Triad parlance as the 'White Paper Fan'. There were two main Triad gangs in Glasgow, the Soi Fong and Wo Sing Wo. When disputes arose, the 'White Paper Fan' would be called on to calm the troubled waters, before or after things became messy.

Wullie was ever hopeful that he might entice this person to drop some kind of information nugget that would help the enquiry. Talk about inscrutable! He didn't occupy his position within the Triad organisation for nothing.

However, I'm sure that he would have been no different from any other villain I've encountered. Irrespective of how far up the food chain they were placed, if it saved their skin they would look to make a deal.

By seeing this man's face and getting to know the vehicles he used, Wullie was ensuring that when I saw him around the city centre I would make a point of stopping him. So many cops give villains too much credit. It infuriated me when I'd hear them say that 'they would never be stupid enough to do that', or 'they wouldn't make such and such a mistake' and, consequently, neglect to stop them in their cars, or from going about their business. My view always was that you make things happen when you show your face around.

That married criminal whose car you've stopped may just have a female (or sometimes male) passenger with him that he'd rather his wife didn't know about. Or, he may have accrued enough points on his licence that another offence would push him over the limit, and he really needs that car, so he may well be prepared to offer up some valuable information. Sure, you'll chase a lot of leprechauns, but at some point you'll catch the one with the crock of gold.

In days gone by, there were occasions when, like the magicians Siegfried and Roy, one could harness the leprechaun with the crock of gold by means of a little misdirection.

Hypothetically, a criminal who had intimated he would never speak to the police may have had his view altered had he found himself placed in the following circumstances.

If we call our criminal 'James', although the term 'criminal' is rather inaccurate because, although he possessed a great deal of criminal information, he himself had very little in the way of 'form', which is police speak for criminal convictions.

Let's say, I had encountered 'James' in the course of my duties and had tried to 'sign him on', which is again police speak for the recruitment of an informant, but 'James' declined, indicating that, no offence, but he'd never speak to the police.

Undeterred, he may have been asked to meet for a drink and 'James' may have agreed saying, 'I like you and your patter is good, so I'll go for a drink, but there's no way I'll talk to you'. James may have been under the misapprehension that the CID officer was on duty, so wasn't drinking (albeit he was teetotal anyway), but, 'Hey, that was no reason James couldn't have a couple of drinks'.

After a couple of hours of convivial chat and a final attempt to sign James on, which was rebuffed good-naturedly with a, 'You're determined, I'll give you that,' the detective indicated to James that he had to get back to work, but finished by giving James a little analogy.

'James you buy house insurance because you hope the house never burns down, but it is reassuring to know you have it just in case.' With that parting shot, he headed back to his office, in the hope that he would shortly receive a phone call about James.

After the officer had left, James got into his car, but hadn't driven any real distance before lo and behold he was 'blue lit' by two friendly, neighbourhood Traffic Officers who, coincidentally, happened to be well-known to the detective. James was breathalysed using the old glass tube containing crystals and plastic bag method, which involved the suspect blowing into the bag, and if the crystals turned green, it meant the person had failed the test and would be arrested, conveyed to a police office, and a more accurate procedure commenced to determine the blood-alcohol levels in the system.

Now, the officers would ensure James remained seated in the driver's seat when stopped and would hand him the bag and tube while they stood at the side of the car. James seated in his car would hand the bag back to the police officer once he had blown into it. Consequently, the officers' torsos, hands and head would, in turn, be largely out of sight to James when they took the bag and tube from him. This meant James wouldn't be able to see the colour of the crystals and wouldn't actually know whether he'd failed the test.

The officer broke the bad news to him. 'I'm afraid you've failed the test, sir. You're under arrest.'

Now, in poker parlance, we arrived at the crucial 'show and tell'.

James could either accept he was heading to a police office for suspected drunk driving, or . . .

'Do you know so and so in the CID?'

I think perhaps he'd caught a whiff of smoke and realised his house had just caught fire.

'Aye,' was the nonchalant reply from one of the Traffic Officers. 'Why?'

'I was with him just before I got pulled over. Could you no maybe contact him?'

James was very grateful for the detective's help in quashing a possible drunk-driving charge, albeit he had never actually failed the breath test, nor did he ever know that his stop by the Traffic Officers hadn't been his random misfortune (although he may now). In return, he provided a wealth of criminal information on murders, robberies, firearm recovery and long firm frauds.

11

THERE'S A RIOT GOING ON

January 1987 began in riotous fashion...literally. HMP Barlinnie exploded following weeks of escalating tension and, as with so many flashpoints, began with a fight.

It would appear that with two inmates involved in a fight, a third, Sammy Ralston, allegedly tried to either intervene or join in. For his troubles, he was escorted to the 'silent room', which was contained within a building known as 'the Wendy House'.

Prisoners, believing that Ralston had endured a beating at the hands of prison officers, began to protest, and the protest quickly morphed into a physical confrontation with prison officers. So violent did the protest become that some officers locked themselves into cells only to be faced with prisoners threatening to 'burn them out'. Some managed to escape, but, finally, in what must be a prisoner officer's worst nightmare, five guards were taken hostage.

Along with other Squad members I was seconded to the enquiry and I suppose I contributed as much as any police officer to the overall enquiry, which wasn't actually that much. The police role amounted to evidence-gathering, which would allow the submission of relative criminal charges against the individuals involved, once the incident had (hopefully) reached a safe conclusion. The resolution to the conflict lay predominantly with the Prison Service.

There appeared to be eleven prisoners holding the officers hostage although a twelfth prisoner was subsequently charged. He claimed, rather bizarrely, that he had taken Valium stolen from the prison pharmacy and had slept throughout the rioting. This twelfth male was never seen on the roof during the protests.

Five officers were originally seized, but three were taken to the loft space and from there to the roof. The prisoners masked their identities initially, and shouted their protestations from the roof, concerning the Prison Governor, alleged brutality within the system, and how they wanted to negotiate. All of which was seized on hungrily by the gathered media.

An attempt was made by a 'riot squad' consisting of forty prisoner officers in riot gear to rescue their colleagues, but this faltered and failed when the officers tried to ascend the stairwells. The prisoners in classic battle tactics held the higher ground and had, in the interim period and through wanton destruction, armed themselves with concrete, bricks and slates, which they rained down on the officers.

It was brave of the officers to attempt the rescue, but if I'm correct some of the group did not have formal riot training, which may have been a contributory factor in the unsuccessful attempt. They were forced to flee, leaving behind riot shields, batons and various pieces of equipment which the rioters retrieved gleefully.

The previous year a similar type of riot had taken place at Perth Prison and the then Prime Minister, Margaret Thatcher, had authorised the use of the SAS to free the officers who were being held hostage, and they utilised their arguably greatest weapons – stealth and surprise. In the early hours of the morning, when the prisoners were at their most tired and vulnerable, they stormed the roof and disorientated the rioters, tossing stun grenades and 'flash-bangs'.

Thereafter (according to the rioters), the SAS proceeded to dispense some ultra-violence using batons. At the time, the use of the SAS was not acknowledged, although the prisoners realised who had overcome them. Naturally, through jailhouse means of communication, this had filtered down to other prisons.

Consequently, the Barlinnie rioters were in possession of this information and were openly challenging the authorities to send in the SAS, in the belief that forearmed with knowledge, equipment and fuelled with stimulants from the pharmacy, they were in a better defensive position. They may have had a point as the terrain was favourable to the rioters. It was January and bitterly cold, and the roof was a slippery proposition, although that didn't seem to inhibit some of those on the roof, some of whom scampered about the angular roof areas with the agility of a monkey or a trapeze artist.

The prison authorities had left the heating on in the loft space but otherwise the temperatures were sub-zero. Consequently, the authorities had little option other than negotiation which, in fairness, would always be the logical option. Any right-minded person would wish the incident concluded without injury to officers or prisoners. I'm sure the hostages' colleagues would have been incandescent with rage and frustration at the sight of fellow officers being paraded like tethered goats and forced to plead openly for help, but given that the rioters had, literally, secured an advantageous position, the authorities faced little other option.

Part of our remit was to identify the rioters and through the collation of criminal histories and intelligence, supplemented by interviews with family members, attempt to profile their likelihood of physically harming the hostages.

There were some violent and nasty pieces of work including murderers among them, but some (un)likely lads too. I was able to identify Hugh Twigg from the Easterhouse area, as a couple of years previously I'd travelled to England, where he'd fled to avoid arrest under warrant. He most certainly was not Gangster Number 1, that's for sure.

Be that as it may, any hostage situation has the potential to escalate towards violence, but thankfully the hostages were released in staggered fashion, with the final hostage released in exchange for hot food and (non-alcoholic) beverages. As part of the agreement to end their protest, the hostages made three demands which were acceded to:

- unbiased legal advice;
- independent medical examination; and
- access to family and relatives visiting the prisoner after the siege.

When they were off the roof and ensconced in individual cells, I was taken, along with others from the Squad, to question them regarding their presence on the roof. To reach the cells we were led – (Wellington) booted and suited – through B Hall. If someone had told me it was the aftermath of a B-52 strike I wouldn't have argued, so great was the devastation. That human beings, armed with little more than hands and anger, could have wrought that damage was breathtaking.

Floors were flooded, hence, the Wellingtons; stairwells had collapsed; there was twisted metal where there'd once been handrails; cell doors had been wrenched off and pitched over gantries; great gouges of brickwork were missing from cell walls; not a sink or toilet was left in position. To paraphrase an old *News of the World* advertising slogan, 'All human rage was here'.

Little wonder the rescue attempt by colleagues had faltered. The *60 Minute Makeover* team would certainly have struggled to hit their deadline.

We were accompanied by some Scene of Crime photographers who also videotaped our interviews with the prisoners to document that they had no injuries. Of course, the responses to our questions weren't exactly expansive. One prisoner I spoke to, Ernie Barrie, was only too willing to tell us that he hadn't participated in the hostage-taking or rioting. Instead, he claimed to have used the opportunity to stage his own protest independent of the others.

He had proclaimed loudly to be innocent of the crime for which he'd been sentenced, namely robbery. As it transpired latterly, following a *Rough Justice* type television programme by the BBC, the Appeals Court believed him, and he was pardoned for that particular crime. He seized the opportunity of a fresh start with both hands, by murdering someone years later and being given a life sentence.

Along with a Detective Sergeant Mike Johnston I was tasked with interviewing two of the three prison officers who had been rooftop captives. We first spoke to a younger man in his twenties. It had been a horrific experience for him, but we had to note the statement, even though we emphasised several times that we could take it in stages or over the course of days if he preferred, but he wanted it over and done with. It took us somewhere in the region of five hours to conclude and we actually had to swap over the task of noting it, as our hands cramped.

The mind is a wondrous instrument. I believe that many boxing matches or races are won in the mind before any physical contests even begin. The mind can limit pain, and when the body is physically at its limit, can summon unknown reserves to transcend seemingly hopeless conditions. I'm sure, conversely, that the mind, if not controlled, has the capacity to inspire abject terror, hence the use of psychological warfare. The implied threat of all facets of physical harm can have as much, or an even more devastating, effect than actual torture.

We spoke to our second interviewee at a police station on the north side of the city. He had been the last hostage to be released and, indeed,

75

had refused the opportunity to be released earlier, when he'd given his place to another officer who he felt was not coping with the ordeal. Although unable to appreciate what the officers had endured, one could understand how this man's control of his mind allowed him to deal with the situation. He had a composed, calm demeanour and his facial features indicated strength of character.

Again, Mike and I had to swap writing duties in a statement that ran to over eighty pages, but which was crucial in assisting in the compilation of charges against the rioters in relation to their treatment of the hostages.

My involvement in enquiries such as this was one of the reasons I'd wanted to join the Serious Crime Squad, and it reaffirmed my belief that I'd made the correct decision to apply. Had I remained at Division, my opportunities to participate in unique major enquiries may well have been limited by Divisional boundaries, but in what was to be standard fare in my police career, I'd have plenty of rough to abrade the smooth.

12

'SOMETIME, LITTLE BLOOD'

The first of April brought the report of a murder and sadly it wasn't an April Fool's joke.

We had just begun our night shift tour when we were asked to assist Divisional Personnel over at Drumchapel. A twenty-year-old boy had been murdered at the Linkwood Bar. We assisted by canvassing for witnesses and noting statements from customers who had been in the pub, although it appeared to have happened in the car park just outside the pub.

Given we were night shift, we could only provide initial assistance. A day shift team would continue the enquiry, but the reason I mention this particular murder was because it was the first time I'd seen such a wound. After the body had been photographed 'in situ' by the Scene of Crime photographer, the pathologist who had been called to the scene conducted an initial examination.

The only visible wound was a small puncture, almost indiscernible, high up on the torso and slightly off-centre, but the heart had been pierced and the young man hadn't travelled more than twenty yards following the stabbing before collapsing and dying. From the blood loss, or rather the distinct lack of it, I finally understood the casualty surgeon's remark to me as he'd left the murder scene in Springburn those years previously.

The dichotomy that represented the frailty and resilience of the human frame always amazed me. On one hand, you'd witness a life lost to a wound one almost struggled to find. Conversely, a victim would survive a grotesque butchering, although in the latter cases, survivors owed their lives almost completely to the interventionist skills of the surgeons and medical staff that had treated them.

13

BROTHERS AND ARMS

Five nights later, on the same night shift week, I continued to broaden my experiences. This time it extended to ascertaining just how many people could cram into a ten feet by six feet toilet area.

At least, that was what it appeared when we attempted to question the patrons of The Vulcan Bar, a Springburn pub, after Stephen McGovern and his cousin James, had been shotgunned in the face while in the pub. If we were to believe the customers, just about all of them seemed to have been in the toilet when the shooting occurred. It is a pity they hadn't forewarned *The Guinness Book of Records*, as they may have collected an award for their effort. The certificate would have blended nicely with the very trendy blood-dappled walls. The shooting apart, the pub could have been renamed 'The Flying Tumbler Lounge'; a ski resort it wasn't.

Stephen was twenty years old and James fifteen at the time, and the next logical question would be, 'What was a fifteen-year-old doing in a pub at eleven o'clock at night?' And on a school night at that.

The McGovern family were a criminal enterprise who had managed to prosper in the early 1980s as a result of their having travelled to Continental Europe, shoplifting and 'dipping' tills*. Once there, they'd use the equivalent of registered post or recorded delivery to post their gains home to Scotland, so had no incriminating evidence in their possession when passing through Customs. It had proved very lucrative.

Cy McWilliams, a senior officer stationed at Baird Street, had hounded them and had some success owing mainly to Cy having an informant in their midst. Once Cy, who had been a detective most of his police

---

* Thieves working as a team and using distraction methods on a staff member which allows an accomplice to steal from the cash register.

career, transferred back to the CID within another Division, a lot of the information he had been sourcing was lost.

Their criminal enterprises continued to prove very lucrative in the intervening years. That they had managed to flourish was, in my opinion, partially the result of a police *laissez-faire* attitude, albeit a reluctant one, on the part of the working officers.

The fact that they weren't hounded and hassled at every turn had its origin in a strange policy, operated by sections of the senior management within the Division in which the family lived. In a chicken and egg scenario, the policy in turn derived precisely from working officers attempting to disrupt the family, as well as other up and coming 'names' on the circuit such as Russell Stirton and Paul Ferris.

Both Ferris and Stirton would subsequently become known to the general Scottish public through a combination of police involvement and high profile media articles. Both spent their formative years in tough Glasgow housing schemes. Stirton amassed a fortune from the importation of pornography and alleged drug involvement. Through legal recourse he is currently demanding the return of circa £5 million in assets seized by Scottish prosecuting authorities under the Proceeds of Crime legislation.

Ferris stood trial for the murder of a former childhood friend who was the son of a notorious Glasgow gangster. When shot dead the victim had been on release from prison a few short hours. At the end of the trial – which at that time was the longest running in Scots Law – Ferris was found not guilty. He currently classifies himself as a security consultant.

Russell Stirton, who married a McGovern sister, took part in a BBC documentary in which he claimed that a Drug Squad officer had handed him heroin and asked him to 'plant' the drug on someone. The only fly in that ointment was that Stirton had no audio evidence to substantiate the claim and, strangely, he was out of sight for a full two minutes between meeting the officer and returning to the camera crew with this wrap of heroin.

The officer alleged to have handed this wrap to Stirton gave evidence at a subsequent trial involving Paul Ferris, who was charged with possession of a sawn-off shotgun. The officer's evidence, that he had never handed anything to Stirton, was accepted for what it was – the truth.

Paul Ferris had gone on trial with a plain-clothes officer from Baird

Street Police Office, jointly charged with possession of a sawn-off shotgun, with Ferris claiming that he was a victim of the police. He was not believed and was sentenced to three years in prison for the firearm charge.

Now it is a given, that a hard-working officer will always draw complaints from the criminal fraternity if he is doing his job properly. I'm not talking about complaints of assault or incivility, but of constantly hounding and trying to disrupt their criminal dealings. I've been the subject of such complaints from various criminals, including Tam McGraw, when he didn't like the idea that I saw him as the target rather than him give up some minnow trade-off that he fed other officers. It is a tactic employed by criminals under threat and pressure from hard-working officers, to lodge a complaint against them in the hope that it deters the officer(s) from continuing their attempts to pursue and disrupt.

In the case of the McGoverns and Stirton, the end result of the claims and counterclaims of underhand tactics, alleged frame-ups and attempts to tape-record police officers was that the senior management decided that officers drawing complaints from these high-profile criminals would be subject to transfer to other Divisions. That was whether there was substance to the complaint or not.

Given that these transfers were generally to Divisions far from where they lived, officers began to wonder if it was worth the hassle and, in many cases, did not carry out the stops, checks and searches that *may* have provided an opportunity to slow or disrupt the criminals' climb to prominence. When that sort of policy flourishes the resulting effect is that you turn around one day and find that the shoplifters and car ringers have suddenly become major drug dealers within the city. They have also managed to construct so many cut-outs between themselves and the filth they pedal, that it is extremely difficult to build a case against them.

Within the Vulcan Bar any potential witnesses were holding their peace (although, I'm sure there were a few who wished they'd been holding 'a piece' when the shooting started), and we were unable to access either of the brothers as they were undergoing surgery. They had been conveyed to the Glasgow Royal Infirmary for initial assessment and treatment, but had been transferred from there to the plastic surgery unit, then located at Canniesburn Hospital.

I knew a woman who had connections to the pub so I called her but

I had to first find a phonebox to make the call as, in the 1980s, mobile phones were a rarity restricted to stockbrokers, and the size of breeze blocks. Once I'd found a phonebox on Springburn Road and called her I found she'd already heard about the shooting. She could tell me that there had been at least two involved and that they were from the Milton and Balornock schemes.

Pat Durkin, my Detective Inspector at the time, knew I was from Balornock and that I knew it like the back of my hand, so that was where I was dispatched, along with another officer to check for the suspect's car and see whether he was home. The suspect lived near a pub called The Cairn. He wasn't home and there was no sign of his car, so we decided to check the surrounding area.

As we drove down Wallacewell Road, we saw that one of the other McGovern brothers, Tony, obviously had the same idea. He was standing beside a dark-coloured BMW on the opposite side of the road. His own car was parked behind it.

When he saw us Tony threw something that glinted into the BMW and the car sped off. By the time we could get turned around and pull up beside Tony he was leaning nonchalantly against his own car. The BMW was well away.

It had raced up a short service road that led into the Barmulloch area which opened up endless opportunities for secondary escape routes. We put a look-out broadcast over the radio for officers in the area, but the best description was for a dark BMW and it wasn't traced. These days, police broadcasts are encrypted, but then they could be picked up by taxis and ordinary car radios tuning into the police frequency.

I knew there was no chance of Tony being honest with us so there was no point in insulting either of us.

'Let me guess? Would that have been a tool that you threw in to the BMW?' I deliberately used the word 'tool'; the slang for a firearm.

'Aye, a spanner. I had a problem with ma car.'

He was average height, of slight build, with fair hair cut in a wedge style popularised by the boy bands of that period. He didn't smoke or drink but until his death, in 2000, he always had a top-of-the-range type car.

'Is the car okay now?'

'Aye, fine.'

'I'd better check it to make sure. I wouldn't like to see you stranded.'

'No need. It's fine.'

'I know there's no need, but I'm going to. So give me the keys.'

He handed them over but there was nothing incriminating in it, as I knew there wouldn't be. Unfortunately, when I was handing his keys back I dropped them down a street drain. I apologised for being so clumsy and told him that as we'd been instructed to remain in the area all night we weren't in a position to offer him a lift.

I did tell him, however, that if he gave us the name of his pal in the BMW I'd have a police unit call at the house and let whoever owned it know he needed a lift. Surprisingly, he didn't take up the offer. He flagged down a black hackney taxi and off he went.

The car was still there at 6 a.m. when we called it quits.

Both shooting victims survived. James suffered horrible facial disfigurement, while the same shotgun blast blew off part of Stephen's ear.

Sometime later, the same female source gave me the background history behind the shooting. Apparently, the gunman had been with his girlfriend in a Springburn pub, which the McGoverns used as a gang hut. A drink had been thrown over the girl, and when her boyfriend objected he was beaten up.

An elder relative impressed upon him the need to show he could stand up for himself, and arranged to leave a shotgun in the boot of a car near to The Vulcan. The elder relative emphasised that the shotgun would kick when fired, and to make sure the stock was held tightly against the shoulder.

The gunman positioned himself at the same phonebox I had used to call the informant, and took a call telling him whereabouts in the pub his targets were located. He walked in, took aim and loosed the gun. Whether through nerves or adrenalin, however, he forgot about the kick and that sent most of the blast high.

Intercepting Tony that night deprived him of his initial bloodlust, but it appears someone may have decided revenge would be more satisfying when carried out calmly and pre-planned.

Perhaps it was simply coincidence and unrelated, but two weeks later a man in the Milton area almost had his legs literally blown off by a shotgun blast, near his house in Milton. He would probably have lost both legs but for two factors.

Again, a gunman failed to hold the weapon properly, and the kick sent the blast downwards where it struck the pavement and ricocheted into the limbs. The second factor was down to one of those surgeons whose skills I praised earlier.

A few months after that shooting, a regular five-a-side football was interrupted by masked people and a Balornock man was stabbed and slashed to within an inch of his life.

Once again, only the surgeon's skill prevented it being a murder enquiry.

None of the victims were able to assist police enquiries, and the other participants in the match all appeared to have been ball-fixated during the attack, and couldn't describe the attackers. Strange that.

I would have no further involvement with Tony for almost a decade. The next time our paths crossed was when he had a Wild West shootout in the middle of the day (but not quite *High Noon*) in Finlas Street in the Saracen district of Glasgow. Once again a family member was involved, but there was no brotherly love lost this time as it was one of his brothers he was exchanging shots with.

14

'A BASTARD VERDICT'

On 12 April, I was sitting at home watching the *News at Ten* and was shocked by one of their leading stories, which concerned the seizing from the street and sexual molestation of a four-year-old girl in the Hamilton area of Lanarkshire. I watched as Alex Cowie, the Detective Chief Inspector in charge, was interviewed and made his plea for witnesses and information.

That type of crime was and remains one of the most horrible a human being can perpetrate on another. It is especially heinous when the vulnerability and innocence of the victim is factored into the equation.

If my memory of the theological teaching I received is correct, Christ in the Bible forgave adultery, fornication and dishonesty, but said that those who corrupted the innocence of a child would be better off if they had a millstone tied around their neck and were drowned in the depths of the sea. I don't suppose condemnations of certain crime types come much greater than that. In his interview, Cowie indicated that the child had been playing near her home when she had been seized by a lone male and subjected to a sexual assault.

I found myself seconded to the enquiry a day or so later, along with other Squad members. I couldn't (obviously) know it at the time, but as a consequence I was to solve the enquiry (maybe); face a grilling from the Detective Chief Superintendent in charge of the Squad and face an allegation from an eminent QC at the subsequent High Court trial that I'd obtained admissions illegally.

I found that Alex Cowie had utilised HOLMES, the Home Office Large Major Enquiry System; a computerised system which had been tested and subsequently implemented by British Police Forces following the Yorkshire Ripper murder hunt.

Once Peter Sutcliffe had been charged and convicted of the murders of thirteen women, the manner in which the Yorkshire Constabulary had conducted the enquiry was reviewed. The review established that so large was the scale of the enquiry that the 'manual' or paper system, which had been utilised by forces up to that point, was unable to cope with the level of information and lines of enquiry, which such an enquiry generated.

HOLMES was able to quickly cross-reference and disseminate large flows of information. Its use by Strathclyde Police was then in its infancy. Now, it is installed immediately a major enquiry occurs.

Partnered again with Mike Johnston, we found that a man who lived near to the victim and knew her claimed he had seen a man picking the child up in his arms, when she was just a short distance from her house, and carry her to the entrance corridor of flats. He claimed that he presumed the man had been a relative and was joking around with the child, and described him as six feet tall and in his twenties.

This formed the initial focus of the enquiry owing to the fact that there were no other witnesses at that point and the child was hospitalised. A member of what is now known as the Family Protection Unit sat at her bedside and tried to cultivate a relationship with her, hoping that, eventually, the child would trust her enough to speak about the incident.

She was, however, too traumatised by her ordeal to want to verbalise what had happened and this, in turn, would ultimately make it extremely difficult to ascertain a scene of crime, obtain an accurate description of her attacker, or identify him. Additionally, we also had negligible forensic evidence, which in a pre-DNA period compounded the degree of difficulty in solving the crime.

The nearby presence of a travelling fairground was a hindrance to progress as it swelled our list of potential suspects. Fairgrounds, traditionally, draw a cross-section of ne'er do wells.

MO is the 'mode of operation' or 'method of working'. In crimes such as murder, robbery, sexually motivated or series and serial crimes the police will obtain a list of 'MO suspects'; that is, a list of persons who have used a similar method to commit the crime(s) under investigation. The people on these lists will then be interviewed and their alibis checked, in an attempt to eliminate them as suspects.

Cowie had obtained a list of sex offenders and, as one facet of the enquiry, the list would be worked through by members of the enquiry team. Other lines of enquiry involved knocking on doors in an attempt to supplement the sighting of the suspect by the male neighbour.

We canvassed the area where our male witness had indicated the abduction occurred, but failed to locate anyone who could corroborate his version of events. The situation became further obfuscated when various other potential witnesses contacted the enquiry team, claiming to have seen the girl playing alone about one mile from her home at 9.15 p.m., which was the time he'd supposedly witnessed the incident.

Given that these latter witnesses seemed credible, the focus of the enquiry was switched from near her home to the area where these witnesses had seen the little girl wandering alone. This confusion led to a confrontation between Alex Cowie, and the Detective Chief Superintendent, John Fleming.

Alex went on leave – which had been arranged long before the enquiry began – and while he was gone John Fleming requested an update on the progress of the enquiry. At a briefing, he asked which members of the enquiry team believed our initial witness's version of events and who believed the other witnesses. From the Hudson Cairns experience, I knew the confusion that could be wrought by well-meaning but mistaken witnesses, but in this case it so happened that I believed those who claimed to have seen our victim a mile away from the alleged initial sighting.

Fleming decided that those on the team who believed the initial witness should re-interview the witnesses who claimed to have seen the victim a mile from her home, and vice versa. The end result was that on 22 April, almost ten days into the enquiry, our main initial witness and his girlfriend were arrested, charged and appeared in court for wasting the time of the police. This and the fact that our little victim still would not speak about her ordeal (despite the best efforts of the policewoman and the victim's grandmother) meant that things hadn't progressed as we'd hoped.

Shortly thereafter, Mike Johnston began a period of annual leave which was partly the catalyst in my chain of events. As HOLMES was a new concept, I was inexperienced in exactly how the system functioned. Mike though had a better understanding than me. In this system, officers are allocated 'actions' or tasks, which would range from being instructed to take a statement from a witness, to confirming an alibi or eliminating a suspect.

Like other enquiry team members, I'd been given some MO suspects to interview, in order to try and confirm their alibis and eliminate them as suspects. I also had witnesses to interview. Ideally, what should happen by working that system is that if you have the action for a day or so and haven't managed to progress it, then the action should be handed back to the personnel staffing the incident room, with an update, and it can be reallocated.

I had inherited some of Mike's enquiries and, additionally, had some of my own to progress, but being unfamiliar with this kind of set-up, I erroneously (stupidly?) thought that handing back incomplete actions would be viewed as laziness. As a result, I took too many enquiries on board to administer them properly, and was only saved when one of the other detective sergeants from the Squad, who knew the system, realised this and resolved the situation.

This meant that when I knocked on a door in Hamilton to interview a potential suspect I'd had the action to interview him for five days.

I was with a local detective, John Mathieson, and our suspect was a twenty-four-year-old male, but it was his father we spoke with initially. He was, naturally, protective of his son when we explained our reason for coming to his door. When his son came downstairs we introduced ourselves and once more explained why we were there. We asked our interviewee if he could account for his whereabouts when the crime had occurred.

I have to say that I have sympathy for people when they're asked what they were doing a week, ten days, two weeks ago, or whenever the day in question was. I would struggle to tell you sometimes what I'd had for breakfast the same morning, but there has to be a starting point. Often, to try and jog the interviewee's memory, investigating officers will provide a cross-referral point. It may be that a particular sporting event took place, or a certain television programme was showing on the night in question.

When speaking to this man, he gave us a couple of different stories as to where he'd been. We decided that he should be interviewed at length, but to ensure fairness we utilised a section under the then Criminal Justice Act which allowed us to detain and question someone suspected of a crime for a period of up to, and including, six hours.

We drove to Hamilton Police Office and began to interview the male in a room directly across from where the HOLMES was situated. The team there comprised some police officers, supplemented by civilian staff who carried out duties such as statement-typing and indexing.

We interviewed our suspect under caution and after about half an hour he made admissions in relation to the crime we were investigating. Now, these admissions came voluntarily and spontaneously. There was no machine-gun-like questioning, no subterfuge, and no threats. But although John and I should have been more than happy, we were perplexed.

I'd already interviewed someone in the enquiry, who had claimed to have been responsible, but he had no specialist knowledge of the incident, and I wasn't convinced about the veracity of his admissions. I'd examined what he'd told me at length and discovered that he actually had an alibi and had slight learning difficulties so was content, as were the Senior Investigating Officers, that his claims were false.

This time though I just could not be sure, and neither could my colleague. The admissions had a ring of truth about them and had been properly obtained.

I'm not going to try and delude people.

Have I in past interviews raised my voice and shouted? Yes.

Have I issued a threat? Yes.

Have I beaten suspects? Absolutely not, but I am 6'2" tall and weigh about 185 pounds. If you ask me then, have I used my physical presence to stand in a suspect's personal space and disconcert them as an interview technique? Yes, I have.

Did I do any of these things in this particular interview? No, I did not.

It wasn't that kind of interview and John Mathieson certainly did not either. Nor is he the type to have tolerated such behaviour. We took what we had to Alex Cowie, who was satisfied with the knowledge from the interview to make the decision to arrest and charge the suspect. Once charged, the prisoner indicated that he wanted to make a further statement.

Under Scots law when a person has been charged with a crime and they intimate that they wish to make a statement separate from any reply made when charged, it is necessary to obtain the assistance of officers totally unconnected with the enquiry. This assists in ensuring fairness, as anything declared in the statement should be unknown to the officers taking the statement. These officers are not permitted to ask questions of the accused person other than to clarify a point. They are obliged to write exactly and *only* what the accused says.

Cowie arranged for Hugh Pillans, a Detective Chief Inspector from another Division, to take the statement and although sceptical initially, he later told me that as the statement progressed he was convinced we had the right person.

I'm a pretty decisive person. However, for probably one of the very few times in my police career I really didn't know whether I had the right man or not. I had nothing to reproach myself for, as I'd acted in a professional manner, but the very last thing any detective wants is to arrest the wrong man. There have been numerous high-profile miscarriages of justice in Britain, including Scotland, where persons wrongly convicted of crimes have spent decades in prison. I would never wish that on my conscience. 'It is far better ten guilty men go free than one innocent man is wrongfully convicted . . .'

To have an innocent man convicted while a murderer, rapist, child molester or the like is left free to carry out another similar crime is unthinkable.

My uncertainty must have been obvious, because on the journey back to Force Headquarters with three other Squad members, two of them commented that for someone who had just 'burst' such a high-profile enquiry, which had received nationwide publicity, I wasn't exactly bouncing like Tigger.

I told them that I was hacked-off for being unable to convince myself I'd got the right person and for being so indecisive, which was utterly foreign to my nature. I also thought the man may have had slight learning difficulties which added to my uncertainty.

Had the situation arisen nowadays we would have conducted the interview under tape-recorded conditions which would have allowed a jury to hear how the interview unfolded. We would also have had an appropriate adult present to safeguard the suspect's interests. An appropriate adult is someone who is independent of the police and is trained in the questioning of vulnerable people.

A couple of days later, I was told John Fleming wished to speak to me. John Fleming struck fear into a lot of detectives largely following a murder enquiry in Greenock. A seventeen-year-old girl, Elaine Doyle, had been found murdered yards from her home, and he had been the Senior Investigating Officer. It was a protracted enquiry and one which, at the time of publication, remains unsolved.

During a period when the enquiry seemed to be faltering, Fleming had introduced what became known possibly unfairly as the '*Mastermind* Chair'. This stemmed from the television programme where contestants are placed in a chair with a spotlight and, under pressure, answer questions on a chosen specialist subject. At evening briefings, Fleming had a chair in the middle of the room and he would seat enquiry officers in the chair and ask them about their tasks for the day, and about various facets of the enquiry.

I wasn't involved in that enquiry as the murder had taken place before I began in the Squad, but it was still very much ongoing by the time I began my term.

From my experience of John Fleming, I don't believe he used this to crucify any of the enquiry team. I think, given that the impetus had stalled, he was simply seeking to ensure that he hadn't overlooked any potential avenues that would have advanced or reinvigorated the enquiry.

From speaking to officers who worked the enquiry, however, the tactic wasn't a good management tool for several reasons. Some officers were reluctant public speakers and being placed in the chair left them like rabbits caught in the headlights. Others were so apprehensive about their turn that they concentrated on nothing but ensuring that they were prepped for the chair, and missed the information imparted by other teams.

Fleming had a florid complexion and a temper to match if he found out someone had lied about how they'd carried out their tasks, or had been unprofessionally slipshod. I had no problem with that or with him. My view was that he tested you to see if you were of strong enough character to stand up for yourself, or whether you would prevaricate, or worse, lie or simply roll over.

'Come in, Gerry.' No offer of a seat. He got right to it which I liked, but was a foreign trait to so many bosses.

'You had the action to interview the suspect for five days. What took you so long to get to him?'

I was honest with him and explained the reason for the delay. He seemed happy with my answer.

He moved on, and again with no messing about he asked, 'Are you happy enough he's the right man?'

I was as honest again.

'You'll have read the admissions he made. That's what he said and they were obtained fairly. We relayed what had been said in the interview to the DCI.'

'I'm happy with the work you did. Well done.'

End of interview.

He hadn't had a face-to-face with me previously and I'm sure he wanted to satisfy himself that I'd acted properly and professionally. I think the fact that I hadn't tried to fudge or embellish helped him make his mind up quickly. He was an extremely thorough man so I would have been astonished if he hadn't already done all his checking before he even spoke to me.

When the trial came round at Airdrie High Court I gave my evidence, which naturally included the interview and the admissions made by the male on trial. When it came time for my cross-examination by the eminent Queen's Counsel, Lionel Daiches, he put it to me that I had pressured the admission from his client. It was an allegation I could truthfully rebuff, but I wanted to stress just why the allegation was untenable.

I (politely) pointed out that if he felt that to be the case then he had been remiss in compiling his client's defence. His head snapped up almost as if I'd questioned his parentage, but I pointed out that I had questioned his client directly across from the HOLMES incident room, which was heavily populated by civilian personnel. I emphasised that if he was of the opinion that I'd raised my voice or pressurised his client then surely the civilian staff within the incident room would have overheard such behaviour and would, as a matter of course, have been interviewed by the defence team. That finished that line of enquiry.

When the jury finally returned their verdict it was one of 'Not Proven'. Every other judicial system worldwide offers juries only two verdicts to return – Guilty or Not Guilty – except, Scots law. Scots law has a third verdict that the jury may return if they feel that the prosecution has not proved their case beyond a reasonable doubt. Then the jury has the option to return a 'Not Proven' verdict.

In the nineteenth century, Sir Walter Scott, the famous author of books such as *Rob Roy* and *Ivanhoe*, described it as 'that bastard verdict', whereas Donald Findlay, one of the most eminent Queen's Counsel in modern Scots law, is a staunch supporter of 'Not Proven' as a third option. It is an ambiguous verdict. It is unsatisfactory for a victim and/or a victim's family, and similarly an accused walks from a courtroom with his innocence still subject to question and scrutiny.

I know the family in this case were left totally dissatisfied and almost broke the courtroom door following the verdict.

Me? I hate the verdict, but in my heart of hearts and humble opinion it was, in this case, in all probability the correct verdict. We had no forensic evidence, no eyewitness, no proper statement from the victim, and no accurate description of the suspect. What we had was an admission to me and another officer, supplemented by a further admission to officers not connected to the case. The admissions and subsequent statement would have required some supplementary inarguable specialist knowledge, and it was short on that.

15

'SQUODDS' AND SODS

I was thoroughly enjoying my time in the Serious Crime Squad. Most weeks brought a variation of enquiries and incidents. One week, it was the collapse of a clubber who'd been poisoned in an Airdrie nightclub and I managed to trace the person responsible.

It turned out that he had grown tired of someone taking gulps from his beer glass when he was at the toilet or on the dance floor, so decided to top it up with some drain cleaner. He was almost a murderer. Bet it cured the beer thief though!

At other times we would assist detectives from other parts of the UK or Europe, who had enquiries in Glasgow. One such occasion found me back at Balornock with some Belgian officers.

They had sent still photographs of some 'till-dipping' suspects to the Force Criminal Intelligence Office and I'd recognised one, hence our presence at the house. Our Belgian officer had a list of questions to ask, but no evidence to arrest at that point.

We were allowed into the house by the designer-clad suspect, and inside the house was beautifully furnished. Outside, the suspect's car was a limited edition racing green three-litre Ford Capri, which was then a highly desirable machine. He'd never worked a day in his life. Despite asking our Belgian officer if he would like us to pose the questions, he politely declined, believing his English was competent enough to do the job, and by and large it was until he asked,

'Are you a member of a club of international cash register thieves?'

In response our suspect said, 'No, I am no longer a member of that particular club. I let my membership lapse as the renewal fees were far too high.'

He looked at me as he delivered the line in a deadpan Jack Dee type voice and I was thankful I was behind our Hercule Poirot as I tried to turn the involuntary guffaw into a sneeze.

It was also around this time that I had occasion to look after some members of the Metropolitan Police Flying Squad who were in Glasgow to give evidence at a High Court trial, in relation to someone they'd arrested in London on behalf of Glasgow officers. We were chatting and asking each other about what we were working on when one of them happened to mention they were desperate to catch some cash-in-transit armed robbers. They were originally from Glasgow, but had been down in London for a long time and were real villains.

He told me the family name and almost fell off the chair when, casually, I listed four of the family and asked which of them he was referring to. I could give him almost chapter and verse on their family history because I'd grown up near them and played football against them. I hadn't seen them in about fifteen years.

I said half-jokingly that they would have no idea I was in the police and that if we could engineer a 'chance' meeting I could pass myself off as having moved to London, after having just returned from Sweden. We could see if, without pushing things, something came from the socialising.

Given that I'd lived in Sweden for several years it would have stood scrutiny as a cover story. They were really keen on the idea. So much so that they actually phoned their Detective Superintendent there and then and pitched the idea to him. For his part he thought that although risky it had great potential.

However, the idea came unglued when we approached a senior officer within the Squad who almost convulsed. By this time, Joe Jackson and others had moved on and been replaced by others whose idea of risk was having Sugar Puffs rather than Bran Flakes for breakfast. He spluttered that it was far too dangerous and the Chief Constable would never loan an officer to another Force. Within ten years it was common practice to use undercover officers who operated across the various Forces. Ideas in the police move slower than the Edinburgh tram-line project and I'll give you another example how closed-minded they are.

The Detective Chief Superintendents, Superintendents and Chief Inspectors who inhabited the fourth floor of Force Headquarters would retire on a Friday lunchtime to one of the several Indian restaurants situated on Sauchiehall Street. I made the suggestion that it may be worth their considering inviting their counterparts in the Customs and Excise, VAT and Inland Revenue to meet them over lunch. I felt that through informal close contact they may be able to formulate a joint strategy for tackling the main index criminals, who were proving resistant to police investigation alone.

It was again dismissed out of hand. Nowadays, the sharing of information and operating in conjunction with other agencies is common practice, but is now referred to as a 'multi-agency approach'. Those are both absolutely true anecdotes and are not included to present myself as some kind of visionary or forward thinker, but to highlight how ponderous and bureaucratic the police hierarchy often is.

16

METALWORK FOR BEGINNERS

Arthur Thompson eventually earned the nickname 'The Godfather' within Glasgow gangland circles owing to his supposed control of Glasgow, but the influence exerted by him was primarily over the north side of the city. At least that was where John Friel, a plausible Irishman, who operated from the south side of Glasgow, thought Arthur's influence should be restricted when he arranged to have Arthur shot. He had been convicted of cocaine supply in London in the early 1980s and had ties to the Irish Republican movement.

Thompson had a reputation for brutality and had in his twenties carried out work in London for the notorious Kray Twins, who ruled the East End of the capital. He had a barrel chest, a bandy-legged, aggressive gait, and had a scowling countenance that made him look at times like a bulldog chewing half a dozen wasps.

Before he eventually died of a heart attack in the street near to his home, he'd survived almost as many assassination attempts as Fidel Castro. He'd been blown up in his car, run over in the street and, on this occasion, shot. The shooting was brought about largely through the utter incompetence of his son, Arthur junior.

Junior must have been a source of despair to the father and must have caused him on occasion to contemplate DNA testing. He was an overweight, soft-faced boy and would perhaps, on his most aggressive day, have struck fear into a timid hamster. However hard he tried, a gangster he was not.

He'd handed over several tens of thousands to Friel for drugs. The amount, in the usual Glasgow exaggeration factory, ranged from £30,000 to £100,000. Without having the basic brains to check the exchanged merchandise at the handover he drove off happily. When

96

he eventually did check his prize haul he discovered Friel had handed over rubbish.

In fairness to him he wasn't the only victim of a con such as that. Two brothers from Possilpark, who were feared and classed as very street-smart, set up a deal with some worthies from Liverpool, with the meeting place at Carlisle railway station. The brothers had timed things so that they wouldn't be standing about on a railway platform with dozens of slabs of resin and had checked the times of returning trains so that they only had to endure a waiting window of a few minutes.

They spoke to the Liverpool gang who were happy with that arrangement as they didn't want to be hanging around holding a bag of cash following the exchange. On the day, the Liverpool lads opened the holdall, showed them the slabs, gave them one to examine and said basically,

'Right, lads. Let's get it done. We don't want to hang about in case there are choo choo bizzies [British Transport Police] about.'

They gave the brothers the bag containing the cannabis and received the cash in return. The return train to Glasgow pulled in on time and the brothers hopped on, delighted with how smoothly the exchange had gone.

It was only when they examined the bag's contents more closely that they discovered they had two bars of cannabis and several dozen more of brown-painted carbolic soap. I'm told they actually had the good grace to laugh as they had pulled a few cons in their time and could appreciate how they'd been taken in.

In Arthur senior's case, however, this was home territory and amounted to what Asians refer to as a 'loss of face', especially in the village that is Glasgow, and he made it known that he wanted revenge on Friel.

Friel was tall, slimly built with dark wavy hair, and a ready smile and joke. He wasn't a fighter and if you encountered him he was gregarious and would talk for ages, so long as you weren't looking to talk about distinct incidents to elicit information. He'd no doubt kissed the Blarney Stone at some point, because he could regale you with stories, but tell you absolutely nothing.

As well as earning from drugs, he defrauded building societies of tens of thousands along with a female companion through mortgage frauds. I always thought, however, there was something of the night about him. He could be found in and around the area of Glasgow known as 'The Drag', which is the gathering area for the city prostitutes. He also had a flat in Elmbank Street, off Sauchiehall Street, and could also be found in the company of adult but much younger boys.

When in the Squad, I learned that a warrant had been issued for his arrest in relation to mortgage fraud and found him easily in the 'Drag' area. I arrested him, but before transporting him to Stewart Street Police office made a concerted effort to see if he was prepared to provide some information, but he had no interest in taking up the offer.

The last time I was aware of him was in 2000, when working at Maryhill on the Frank McPhie murder. Out of habit I was checking the list of the lock-ups for the previous twenty-four hours when I saw the name, and thought the date of birth looked familiar, but almost dismissed it as the charge was for Drunk and Incapable. The person in custody had been found unconscious by uniform officers in the street near St George's Cross. He had about £600 or so in his possession and they had managed to identify him from some paperwork he had in his possession.

I ran a quick check on the Police National Computer (PNC) and confirmed it was indeed the same John Friel. It is strange how reputations wax and wane because when I mentioned it to the other detectives not one, other than a long-in-service Detective Inspector, had ever heard of him.

I had urgent enquiries, but went quickly to his cell to see what kind of condition he was in. I was hoping that perhaps the passage of time or consumption of alcohol may have made him more amenable to an approach. He was almost comatose so I arranged with the duty officer to try and hold on to him until I got back, or if he was released to have an officer from the CID at least have a word with him. However, as often happens in the police, come shift changeover the message was lost and with it an opportunity. He went out of the door without having been spoken to.

At the time of his feud with Thompson, however, he knew he didn't have to fight him physically. He had assistance to combat the threat to himself, and as with so many dangerous individuals he didn't talk about what he intended to do, or issue threats. He just did it.

Thompson had a workshop in Carmyle, in the East End of Glasgow, and was working there one day when what was later described by one of the work crew there as a 'tall, lean, muscled male with an Irish accent' walked in, and asked to speak with him. On Thompson being pointed out the male began to produce a gun from his inside pocket of which, the workman said, looked as if the barrel went on forever. He promptly aimed it at Thompson and it misfired. He tried again and it misfired again. He looked to see why the gun wouldn't function and it suddenly went off; the bullet struck the ceiling and ricocheted into Thompson's groin. Exit the assassin.

Thompson got himself to a private hospital – the Nuffield Clinic – and tried to convince the doctor that the piece of metal in his groin area had come from a faulty lathe at the workshop. The police were notified when the surgeon noticed the piece of metal lathe had a .45 calibre look to it. Of course, Arthur was less than expansive but his workman, still in shock, was caught in time and gave his version of events.

Word came in that the person responsible was an Irishman who had served time for explosive offences, and who intelligence believed provided physical training for IRA Active Service Units. Along with other officers, I was dispatched by Joe Jackson to bring him in. We forced the door of a flat in the Kings Park area near Hampden Football Stadium at about 5 a.m. The suspect awoke to three .38 Smith and Wesson revolvers pointing at his head and cops screaming at him and ordering him to get up (slowly).

Now I'd imagine that if you woke me in that manner I'd probably be a stuttering wreck, or you'd need a defibrillator to revive me. With him you would have thought he had been wakened by the maid bringing him his breakfast. He wasn't one to scare easily that's for sure. You could see he was lean as whipcord. I put handcuffs on him and we took him to Shettleston Police Office which covered the area where the shooting had taken place.

Our man would not give you the time of day. Gregarious like Friel, he wasn't. I once read a document issued to IRA members and it outlined every single tactic that could or would be employed by interrogators, and emphasised the absolute necessity to remain silent. It warned members that saying anything whatsoever was like a cat playing with the end of a ball of wool. Once the cat had a loose end of the wool very soon it would unravel the whole ball. In fact, the document's title was *Whatever you say, say nothing.* Our man must have memorised it.

We made arrangements for an identification parade to be held at Shettleston and astonishingly Arthur Thompson agreed to attend. Not so surprisingly, he had other reasons for attendance. He was asked prior to the parade whether he intended, if he recognised his assailant, to identify him.

It was a snort more than a reply. 'I'm here just to make sure you've got the right guy and get another look at him.' At which point what would have been a futile parade was called off, and with no other evidence which would have allowed us to detain our suspect any longer he was told he was to be released.

He was offered an armed escort down to the ferry to Ireland which left from Stranraer and to be taken out of the side door of Shettleston office. You'd have thought he'd been asked to smell dog dirt the way he wrinkled his nose.

'If I'm free to go, I'm walking out that front door on my own and going back to my flat.'

I watched him stroll out the front door and down Shettleston Road before hailing a taxi. A very cool customer. There may have been a few reasons why, but Thompson never took any revenge on Friel.

During the Hanlon and Glover murder enquiry, which ran in tandem with the enquiry into the murder of Arthur's son, I had it confirmed that Arthur senior was a Security Service asset, so he may have been advised to desist by his handlers.

Or, it is possible that he may well have been concerned that Friel, with his Republican connections, may have been too hot a potato to engage in a war. Or, he may well have decided that being king of one particular hill beats being dead at the bottom of all of them. Either way, both he and Friel eventually died of natural causes.

My next dealings with Arthur Thompson followed the murder of his son and, rather ludicrously, involved issuing him a 'threat to life warning'.

17

AN ANGEL'S FINGERPRINT

The Crinan Canal, near Lochgilphead in Argyll, is picturesque and a tourist spot, which only compounded the horror that occurred on 6 May 1988. A woman enjoying a mid-afternoon walk there saw a plastic bag floating on the surface of the canal and noticed movement from within. She presumed that it may well have been a kitten or kittens that someone intended drowning, and brought the bag to the banking. One can only imagine her shock and dismay when she found the bag contained a baby girl only several hours old.

The woman naturally sought medical assistance and the newborn was rushed by escorted ambulance to the Sick Children's Hospital at Yorkhill, but after several hours of treatment she died.

The resultant post-mortem examination revealed the baby had suffered a head injury and that, allied to the circumstances of her discovery, launched a murder enquiry. Adam Hay was the Detective Chief Inspector with responsibility for the area of the find, and led the enquiry.

Argyllshire had very low crime levels and, consequently, only a few detectives worked the area. The CID staff comprised a Detective Inspector and Trainee Detective Constable, who worked from Lochgilphead office, while Campbeltown, which lay thirty miles further north-west, had a Detective Sergeant and a Detective Constable.

Hay requested the assistance of the Serious Crime Squad and, along with other officers, I found myself driving the very scenic route around Loch Lomond to Lochgilphead. An incident room had been set up within Lochgilphead Police Office, and initial enquiries had begun when we arrived. As with all major enquiries door-to-door was a quintessential tool in trying to source witnesses, and having little else to go on, the witness canvass was initially situated in and around the area of the canal.

Initially, I found myself partnered with Mike McKenna, and if our presence there hadn't been the result of such sad circumstances it would almost have been idyllic given our surroundings and the beautiful spring weather. Indeed, at one point, Mike joked that the area was so appealing that once we'd completed the door-to-door enquiries he hoped Adam Hay extended them to croft-to-croft and glen-to-glen.

By chance, I was able to assist with a first clue which would eventually prove absolutely crucial. The baby when discovered had been wrapped in a bloodstained, pink, woollen blanket and a sports type top which read 'MOM Motors'. Also in the plastic bag had been a bloodstained bed sheet, towel and a pair of pants. The top within the bag appeared, to all extents and purposes, to be a motor cycle top.

My brother-in-law was a keen motorcyclist, so I called him and without going into detail asked him if 'MOM' meant anything to him. He came up trumps immediately, telling me it stood for 'Mickey Oates Motors', motor cycle specialists based in Glasgow, so that gave us the first enquiry lead.

A call to their Glasgow base quickly established that the top in question was a special edition, but the owners couldn't say exactly who had been the recipient of the top other than members of the motocross fraternity in general.

In the initial stages of the enquiry, we travelled to and from Glasgow to Lochgilphead daily, but after a couple of days it became obvious that to alleviate the possibility of driver fatigue and maximise working time we would have to relocate temporarily to Lochgilphead. We spent the next eight days or so based there without too much progress, although the enquiry had received national publicity. Even displaying the top, which the baby had been wrapped in, on television hadn't drawn the hoped for response.

At that time, the Serious Crime Squad operated a five-week night shift cycle and it was my and Mike's turn to work it so we found ourselves back in Glasgow and divorced from the enquiry. When, after several weeks, there had been no real progress made there was a gradual withdrawal of most of the other operational officers who'd been seconded from the Squad.

From the very outset of the enquiry, Adam Hay was unshakeable in his belief that the solution to the enquiry lay locally, although not all the enquiry team were as certain. Given the area's high volume of transient traffic, and the remoteness of the find there were some on the investigation who felt that the location had been chosen as a means of placing distance between the baby and birth mother.

When the various checks that had been carried out with local doctors, Health Centres and Health Boards hadn't uncovered any pregnancies, which would have provided the answer to the puzzle, it gave the latter view some credence. Additionally, we had witness sightings of a 'hippy type' couple who had been seen a short time before the discovery of the baby. The couple had been seen carrying a bin liner.

In Glasgow, and carrying out night shift duties with Mike, I thought the Crinan Canal find was an enquiry I would have no further involvement in. I was wrong, although it would be several weeks and the result of some good detective work by other officers before I would find myself back in Argyll. Before that, however, I was given cause to reflect on the randomness of fate and injury.

At that time, owing to the shift patterns worked by Detective Officers in Glasgow, there were no Divisional CID officers on duty from 2 a.m. until 7 a.m. on the Monday morning. As a consequence, any incident which necessitated the attendance of a Detective Officer during those hours fell to Serious Crime Squad officers.

That resulted in Michael and I being asked to attend Cambridge Street in Glasgow; a department store occupied then by Littlewoods, and now by the Irish firm Dunne's, where an attempted break-in had occurred. Littlewoods, as with all retailers, had a window display, and this one held faux-type ski jackets. The method of entry had been crude. A large plate-glass window had been smashed and an attempt made to grab the jackets from the display.

It didn't require Sherlock Holmes to see why the attempt had been unsuccessful. The arterial blood spray told us everything we needed to know. When the window had been smashed the glass had shattered and left the top half hanging like an unstable stalactite. The resulting vibrations caused by the perpetrators lunging through the window to grab the jackets had brought the jagged upper section of glass crashing down like a guillotine.

Whoever had entered through the smashed window had suffered a horrific injury, but of the injured person there was no trace. The blood trail ended a short distance from the entry point so we took it as a given that the victim had entered a car which, no doubt, was to have been used to carry off the stolen goods.

Mike and I knew that the injured person would require medical attention (immediately) and arranged for Force Control to contact the likely hospitals that someone requiring urgent medical care might head to. Stobhill, Glasgow Royal Infirmary, the Western Infirmary and the Southern General were the only real possibilities given that the injury most certainly involved arterial damage.

Within minutes we had a match, albeit the smash and grabber had paid a tragic price. The glass had severed his femoral artery and he had bled out and died by the time his transport had reached the entrance to the hospital. For a young boy to lose his life for three or four jackets doesn't bear thinking about.

It did cause me, retrospectively, to consider how lucky I'd been at the situation in Torrance when I'd climbed through a window whose top section of glass had also fragmented in a similar manner to that of the shop window. Both the boy who lost his life and I were motivated, determined; both of us would have been fired with adrenalin and subconsciously weighed the potential risks, but proceeded anyway.

Clearly the dwelling house glass was of a lighter consistency, but having seen several deaths from femoral artery severance I can appreciate that if the glass at the house had sheared and struck my femoral, the same fate may have befallen me.

It would be very easy and pat to say that one person was performing what they perceived to be a good deed, or was arguably on the side of the angels, while the other was maybe morally in the wrong, but life isn't like that. I suppose fate allocates everyone a quantum of luck and when you're overdrawn the forfeit can sometimes be fatal.

It was my daughter's sports day, and I'd arranged to work in the morning and use time owed to me to make sure I got there in the afternoon. It would be another promise broken.

Some weeks previously, a neighbour had held a party and the adults, fuelled by too much alcohol, had been playing on the child's swing and broken it. Their parents had told them that Sammy the Seagull had been responsible. As a means of explaining having to miss the school sports and my hurried departure, I told my daughter that I was going to arrest Sammy the Seagull.

There had been a development in the enquiry at Lochgilphead.

During the time Mike and I had been night shift, Adam Hay had used the information I gleaned from Mickey Oates Motors concerning the shirt and had sent officers to Motocross meetings. He wanted competitors quizzed about how one of the limited edition shirts came to be in the Lochgilphead area.

It was sound procedural detective work, although on the surface it seemed like one of those 'needle in a haystack' tasks. At one of the motocross meetings two of the enquiry team found the needle. One of the competitors recalled that after a meeting held in Argyll two years previously, he and a friend had attended a locally organised dance.

They had been staying in a caravan and hooked up with two local girls, and he had given one of the girls a similar top. Unfortunately, try as they might, neither he nor his friend could recall anything about the girls that would have advanced things. No names, descriptions, phone numbers. *Nada!*

We checked and it turned out that a local couple arranged a dance every other year, and so the next step was to ask them for names of locals who had been at that dance. A ludicrous request one would have thought, but they were able to supply us with close on seventy or eighty people. That left us with the task of tracing and interviewing as many of those people as possible, in the hope that something would emerge.

On my return to Lochgilphead I was partnered with 'A', as Mike had remained in Glasgow working another enquiry. I was more than happy because we liked each other and, more importantly, he was good to work with. He had pretty much the whole package: educated, intelligent, but full of common sense (in the police they don't always go hand in hand), tough and intuitive. I always enjoyed working with him.

We were given a list of some fifteen names to work our way through, but by the time we regrouped at the office to debrief at about five in the evening we were full of frustration. We hadn't managed to interview a single soul on our list. Argyllshire at that time was enjoying a boom in employment thanks to the presence of a large Health Board, and the Forestry Commission. Every potential interviewee we'd gone to see had been at work.

We'd put in some seventy-five to eighty miles and had had absolutely no joy. Adam Hay wasn't there. He was home on annual leave which he'd delayed several times already as a result of the enquiry. The local Detective Inspector was in charge in his absence.

Consequently, we had nothing to contribute at the briefing, but no one else had managed to obtain anything of note either. We told the Detective Inspector that we wanted to revisit some of our interviewees in the evening and were met with the usual cynical 'Yeah yeahs' from the other teams, suggesting we were looking to manufacture overtime.

On most other occasions, they would have been absolutely right, but the fact that we'd driven those miles and got nothing made us want to derive something from what we perceived as a wasted day. We were given the go-ahead, and chose five interviewees who lived farthest in distance from our base, as we didn't want to drive those distances the following day and miss out again. I remember jokingly saying to 'A', 'A bad start is a good ending.'

The village of Furnace lay about fifteen miles away so we headed there. Fifteen miles sounds nothing but owing to the road layout and the fact that our list of interviewees criss-crossed the rural region it took longer to reach than one would expect.

We were met by the mother of our interviewee who showed us to the lounge area of the house where we found a girl, aged about twenty, asleep on the floor in front of an open fire. Her mother woke her, and after initial introductions we asked her about the dance and her attendance at it. She admitted being at the dance, but that was as far as she could recall. She didn't seem able to advance things, and was of no assistance when we showed her a photograph of the motorcycle shirt.

She didn't seem able to help, although she appeared to be trying, but something wasn't quite right. Sure she had been wakened from a sleep, but it was her indifference, or lack of interest in an enquiry that had made national news, and was most certainly big news in such a rural community, that aroused our suspicions. Almost every person we spoke to was desperate to know how the enquiry was progressing. I looked at 'A' and he had the same thought, so we politely asked her mother and father if we could speak to their daughter alone.

We began again, but with the pressure elevated ever so slightly. Eventually, she admitted being one of the two girls who had hooked up with our motocross pair and gave us the name of her friend and where she worked. She added the caveat, however, that she'd seen her friend barely a week before the baby had been found in the canal and there was no way she could have been pregnant, as she hadn't displayed the least sign of pregnancy.

I wanted to satisfy myself that our interviewee hadn't been the mother of the child, but 'A' was keen to be off and once outside, I quickly found out why. The girl named by our interviewee worked at a local hotel. He recalled having spoken to her when having a beer after work with some of the team, on the third day of the enquiry. The girl had been making typical barmaid chat until she had asked what had brought him to the area. When he'd explained, he said the girl had become rather frosty.

At the time, he assumed she may have held a dislike of the police, and if so that certainly wouldn't have made her a member of an exclusive club, and he hadn't given the matter too much more thought. Now, however, the pieces fell into place.

'That's the mother. She's got the same philtrum as the baby. I should have put it together earlier.'

The philtrum is that groove that runs from below the nasal septum to the top of the upper lip. The length is defined by genetics passed down from parent to child. It serves no purpose anatomically, but Jewish folklore attributes to it a mythical quality.

It is believed that while in the womb a baby is visited by an angel to 'shush' it. This is because the baby, in its innocence, knows of heaven and its secrets. The indentation is caused by the angel placing a finger there to cause the unborn baby to forget those secrets.

'How the hell can you make that quantum leap?'

'Because I saw the photos of the baby pre the post-mortem and now when I visualise that girl, she's the mother. They've got the same philtrum. Trust me.'

It was an astonishing piece of intuitive detection. 'Some make' was all I could muster, but I knew him well enough that I did trust him and would have with my life. If he called it that way then that was good enough for me.

As quickly as we could we returned to the office, and laid it all out for the Detective Inspector, and what appeared utterly logical to me seemed ridiculous to him.

When the 'same philtrum' theory was proffered, the facial expression on the detective inspector's face was one of utter bewilderment, and he looked at us as if questioning our sanity. He lived locally and knew many of the community he served. The girl in question was either known to him personally, or else he knew some of her close relatives.

He told us that she'd been interviewed twice in the area canvass. She'd been interviewed firstly during initial house-to-house enquiries and most recently two nights previously, when the area had been revisited. On both occasions she'd told interviewing officers that she had no information that would assist the enquiry, but that if she heard anything she would contact the incident room.

'So what?' was our response.

We told him that the girl was, as we spoke, working at a local hotel and we wanted to go and speak to her. By this time it was about 8 p.m. and the Detective Inspector, I think, wanted to revise the information and perhaps contact Adam Hay for his view. He said things could wait until the morning. We wouldn't be swayed, however, and persisted.

'Look, we're determined to speak to this girl, and if nothing else she hasn't been truthful in the house canvass, so what's the harm in letting us go over and have a word?'

At the hotel, we asked to speak to the girl who was waitressing in the dining room. We conducted our interview, separated from the diners only by a French screen. Owing to the information to hand we administered a caution before any questioning began. 'A' questioned, I studied the body language. Initially, she stonewalled all the questions.

After a period, 'A' gave me a surreptitious signal to assume the role of interviewer. Any interview requires a dynamic. Two people asking questions spoil the rhythm of an interview and can result in both interviewers speaking over one other and causing it to descend into farce.

I was purposefully more forceful in my questioning than he'd been. He'd adopted a coaxing more sympathetic approach but realised that it would require shade to offset the light. There was no shouting or aggression. It was basically:

Look, we've a statement placing you at that dance and later being given a shirt similar to the one wrapped around the baby. You've been interviewed twice and denied having any information that would help us. Why act that way unless you're covering for someone, or you're the mother of the baby?

She let out a wail and then followed the story. Her boyfriend, who was a fisherman and worked away for days on end, had got her pregnant but didn't know. She had managed to conceal her pregnancy even from her family, until finally giving birth in her upstairs room in the family home while her father and brother, unaware, watched television downstairs.

She told us that after delivering the baby she had dropped it and the baby's head had struck a bedside cabinet causing the head injury and in a panic she had put the infant in the canal. We wanted specialist knowledge and asked what she'd done with the afterbirth. As if to compound the whole tragic episode she said, 'It's in my room in a black bin bag.' This was six weeks after the infant's discovery.

We detained the girl under a Section which affords the police a period of six hours to conduct further enquiries, to establish whether there is sufficient evidence available to substantiate a charge, and took her back to the office and updated the Detective Inspector. There was a real look of surprise on his face because we'd hardly been gone a half hour and after six weeks of intensive enquiry, for an incident which had received national publicity, it probably seemed too good to be true.

Owing to the evidence we had accumulated we convinced the Detective Inspector that it would be folly to allow the detention to continue as we had sufficient evidence to arrest and charge the girl. We felt that having retrieved the afterbirth, and allied to her admissions that it might prove detrimental to the enquiry if we attempted to question her further, the Detective Inspector agreed, and not only did we arrest her but charged her also.

Nowadays, it is common practice, in fact the norm, for Detective Constables and Detective Sergeants to arrest and charge murder suspects. Then, however, the old system prevailed whereby Detective Chief Inspectors and Detective Superintendents arrested and charged. I stand to be corrected, but I believe we broke the mould and that was a first in Strathclyde.

When the Detective Inspector phoned Adam Hay at home to tell him the enquiry had been resolved and that we'd arrested and charged the girl, he went stratospheric, and I think tore strips off him on the phone. He told him he was heading straight up.

When he told us Adam was en route and on the warpath it didn't faze us in the slightest. Apart from the fact that both 'A' and myself were strong characters and more than capable of fighting our corners, we knew our procedures had been sound, and the charge we had libelled had been structured properly.

When Adam Hay appeared we let him blow off initial steam and then explained calmly what we had done and why. He was more than happy by the time we'd finished. He'd also been proved 100 % correct in his unshakeable belief that the answer lay locally and near to the infant's discovery.

A plea was later accepted to a reduced charge of culpable homicide.

My wife and I had suffered a full-term stillbirth about a year before this enquiry so, for my part, I wasn't as full of Christian charity for the girl at the time as perhaps I should have been. I found the story a bit too convenient. I couldn't understand how someone who had a steady boyfriend, came from a stable background and found herself pregnant couldn't have acted differently, or told her family and avoided so much pain and heartache.

Retrospectively? I've made more than my share of mistakes and haven't behaved in an exactly saintly manner throughout my life, so I don't get to judge.

18

A LOST BOY

On 17 September 1988, a five-year-old boy, Stephen McKerron, began what was supposed to be a week's holiday at Butlin's. He had been taken out of school a few days before the official break and was with his aunt and uncle. Within half an hour of his arrival there he had gone missing.

I was among a group of Serious Crime Squad officers dispatched to assist in the enquiry. There may have been the initial concern over whether there was the possibility of foul play, but that quickly faded as we interviewed various witnesses.

At about 6.30 p.m., one had seen Stephen climbing a perimeter fence at the camp which was six feet in height. Thereafter, at least four motorists had seen a boy fitting Stephen's description walking alone on the road towards Ayr, dressed only in a t-shirt, tracksuit bottoms and training shoes.

The area of the camp was surrounded by cliffs, seashores and fields and, additionally, although the sightings suggested Stephen had left the camp there were still 1,200 chalets, 400 caravans and outbuildings which would require to be searched. Logistically, it was a search nightmare.

Owing to some 3,000 day trippers at the park at the time, plus the week-long residents, we were drafted in to assist in the mass canvassing for potential witnesses.

I was again partnered with Mike McKenna. Mike fitted the Hollywood stereotype of the detectives one would see in the 1950s movies. He was almost six feet tall and burly, and resembled in looks and physical appearance the actor Tom Sizemore.

Michael was a good interviewer of reluctant witnesses or the lying variety, as well as suspects. People empathised with him because he was amiable and came across as a punter with no airs or graces. Watching him with suspects always improved my reading of body language.

In the 1980s, so many people smoked and now, when I look back, it fills me with dread when I think of the hours I've spent in interview rooms or in cars with witnesses, suspects and colleagues, all generating huge clouds of smoke. Given the volume of smokers, cigarettes were a valuable part of an interviewer's armoury both as an ice-breaker or enticement.

On entering the interview room, Michael would take his jacket off and take out the pack of cigarettes and his lighter and leave them untouched between himself and the suspect. He would start his interview and ignore the cigarettes, but watch for the signs of the suspect or lying witness becoming edgy or uncomfortable when the questions became difficult.

Invariably, their eyes would start to flick towards the cigarettes. Nicotine is as much a drug as heroin and when placed in a pressure situation the craving for the crutch provided by the nicotine often proved unbearably strong.

The lips would be licked and then, 'Could I get one of your cigarettes?'

Michael would usually respond with something like, 'You can have a cigarette, tea, coffee, or a cooked breakfast if you like, just as soon as we get to the truth.'

The pack and the lighter on the table was such a simple tactic, but effective psychologically and that really is what an interviewer looks for, a psychological edge, because in so many cases you are attempting to persuade people to say things they would rather avoid saying.

The more we worked the enquiry, the more it became fairly clear that the missing boy was not the victim of a crime, but lost outwith the confines of the holiday camp. Several times Michael and I, when given certain enquiries, would delay them and drive around the surrounding area in the forlorn hope that we'd see or hear something that might lead us to the child.

One particular day, we had an appointment to speak to a Procurator Fiscal Depute at Glasgow Sheriff Court, on a matter unrelated to the Ayr enquiry, and so we let the Incident Room which had been set up at Ayr Police Office know that we would be delayed. The Depute in question was in court and the court officer told us he would not be free for half an hour.

To kill some time we popped in for a coffee to what was then the Force Training Centre, adjacent to the Sheriff Court Building. There were always cops within the canteen area as all the various courses naturally emanated from the Training Centre.

We were speaking to a sergeant we knew and he asked us what we were working on, and on finding out it was the missing boy at Butlin's, which was national news, he asked us what our search parameters were. We told him and, in response, he told us a story about a boy of similar age who had become lost on the Ochil Hills and, alone and on foot, had traversed a far greater distance than that which had been designated as the search area by the senior management. I asked him if he was sure of his distances and terrain. He was experienced and competent so it was perhaps a patronising question, but I wanted to be absolutely certain.

The response I got (and deserved) was, 'Well I was only part of the fucking team looking for him, Gerry.'

At the briefing at Ayr, armed with the information the sergeant had given us in Glasgow, I asked the Divisional Commander in charge of the area covered by Butlin's how we had established the search parameters.

'That was the advice we were given.'

'I think they're too narrow.' And I relayed the Ochil Hills story.

He became flustered and then said, 'That's what the boss decided,' and indicated towards John Fleming. John Fleming was the Detective Chief Superintendent and held exactly the same rank as the Divisional Commander, so I found it strange that he referred to him as 'the boss' and deferred to him.

I'd already faced Fleming following the child rape in Hamilton and been open with him. He always liked workers and I felt I had his respect.

Now, at Ayr, with the whole enquiry team assembled, including uniformed personnel and CID, I asked him the same question I had put to the Divisional Commander. How had we established the search parameters?

I got the same answer, 'That's the advice we were given'.

'Yes, I understand that. But surely the story I've just recounted would cause us to reconsider the established search parameters.'

'That's what the expert told us.'

'Would it not be worth a reassessment given the new information?'

I could sense those around me trying to create physical space between them and me, as if ensuring disassociation with my comments.

'We've taken the advice of the expert.' His tone was as sharp as a razor.

The 'expert' was a consultant paediatrician. Now, when my wife had been expecting our first child, she had been taken into hospital where she was seen by a paediatrician who told her, mockingly, that she shouldn't be wasting time with false pregnancy pains and was nowhere near ready to deliver. A half an hour later I was holding my son, so it is fair to say I had a healthy cynicism when it came to his 'expert' opinion.

I ventured, 'Well, what about consulting a topographer rather than a paediatrician? Would someone like that not be more relevant?'

I was fixed with a look that could have fried me and told,

'That is the area we're going with.'

As he said it Mike, who hadn't distanced himself, slipped a note in front of me that read 'Fucking leave it'.

After the briefing Mike pulled me aside.

'Are you trying to get yourself kicked off the enquiry?'

'What are you talking about? What I said was valid.'

'Of course it is, but they aren't going to change their minds, no matter how you present it. They've made their mind up, and if you'd pushed it anymore and tried to show what a smart bastard you were, you'd have found yourself up the road and allocated other tasks. Simple as that.'

'But that's bad management, to entrench yourself like that, and even worse . . . they're wrong!'

'No, that's the way it is, and nothing you said would have changed that. Do you think they are going to alter their whole incident strategy and admit they're wrong this length of time into the enquiry just because you tell them?'

On 3 October, fifteen days after going missing, Stephen was found dead, huddled in a ditch, by a hill-walker. He was six miles from the holiday camp; a mile outwith the search area.

A national newspaper posed a series of questions to the police regarding the manner in which the search was conducted. They asked: Who had the police taken guidance from regarding the search area, and how was the distance established? Why had it taken three days to utilise a helicopter fitted with infra-red equipment? Why was the helicopter's search area using the infra-red equipment restricted to the search area? Was there a conflict of opinion between uniform and CID?

In response to the latter question, the police answered, 'Absolutely not.'

There were a few unsatisfactory responses to the other questions.

I don't know whether the question of conflict referred to my questioning or not. If it did the information certainly never came from me. I've never spoken to journalists and I would never leak information on an enquiry. I've always found that contemptible.

Whatever the source, the questions were valid, but if, as the saying goes, a chain is only as strong as the weakest link then this particular chain was weakened from the very outset.

Why didn't Stephen's aunt and uncle keep a closer eye on him? They'd only arrived at a strange place and he was away from his parents.

Why didn't whoever it was that watched a five-year-old climb a six-feet fence not intervene?

How could four motorists watch a small unaccompanied boy walk along a road and not stop to see if everything was okay, or at least contact the police?

Why did the police stick to five miles as a search area and take three days to bring in the equipped helicopter?

Why wasn't I more aggressive in emphasising that the search area was too narrow?

I thought we were wrong in our search parameters then, and still do now, but I'll counter-balance that statement.

There were future Deputy Chief Constables, Assistant Chief Constables, Detective Chief Superintendents and various other soon-to-be senior ranks present at that enquiry. Not one of them opened their mouths when I made my pitch. Given the ranks they ascended to and in comparison to my eventual rank then, they must have believed the strategy to be correct because they would have surely been of strong enough character to have opened their mouths if they had agreed with me. Don't you think?

Why do I think Stephen ran away from the camp?

I always felt he was simply a little boy who was away from his mum and dad and missed them, and was homesick, and was trying to make his way home, which probably makes the whole incident even sadder.

19

A CAUTIONARY TALE

I was home one February afternoon in 1989, when I was contacted by Jimmy Crawford, who told me to be in the office for 6 p.m. that evening and to pack an overnight bag. He wasn't for enlightening me as to why and, for my part, that didn't bother me greatly. My view was that it meant one more adventure. Jimmy, at that time, was a Detective Inspector in the Squad, but I had known him since I joined the police when he'd been a Detective Sergeant at Kirkintilloch.

Jimmy was small, with immaculately barbered hair and a mischievous face. He played shinty, which is a tough, physical game.

Ever since I'd known him, Jimmy had always been a worker, but you had to realise that he'd steal your informants, information or captures if he had the chance, but was a nice guy to be done over by. I'd only worked with him for a short period at Kirkintilloch, before he'd been promoted, but always enjoyed it. Nicol, Stobo and I had been on the opposite team from Jimmy and his crew, and there was always healthy rivalry.

When I got into the office that evening I found out the reason behind the 'Secret Squirrel' routine. It was a terrorist enquiry. Special Branch were in receipt of information (which probably emanated from one of the Security Service sources in Northern Ireland) that a group in Scotland, affiliated to the Orange Order, had sourced explosives and were planning to transport them to Loyalists in Northern Ireland, where they could potentially be used to bomb and maim.

Special Branch would probably be regarded as the equivalent British Law Enforcement agency to the FBI. I regarded them in a similar fashion to how American police officers regarded FBI officers i.e. not real police officers.

Most CID officers regarded their Scottish Special Branch counterparts as failed detectives, which stemmed largely from how they were recruited. They would be plucked from the ranks of the detective division or uniform before they could involve themselves in cases of note or give evidence in court and, consequently, have their faces recognised. They didn't report cases, give evidence in courts of law or exercise their powers of arrest, as this would compromise their anonymity.

I, personally, didn't hold them in high regard, but then my view of their competence may have been somewhat coloured by one of my earliest days in the Squad.

We were waiting for a replacement clerk, as the previous clerk had retired, so the position was filled on a daily rotational basis by an officer who had paperwork to compile. Having just arrived from Division I still had Divisional paperwork to be addressed, so I caught a turn. One of the administrative tasks involved the sorting of any mail that arrived at the Squad office. The post generally arrived in either buff or orange envelopes, and these would be redirected to the intended recipients.

One of the envelopes was unaddressed so naturally I opened it to see if the contents would provide a clue as to whom it should go. The envelope contained the names of Special Branch informants, what their previous code names had been and what their replacement code names were to be.

Initially, I was certain it was a joke being played on the newcomer, or, perhaps dosed with paranoia, a test. Maybe, given my name and Southern Irish heritage, someone wanted to see what I'd do. No one could be that stupid or careless with such highly sensitive information, surely?

As it transpired they could and had been. I spoke to Iain Mackay and showed him the list. He needn't have reminded me, but did anyway, to keep the breach of security between myself and him, and quietly returned the list to his counterpart in Special Branch.

On this particular campaign, I was to head to the Isle of Mull along with Jimmy to detain Lawrence Hodge, under terms of Section 12 of the Prevention of Terrorism Act 1984, in relation to an ongoing enquiry in Tayside. Hodge was an employee of the Forestry Commission, and part of his duties involved the use of dynamite and fuses to blow out tree stumps. There was just one problem – he was allegedly using his job to smuggle excess explosives to Orange Order colleagues.

As with the enquiry at Lochgilphead the journey to the west coast of Scotland unveiled scenery that a Hollywood director would have given his eye teeth for. We were to rest up at a hotel at Oban, near where the *Harry Potter* series were filmed, catch the ferry to Mull the following morning, and detain the male under the Prevention of Terrorism Act.

Rest up?

The central heating in the hotel broke down, and workmen banged and hammered on the piping throughout the night and, additionally, the fire alarm had a mind of its own. The only thing missing was a stag party.

We were bleary eyed and bad-tempered on the boat journey the following morning. Our mood didn't improve when we discovered that our suspect was working on site at a part of the island known as Tiroran, which turned out to be halfway up a boggy hillside, which we had to negotiate in city suits and shoes.

If the suspect had been so inclined he could have rolled a stick of dynamite down the hillside, and smoked a cigar while he watched it take us all out. Eventually, through clinging on to roots and branches we reached where the suspect and his workmates were.

Once we'd identified Hodge, Jimmy and I detained him under the Prevention of Terrorism Act (POTA), and returned to the small police office at Tobermory. Under the POTA we were obliged to record and notarise every contact with the suspect commencing with the minute we detained him, in what is known as a Prevention of Terrorism Log (POT Log).

We had been accompanied to Mull by Eric Stewart, a forensic scientist, and Eric initially 'swabbed' Hodge's hands for explosives' traces, although given his employment that would not be particularly damning.

As Jimmy and I were placing Hodge into a detention cell he asked to speak to us, and given the tone of the request we knew it wasn't to ask for a cup of tea. Jimmy reminded Hodge that the caution that had been administered to him when we'd initially detained him was still applicable. We didn't want him to be in any doubt concerning his right to silence.

Hodge wanted to put over his side of the story.

He claimed that a 'mate' had asked him to get some gelignite and he'd taken it from his workplace. He told us he'd secreted it down the Wellington boots he wore to work. His friend and another man had come to Mull, and he'd handed over nearly a dozen sticks of gelignite and a couple of detonators. Hodge claimed that he knew the explosives were 'going across the water'.

'Across the water' is how people in Scotland refer to Northern Ireland.

He seemed so matter of fact in his admissions; so much so that I wondered if he had actually grasped the potential for murder, misery and mayhem that could have resulted had the explosives reached Northern Ireland.

At the conclusion of the interview, which had been recorded in the POT Log, we read his admissions back to him, and he agreed with what had been recorded. The admissions were timed, dated and initialled by the suspect, as well as by Jimmy and me in such a manner that no one could subsequently attempt to imply that anything had been added or subtracted post-interview.

When Hodge admitted that he had secreted the explosives down the Wellington boots, I asked Eric to swab the inside of his boots for the presence of explosives. A positive result for their presence would act as corroboration for his admissions.

Now with him under arrest, we began the journey to transport him to Dundee where all the suspects in the enquiry were being detained. At a point on the journey, our prisoner pointed out an area we were travelling through and said, 'My mother lives up there.'

It was said so nonchalantly that I couldn't help think that this guy had no idea how grave his situation was. He was under arrest for alleged terrorist offences, and given the political climate at that time and how acts associated with terrorism were perceived, he could well be facing a lengthy prison sentence. Bizarrely, here he was pointing out his mother's home.

Once we had deposited him in Dundee I didn't see him until called to give evidence at his trial at Perth High Court, where he was seated in the dock with five co-accused, all charged with varying offences under the POTA.

I presented my evidence and awaited the cross-examination by the defence counsel. I was questioned on various facets of testimony. I felt on reasonably solid ground as there was little that could be alleged in relation to the veracity of admissions, since the initialled entries in the POT Log pretty much provided incontrovertible proof.

The probe when delivered seemed initially innocuous. I was asked about the nature of the caution administered. It was a clever tactic but then those who practice the Law in the highest courts in the land are generally sharp of mind and cunning strategists.

I had read out the admissions Hodge had made and initialled, and they were potentially damning to the defence, but if they could cast doubt on the caution then that could, in turn, render the admissions null and void.

Now, I enjoyed giving evidence in a Court of Law. That may surprise many officers who find the whole process stressful and harrowing, but like numerous officers I worked with throughout the years, I found it a challenge and an integral part of my duties as a police officer.

Indicating that I enjoyed giving evidence does not in any way mean I was without nerves or unconcerned by the process. On the contrary, I defy even the most sanguine person not to be apprehensive when walking to a witness box. Irrespective of how many times I presented evidence in the various levels of courts, from the District to the High Court, I had butterflies in my stomach.

I viewed it as similar to a football match though; you utilised the adrenalin induced by the nerves to sharpen the senses, and then turned the valve off before the nerves got the better of you and ruined your evidence presentation.

I always tried to prepare properly for the trial. In advance I refreshed my memory from my notebook, fixed the sequence of events in my mind, and tried to put myself in the position of the defence and anticipate what questions they would ask. As with most tasks, the more thorough the preparation the less chance there is of failure.

That said, it is undeniable that the average officer is neither as educated, nor as well-versed in the law as a High Court practitioner. That's the reason their services cost upwards of £2,000 a day.

I was in the High Court, in a high profile trial and faced by five of the most learned legal minds practising criminal law in Scotland, so you'd best believe the adrenalin was coursing and sharpening my mental capacity. It was a casually baited but potentially lethal trap.

A caution is crucial in the questioning of anyone suspected of a crime. It basically informs a suspect of their right to silence. In the United States it is known as 'Miranda Rights' and the use of that phrase in television and films will be familiar to most people.

When I was asked what form the administered caution had taken I realised where the defence hoped it would lead. They were hoping that I would contradict the evidence given previously by Jimmy Crawford. If they could demonstrate that Hodge had either not been properly cautioned prior to questioning, or had failed to understand that he had a right to silence then any admissions made could be rendered inadmissible. I took a second before formulating my reply.

I stated that there were several ways one could word a caution and gave examples of this. There is a standard method which, again, is familiar to lay persons from police television dramas. The officer will say, 'I must caution you that you are not obliged to say anything, but anything you do say will be taken down in writing and may be used against you.'

I continued, however, and in evidence indicated that there were variations on the wording of the caution. Some officers worded the caution, 'I'm about to caution you. You do not have to say anything in response to that caution, but if you do so, anything you say will be noted and may be used in evidence.'

I highlighted further slight variations on the wordings that could be used when administering a caution, none of which nullified the legality of the caution. I finished by emphasising that the crux of every caution must be that it had been properly given and properly understood.

I took my time and was deliberate with my explanation, mainly for the benefit of the jury members who would decide the guilt or innocence of those on trial. I wanted to ensure there was no doubt in their minds that any nefarious methods had been employed in securing the admission. His Lordship and the defence would know better than I the logic of my explanation. The answer must have smothered the probe at source because after my explanation there was no further cross-examination.

As I was being escorted from the witness box a uniformed sergeant performing court duties followed me out and congratulated me on the quality and strength of the evidence I'd presented. That pleased me greatly.

All six on trial were found guilty of various offences, with Hodge receiving a sentence of eight years.

20

'A SALUTARY LESSON'

That same month I became involved in a murder that almost never was.

Denis Mair, was the Detective Chief Inspector at Stewart Street Police Office, which covered Glasgow city centre. He'd been my Detective Inspector a year previously in the Squad, prior to his promotion. I'd enjoyed working with and for Denis. He had a full head of greying hair, but it sat in such a manner that I used to joke with him that it was a hairpiece. He loved a laugh and to laugh, and was a degenerate supporter of Motherwell Football Club.

He'd requested the assistance of the Squad for an incident which had occurred the previous night in St Enoch Square, and which had resulted in the death of a thirty-two-year-old man. The death was being treated as murder.

St Enoch Square is literally that, a square which has an underground railway station at one end and is bordered by shops, pubs and restaurants. During daylight hours it is extremely busy and well-populated, but at night obviously less so. Nowadays, it is a traffic-free zone and a pedestrian precinct, but then it accommodated a taxi stance, and a bus terminus.

There were benches which, later in the evening or at night would be used by drinkers. From the information gleaned initially our deceased had been sitting drinking when an argument developed, and as he began to rise a witness thought he had been punched or stabbed. There was no obvious wound on the victim, but it may well have been the case that if punched, he had struck his head and suffered a subdural haemorrhage. The cause of death would hopefully be established at the post-mortem, which Denis had arranged for later that morning.

The name of a possible witness had been obtained but we had no address, so I phoned a contact at the Department of Social Services (DSS) and gave him the details of the potential witness. In those days, prior to the Data Protection Act, it was far easier to channel information between government bodies and I'd worked with the same contact several times on joint enquiries.

My contact not only came up with a possible address for the witness, but told me he was scheduled to attend that same day at the DSS office situated on Pitt Street, directly opposite the main entrance to Strathclyde Police Force HQ (FHQ).

I told Denis what I'd got and he arranged for me, Gerry Boyle who was my Detective Sergeant in the Squad, and one of his own Detective Constables, George Adair, to pick up the witness when he emerged from the DSS and follow him.

We watched the entrance from a second storey window in Force HQ, and were contacted by a member of staff from the DSS, who let us know what our target was wearing and when they were leaving. We followed him through Glasgow city centre, down Jamaica Street and over the suspension bridge towards the Sheriff Court. By this time we'd been contacted and told that the suspect was thought to be living near Maryhill, so when our 'lead' continued towards the south side of the city we decided to take a chance, grab him and speak to him.

We should have used that tactic a lot earlier as it would have saved us shoe leather. He realised the severity of the situation and quickly told us where the suspect was – a flat in the St George's Cross area of Glasgow.

Thankfully, he was also able to provide the exact flat number as the complex was a rabbit warren, with walkways the length of football fields and sitting six storeys high. We listened at the door and there was movement from inside. In response to knocking and declaring ourselves as police officers we heard what appeared to be scurrying. I thought he might be intent on running so, given it was such a serious enquiry, I kicked the door in.

He knew exactly why we were there and began making admissions before we had hardly begun the formalities. We quickly cautioned him, but he was like a leaking tap. He couldn't be turned off. He told us he had been drinking and had an argument with the deceased, who had been sitting on a bench in St Enoch Square. As the deceased began to rise he'd stabbed towards him with a knife, which had gone into the deceased's nose. Our suspect then ran off towards the nearby River Clyde where he had disposed of the knife.

It seemed absolutely accurate and was, as they say, 'an open and shut case', albeit that appears such a casual and dismissive phrase to describe the loss of a human life. For our part, we were pleased with the job we'd done and conveyed our prisoner to Stewart Street Police Office to update Denis.

When we got there and told Denis that we had the person responsible, he burst that bubble big time. 'It's not a murder the pathologist has indicated it was natural causes.'

I think in unison we responded with, 'What?'

Denis continued, 'He had a brain haemorrhage.'

Now knowing Denis to be a joker I looked at him, half expecting some macabre punchline, but he was totally serious.

'The post-mortem gave the cause of death as a brain haemorrhage.'

I told him, 'Denis, the guy we have at the office has admitted having a knife and stabbing the dead guy up the nose as he rose from the bench he'd been sitting on.'

We went through to Denis's office where he made a call to the Forensic Medicine Department at Glasgow University and spoke to one of the pathologists who had carried out the post-mortem, Dr John Clark. Dr Clark had carried out the procedure, along with Professor Alan Watson.

To establish fact, Scots Law requires corroboration in cases of a criminal nature. That corroboration can be provided by two witnesses or, say, a single witness and other substantive evidence. As a consequence, in a case of a suspicious death, the post-mortem examination will be undertaken by two pathologists.

Some years later, I undertook a forensic medicine course at Glasgow University, and Professor Watson was the chief organiser and lecturer on that course. He was a slim man with sharp features, spectacles and greying hair. He had conducted the post-mortem examinations on an IRA Active Service Unit that had been shot dead by an undercover SAS team on Gibraltar. Subsequently, he had caused great controversy when at the fatal accident enquiry he described their killings as 'frenzied'.

In contrast to other pathologists such as Marie Cassidy and Mike Curtis, I found him to be rather aloof, but that may well be a common trait in those who are Regius Professor in their field of study at a

University. He was a published author of a book on forensic medicine and lectured on the Detective Training Course at the Police College.

Dr Clark, told Denis that at the post-mortem Professor Watson had noticed a slight 'nick' at the nasal cavity but did not believe it to be worthy of further investigation. Now, given the admissions made by our suspect, Dr Clark told Denis he intended to re-examine the corpse.

He and Professor Watson performed a closer wound inspection and found that, as per our suspect's admissions, the knife blade had penetrated the nasal cavity and pierced the brain, simulating a brain haemorrhage.

It is very possible that if we hadn't acted as speedily as we had done, and reached the suspect so quickly then when eventually apprehended he may well have faced a different line of questioning. Given the result of the initial post-mortem, he may have been questioned as being a witness to a sudden death and not murder, and may have evaded prosecution.

Amazingly, given the debris in, and poor visibility under, the River Clyde, the underwater unit managed to recover the murder weapon after our suspect led us to where he'd disposed of the knife.

While researching the book I contacted Dr Clark. After introducing myself, I only had to say St Enoch Square and he knew immediately the enquiry I was referring to, even given the passage of twenty years and the hundreds of post-mortem examinations he would have conducted over the intervening decades. He was even able to access his autopsy examination notes, and could tell me that the deceased had 260ml of alcohol in his blood at the time of death. The incident had been, to quote Dr Clark, 'a salutary lesson'.

That single initial oversight may have been more valuable to Dr Clark than dozens of hours of lectures or classroom theory lessons. The public are now saturated with programmes extolling the wonders of forensic science but which often overlook the most crucial ingredient – the human factor. Pathologists, forensic scientists and most certainly police officers are far from infallible. They're human beings trying to do a professional job of work, but they will make mistakes.

I've always maintained that when there is a publicised mistake or oversight by a police officer in their working lives, a great many officers could look at the error and, if brutally honest, say, 'There but for the grace of God . . .' Policing is the greatest profession ever for learning from others' mistakes and for on-the-job training.

Unlike the television or cinema, cops, pathologists and scientists don't solve every crime; DNA identification isn't produced within half an hour of a crime scene examination, and suspects don't break down and confess when presented with some tenuous piece of evidence.

I've been fortunate to have been on enquiries with detectives from Las Vegas Metro, and been present when they've summoned the assistance of their Crime Scene Investigators to violent crime scenes. They weren't Gil Grissom nor did they resemble any of the characters on those types of shows. They were the same as our own forensic scientists and scene of crime examiners – ordinary people carrying out their difficult and often gruesome job in as thorough and professional a manner as they could.

21

BRISTOL ROVERS

If there had been any other senior detective officer or, for that matter, just any senior officer other than Joe Jackson on call in June 1989, when the rather incredulous Drug Squad officers rolled out their story, the murder would have remained unresolved. It was to be a murder that was to proceed without the discovery of a body, and in playing my part in achieving a successful outcome, lead to me being dispatched by Joe to London and Bristol (three times in the latter's case).

Drug Squad officers would have made good horse traders or performed well on the game show *Let's Make a Deal*. Whenever they raided a house or seized drugs, and following the search of the premises, they made their pitch.

They were always looking to move higher up the drug supply chain. If the person could move them further up that ladder, then the possibility existed that they could speak to the Procurator Fiscal when submitting the case. In theory, everyone benefited. Often, it was a successful ploy and sometimes, it wasn't. On this occasion, when they spoke to the occupants of the flat, I'll bet the equity on my mortgage that even the most optimistic among them could not have imagined where the response would lead.

'How would it go if I told you about a murder?'

'What? Like a murder that we haven't solved?'

'No, like a murder that nobody knows about.'

The tale that unfolded thereafter left them in disbelief, hence their presence on the fourth floor of police headquarters, Pitt Street, repeating it to Joe Jackson. Joe was no longer at the Squad. He had been transferred to Govan, but as fate would have it he was the 'on duty' Detective Superintendent that Saturday morning. Came weekends Detective

Superintendents took their turn on a rota to report to Police HQ and review the various serious incidents that occurred over the weekend, throughout the Force area.

When the Drug Squad officers had made their pitch to the male and female whose house they had raided the couple had offered the following: a drug courier had allegedly travelled from Bristol to Glasgow and had been murdered there by three guys; one was allegedly Spanish and an ex-Foreign Legionnaire, and one, a nasty character from England. They'd supposedly dumped the body on the Fenwick Moors.

By this time, Joe would have heard most stories in his service and been able to relate quite a few, but this was a topper. What reduced the story's plausibility factor, on initial hearing, was that the police had not the slightest piece of information to substantiate it: no intelligence; no rumours; absolutely nothing. Well, that may not be strictly accurate. What probably no one else who worked the enquiry knew – and I would include Joe in that – but what I've learned in the interim years is that it wasn't the first time that that information was proffered.

It appears that the duo offering up the information to the Drug Squad had, in the previous couple of months, attempted twice to bargain the self-same story. The officers who had dealt with them on those occasions, however, had dismissed it each time as *Fantasy Island* material. They had made some initial enquiries and failing to find anything to substantiate it had written it off as nonsense.

Fate, however, has indeed a strange way of manifesting herself. I'm in no doubt whatsoever that if those officers that had initially dealt with the informants, had accepted the story at face value and approached some other boss, then that murder would never have been resolved. Consequently, three people, at least two of whom were nasty, nasty bastards, would have escaped justice.

Joe arranged for initial enquiries to be conducted and, I believe, even spoke to the duo and was satisfied that, although bizarre, their information had credibility.

He also realised shrewdly that given the nature of the enquiry he would best be served by seconding officers from both the Drug Squad and Serious Crime Squad ,and have them work in tandem. He also cherry-picked officers from the local CID.

We operated initially from Kilmarnock Police Office owing to it being the closest in proximity to where the murder had been committed. I suppose, technically, the enquiry should have been passed to whichever Detective Superintendent oversaw the Kilmarnock area, but knowing Joe, once he had convinced himself there was substance to the story there wasn't a hope in Hades he would relinquish control.

At Kilmarnock, on the Sunday, he had me contact the police in Bristol. Officers from that office fell under the auspices of Avon and Somerset Constabulary. I spoke to then Detective Inspector Bill Davis. There was a bit of confusion initially as they had a missing person by the name of Wayne Lomas, and thought that may have been who we were enquiring about.

We eventually established that it was Paul Thorne we were referring to, and he confirmed that he was involved in the periphery of the drug scene and had been listed as a missing person since November 1988.

Later in the day, Joe told me he was sending me to London and Bristol, together with a local Detective Sergeant Alex Patterson. Joe knew Alex and although I hadn't met him prior to that enquiry, he was one of those people you take an instant liking to. Alex was the type that would be smoking a cigar when the canon shot was flying around your ears. He was very relaxed, calm and measured, but thorough. He appeared serious but had a lovely dry sense of humour.

I was quietly pleased that Joe had chosen me to travel down. Hugh Aitken, who was my current Detective Inspector in the squad, once told me that disregarding the gulf in ranks he saw a great many similarities in the characters of Joe and I. Joe may well have held a similar view.

Our visit to London was firstly to trace a female associate of Paul Thorne and try and gain some background information. We had no joy at the addresses we tried but the Metropolitan Officer that Joe had arranged to assist us checked the local office which covered our potential interviewee's main address. He found she was currently enjoying police hospitality on a charge of soliciting. We had a captive audience.

Unfortunately, the lady wasn't for playing. She was cold, tired and hungry . . . and banged up. The reception we got from her was as cold as a stepmother's breath.

'Hello. How are you doing?'

'Take a wild fucking guess, genius.'

'We're down from Scotland. We're looking to speak to you about Paul Thorne.'

'I couldn't care if you're down from Littlewoods Pools. You can fuck off.'

I thought I'd try a different tack.

'That money your folks spent on Swiss Finishing School was a good investment.'

Just a flicker of a smile and then she said, 'Keep trying.'

So I did.

'There's this guy walking along the street and the hooker stops him and says, "Would you like to have sex, big boy?" The guy says, "I'd love to, honey, but there are three reasons why I can't. Reason number one, I don't have any money." And the hooker interrupts him and says, "Stick the other two reasons up your ass."'

Being a working girl she got it and laughed out loud.

'Did they bring you over from the Palladium?'

I then really threw her and started singing, 'You made me love you'.

Throughout, I could see Alex's shoulders shaking as he suppressed the laughter.

She said, 'You're different, that's for sure. What's your name?'

I told her.

'You got a cigarette?'

I always had cigarettes, although I never smoked. Most CID officers kept cigarettes, as well as matches or a lighter in a drawer at work. They were always handy ice-breakers at interviews. I gave her a cigarette and lit it for her.

'Do you want a cup of tea and a bacon roll?'

That was all it took and, in return, we managed to obtain very good background information on Paul Thorne.

We caught the train to Bristol and made contact with the lads from Broadbury Road Police Office, who proved a first class group to work with. Led by Bill Davis, the Detective Sergeant was Jeff Stratford with Detective Constables, Steve Broad and Ken Smith. By the time we'd arrived at Bristol it was early evening and they had finished work for the day.

They took us out to a cricket match their office was having against local rivals. Alex and I found ourselves, on a gorgeous evening, at a cricket pavilion, having sandwiches and a cold drink, discussing a suspected murder and all that murder entailed. Meanwhile, a cricket match was ongoing fifty yards away. It seemed absolutely in keeping with such a bizarre enquiry.

When we returned to Kilmarnock, Joe was really pleased with the progress we'd made and Alex naturally told him about my serenading the hooker. That, of course, tickled Joe and he said, 'Just don't try sticking me with a bill for her services, Sinatra.'

Joe sent me back down to Bristol the following week, along with other officers, to establish who Paul Thorne was, his associates, who he worked for and how he had come to be in Scotland.

Among my tasks was to interview Thorne's mother. He stayed in an area of Bristol called Lawrence Weston. I had to try and glean everything I possibly could from her. Obviously, we had no body and, officially, he was still a missing person, but anything at all could well be significant. I spent a whole afternoon in the lady's home, trying to obtain as much information on her son without imparting anything.

It was uncomfortable. She seemed a decent, ordinary woman and mother, and although her son had become involved in a filthy trade that profits from human weaknesses it wouldn't lessen the impact of the pain for her. She never queried why I was asking some of the questions I did, but she must have suspected. She was as dignified and helpful as she could be. I ended up taking an almost forty-page statement, and the officer with me said, when we left, that it was the most comprehensive statement he'd ever seen taken. It had to be. I didn't want to return home and find I'd missed something and that she would require re-interviewing.

Bill Davis, the Bristol Detective Inspector, had allocated each of us an officer from his CID to assist us with background knowledge on the people we were to interview, and also to help us negotiate our way around Bristol. I was lucky enough to draw Stevie Broad. Stevie was a top guy. He was small, dark and had a good sense of humour. His partner in the CID was Ken Smith, but he was known as 'Bob'. He was small and stocky, with fair hair, and filled in on the enquiry if Stevie had to attend court. Both were rugby fanatics.

They had both been uniformed officers on the frontline during the Bristol riots in the 1980s, when officers used dustbin lids and milk crates to try and protect themselves from the concrete slabs and petrol bombs that were being launched at them. All they had were the old style small wooden batons and no protective clothing. Both said being in the middle of the riots had been an absolutely terrifying experience.

Stevie had actually transferred to the Vice Squad on 1 April and his first task was to take observations on a café in St Paul's, which is where the trouble initiated. The next day he found himself back in uniform as it was a case of all hands to the pumps, and it had been no April Fool.

Residually, the St Paul's area was still regarded as a potential tinderbox, and if officers looked to enter the district they first had to notify the highest ranking officer at their Force Control room. He in turn would carry out a risk assessment and decide whether it was safe for the officer.

Come 7 p.m. on the last night of our time in Bristol I had one more task to complete, to interview a West Indian male who lived in St Paul's. Stevie was trying to ascertain whether it was absolutely necessary as it was a potentially volatile part of the district the man lived in, and it was only he and I. He was understandably reticent, and Lord knows, if I'd stood on those frontlines in the midst of those battles I'd have been the same. It was a strange situation for a Scottish-based officer because we just didn't have potential no-go areas.

The view in Scotland was that we were the police. We dictated what happened but, conversely, other than the miners' strike, Scotland hadn't faced civil unrest on anything near the scale of the Tottenham, Toxteth or St Paul's riots. Call it professional pride. or more likely foolhardiness, but I couldn't for the life of me envisage returning home and telling them I hadn't managed to interview the guy because it may have been unsafe.

The end result found me standing on the doorstep in St Paul's with Stevie Broad. I knocked on the door without first seeking the permission of Force Control. It was opened by a black male. He was a big guy.

In a Caribbean accent he asked, 'Who are you?'

'I'm a police officer. I've come down from Scotland. Who are you?'

'I'm a man,' although he pronounced it 'mon'.

'Well, Mr Man, I'm wondering if you'd give me ten minutes of your time. I'm not here to hassle you or arrest you, and I don't have any warrant, but I'm from Scotland and we both know about English oppression. What do you say?'

A smile and no words, but he held the door open and stood to one side. I quickly accepted the invitation and got more than my ten minutes. He even offered me something to drink. He must have heard those Scotsman stories.

When we left, Stevie said that he couldn't believe I'd just 'brassed my case', and reaffirmed that officers from his Force just would not have done that in that part of the city. For my part, I told him how much I appreciated his going with me, even knowing the potential dangers from past experience. His reply in that Somerset accent?

'English oppression? Oi 'ope we fuck you Jocks at the rugby.'

Later that year, I did manage to get both Stevie and Bob tickets for Scotland versus England at Murrayfield. Sadly for them, that happened to be the year that Scotland not only won the Calcutta Cup but also took the Grand Slam.

Although I explained to Stevie that I found no-go areas difficult to understand as they didn't exist in Scotland, nor were there districts we would be fearful of patrolling, I knew he felt I hadn't walked any distance in his shoes. I could almost hear him saying to himself, 'Yeah, but you haven't policed a full-scale, trying-to-kill-you riot for three nights running.' I was all the more impressed that even given the dangers he'd faced during the riots, and knowing the continued potential for conflict, he was willing to accompany me into St Paul's.

From our interviews with various people it was obvious that Lennox Gayle, a black drug dealer from the St Paul's area, had a crucial role to play in the proceedings.

Gayle was a drug supplier, and had identified Glasgow and the surrounding area as a potentially lucrative outlet for his expanding drug supply. He knew Ricardo Blanco who was living in Bristol. Blanco was Spanish and allegedly an ex-Foreign Legionnaire, although I don't know if that was ever verified. From interviewing witnesses who had dealt with Blanco, he loved to try and portray himself as a Tony Montana type gangster; the character played by Al Pacino in the film *Scarface*.

Gayle also knew John Paul McFadyen, who revelled in the nickname 'Tough Tony'. McFadyen was based in the Rugby area of England. He had a round, mean face and a stocky build. Gayle wanted those two to front the Glasgow end of his business. McFadyen and Blanco hooked up with Thomas Collins, Thomas Currie and Stephen Mitchell from the East End of Glasgow, and who would be valuable to the set-up because of their local knowledge and contacts.

These three would go along with whatever McFadyen and Blanco dictated out of fear or perverse admiration. Blanco and McFadyen, if I recall correctly, had boasted that previously they had brutally tortured a drug dealer until he gave them his stash.

Gayle made arrangements to send Paul Thorne to Glasgow with a consignment of drugs. Thorne would be transporting a kilo of amphetamine sulphate, as well as Temazepam and Temgesic. The value of the drugs was circa £30,000. Thorne would be accompanied by Gayle's then girlfriend. At some point, McFadyen and Blanco, with the tacit agreement of the others, decided that they would have the drugs without paying, and that the best method to achieve that was literally to shoot the messenger.

They drove in a van to the bleak Fenwick Moors in Ayrshire and Blanco and McFadyen both fired a shot into him and made Collins and Currie, who were with them, fire a shot into him, ensuring they were tied through the bloody deed. They had cold-bloodedly planned the murder as they'd stopped en route to buy a shovel. Also en route, they'd stopped at a fish and chip shop as Thorne, having no earthly clue as to what fate awaited him, had indicated that he was hungry. After the murder they joked among themselves that it was a 'Last Supper'.

They buried the body on the Moors and told Gayle that they'd paid Thorne and put him on a train heading back down to England. Gayle's girlfriend had gone back down to Bristol earlier after the consignment had been delivered.

Joe sent me down for a third and final time to Bristol. He needed Gayle in Scotland as he was the conduit between Thorne, Blanco, McFadyen and the others, and had begun the grisly carousel by dispatching Thorne. The Drug Squad officers had done a really good job of compiling a case against Gayle for being concerned in the supply of controlled drugs, although not a gram of controlled drugs had ever been seized. As a result, Joe had been granted a warrant for Gayle's arrest.

Bristol were made aware of the existence of the warrant and conducted an armed operation to arrest him from his bolt hole in St Paul's, at 4 a.m.

I travelled down with Hugh Aitken. Hugh was smallish in height with an open face and a somewhat nervous laugh. He played rugby and football and, as a competitor at either, was as tough as teak. It took four and a half hours to reach Bristol; no speed cameras in those days and in a powerful car. We collected Gayle at Broadbury Road police office and I sat beside Lennox on the journey back. He was a player in his home territory, but he wasn't in his home territory now.

He was confused, disorientated and out of his comfort zone, that's for sure, and that was the way he remained throughout the journey. On the journey back, Hugh and I had a general conversation about what kind of prison Barlinnie was, and the violent men it housed. I had been involved in the enquiry into the riot where prison officers had been taken hostage, and no doubt we spoke about that too.

Being a passenger in the car, Lennox must have been privy to the conversations. Of course, it wasn't intended to deliberately unnerve him but one thing is for sure, by the time he reached Clydebank Police Office, he most certainly realised, 'I'm not in Kansas anymore, Toto.'

That was absolutely fine by Joe, because with Gayle expecting the worst he instead got Joe playing the role of 'The White Paper Fan'; a person who calms the troubled waters in Triad parlance, and is called in to settle disputes. Joe did that with words of reassurance and a vegetable curry. He convinced Gayle to do the right thing and even persuaded him to convince his girlfriend, who was in England, to tell her side of the story. At the subsequent trial, which lasted just short of fifty days, both provided vital evidence. Blanco, McFadyen and Collins received sentences of minimum twenty years.

It was a historic case given the lack of a body, and was a total vindication for Joe. He had fought internal battles with officers more senior in rank but less talented, who believed that not only could the crime not be solved, but stood no chance of being prosecuted successfully.

Understandably, we mounted a massive search in an attempt to find the body but it was forlorn given the area where the body had been buried. Joe utilised the Support Unit, specialist dogs and the Force helicopter. Given that when they had shot and buried Thorne, they had covered the grave with a mattress, the enquiry team hoped that would act as a decent target for the searchers. However, when the actual search area was viewed it was really a hope and prayer.

I took Collins, who had been arrested over a weekend, out in a car to Fenwick Moor, prior to his appearance in court. He seemed to be making an effort to try and pinpoint the area of the murder, but maybe we were nowhere near the true location. Perhaps he thought that if we couldn't find the body he would never be convicted, and was merely looking to mislead.

In fairness, the ability to recall the geography of an unfamiliar area traversed at night alters drastically when viewed during daylight hours. The murder took place on a winter's November night, on a bleak moor, and to try, subsequently, to pinpoint the location of a makeshift grave would test anyone's geographical skills.

Blanco, when eventually released, gave an interview to a newspaper in which he claimed that the whole murder had been McFadyen's idea, and that he had only gone along with the horror show because McFadyen had threatened to shoot him if he didn't. This from someone who was supposedly a tough ex-Foreign Legionnaire and who'd actually had the shotgun in his hands to fire the first shot! If he was so appalled at the whole thing why didn't he use the gun to hold off McFadyen and allow Thorne (who he knew) to escape? He claimed that he fired wide of Thorne, but that also sounds utterly incredible when one factors in his 'Tony Montana' persona.

McFadyen appealed against the length of sentence handed down by the judge, but was unsuccessful.

Lennox Gayle returned to his old habits in Bristol. About a year or so after the trial, he died during a police pursuit, when the stolen van he was travelling in crashed, and the stolen television that was in the back of it married itself to his head.

My mother moved to Ayrshire for the last two years of her life and when I drove down to visit I would often think of Paul Thorne and his mother when I passed Fenwick Moor. He had willingly involved himself in a business that thrives on the greed and misery of others, and for that he'd paid the highest price. His mother, for her part, hopefully drew some comfort from the fact that although she had no body to grieve over, her son's murderers hadn't escaped punishment.

22

HOW TO WIN ENEMIES AND ISOLATE PEOPLE

1989 saw my secondment with the Serious Crime Squad come to an end and I was to transfer to 'E' Division, which, in those days covered, the east end of the city. I knew from having worked several murders and other enquiries in that part of the city that it was a busy division with some very good quality villains living within the Divisional boundaries.

Although I was to enjoy the work and enquiries at 'E', I never actually enjoyed working with the personnel in the CID there. I found the Detective Division very insular and cliquey. They were neither welcoming nor obliging. Around eight of their colleagues had been moved to other duties outwith the Division, following an off-duty incident so, in fairness, they may have harboured some resentment towards the replacement officers . . . of whom I was one.

Whatever the reason, it wasn't somewhere I found to be a comfortable working environment, but ironically found myself involved in some unique enquiries (again), and eventually I was promoted from that Division.

I was initially based at Baillieston Police Office and within a week of my arriving I'd been allocated a robbery to investigate. Although that in itself was nothing out of the ordinary it was the manner of allocation that made me hope for a slice of luck to supplement my determination.

An investigator can be as diligent, determined, conscientious and downright good at their job as they come, but you require a degree of good fortune to be successful. The old story of a general recommending someone for advancement to Napoleon with the words, 'He's very good,' with Napoleon's reply being, 'Yes, but is he very lucky?' was very apt when applied to crime investigation.

As things turned out, not only did I encounter some good fortune in my enquiries but I also drew an Advocate Depute at the top of his game when the case came to the High Court, and that is equally as crucial in bringing an enquiry to a successful conclusion.

The enquiry was also to introduce me to an up and coming gangster who was to threaten my life before coming to a terrible end himself, which is the main reason for including this crime.

It began with three masked and gloved men bursting into a licensed grocer shop in an area known as Garrowhill. The shop was owned and operated by an Asian male and when the robbery occurred he, his daughter and another staff member were working in the shop.

The males were armed variously with axes, knives and wooden batons of some sort. One of the assailants threatened the owner's daughter and the female staff member before assaulting the owner's daughter with a knife and axe, while the other two leapt the counter. After badly beating the owner, they forced him to open the cash registers and fled with about £1,000 in cash.

The owner had gashes to the head and a fractured skull which hospitalised him while his daughter sustained head injuries which required stitching. She was, however, a plucky girl. When she saw the beating her father was being given, despite her injuries, she began to throw tins of creamed rice at the perpetrators. Her father also put up a fierce struggle and the robbers fled, leaving behind a hatchet and a pool cue.

When the enquiry came to be allocated the senior CID supervisor passed it to me and said, 'Let's see how well you do with that dead-end, big city hot shot.'

It was delivered with a smile that couldn't have been any less sincere because behind the smile the unspoken words were, 'Masked and gloved; no witnesses; dead-end; fuck you very much.'

And no he wasn't employing any kind of reverse psychology. For a start, I never needed anyone to motivate me to carry out my investigations and, secondly, he wasn't that smart. I learned that he'd been checking with people he knew in the Serious Crime Squad before I arrived, and had been told that I was a very hard worker, ambitious and a strong personality who didn't suffer fools gladly.

He was one of those lazy types who only wanted a quiet life and did not relish the thought that I might upset the laid-back, cosy environment he'd created. He may have thought that if he kept feeding me difficult-to-resolve enquiries it would frustrate me; that I'd become slightly disillusioned and slump to his method of (non)operating. If so, he couldn't have misread me more.

With the perpetrators having been masked and gloved, identification was going to be difficult and the scene of crime examiner was unlikely to capture any 'lifts'. There was no CCTV or DNA but, hey, if crime investigation was easy everybody would do it.

I visited my crime scene which, strangely, many officers neglect to do. They may have a synopsis on the work carried out by whoever has initially covered the call, and feel they're gaining nothing more from revisiting. I always wanted to get a feel for the scene of the incident and survey the surrounding area, just to ensure nothing has been overlooked by the original attending officers.

I wasn't questioning anyone else's competence or professionalism, it was just that I'd inherited the enquiry and it was now my area of responsibility. Any subsequent criticism, if things were overlooked, would fall on the officer who had ownership.

After I had walked through the shop area, I noticed that several of the items on sale within the shop were bloodstained. The witnesses were uncertain whether they'd managed to injure any of the perpetrators during the struggle so I arranged for the scene examiner to obtain 'blood lifts'. I'd need to have a casualty surgeon (police doctor) obtain blood from both victims to ensure that the 'blood lifts' weren't simply theirs.

On going outside the shop, I looked around to see if there were any areas suitable to canvass for potential witnesses. As I was walking around there were a couple of twelve-year-old boys kicking a ball. I nodded to them and asked how they were doing.

They asked the usual question, 'You CID?'

'Yeah,' I replied.

I wasn't paying too much attention as I was busy making notes on a clipboard about possible exit routes because as it stood no one had seen where they ran to.

'You there for the shop getting done?'

'That's right.'

'I saw wan ae them,' said one of the boys.

Now, he had my full attention. 'What do you mean, saw one? In the shop or outside?'

'Outside. After it. He ran over there and then ran efter the other two, that way.' He pointed a route.

Where he'd seen him running to was towards another shop about twenty yards from the crime scene. I decided to take a look behind the shop he'd run towards and, on doing so, found a sports bag containing a screwdriver, pool cue handle, sawn-off broom handle, syringes and needles.

Now, thanks to having gotten off my backside to work the crime scene and surrounding area I had a secondary crime scene. It might not be a dead-ender after all. With DNA not yet in use in police investigations I would have to hope that any 'lifts' could throw up a match on the fingerprint database. I had been lucky speaking to kids about the fire in Waterside seven or eight years previously, so perhaps lightning would strike twice.

I decided to see if I could push my luck and walked the direction the three had taken, which was a pathway that ran for several hundred yards. I was hoping that something may have been discarded. In a street across from a dual carriageway, which leads from Garrowhill to the Easterhouse scheme, was a row of houses. I walked the length of those houses trying each door in the hope I'd find a witness. Again I was fortunate because I spoke to a couple who had seen three males similar in description to my suspects running across Edinburgh Road.

The witnesses thought the three appeared distressed. I arranged for them to show me exactly where they'd first seen the three and their route until they'd lost sight of them. I walked the route they pointed out looking for any likely places they may have discarded weapons or masks. On checking a bush, I found a pair of tights cut off at one leg and a pair of gloves. There was hair and what appeared to be blood within the stocking mask. Potential gold dust.

What I needed now were names. In all likelihood they were junkies from nearby Easterhouse, but that wasn't an exclusive club. I circulated the descriptions, making sure the CID at Easterhouse was fully aware. I got a response from a young Detective Constable who thought one of the descriptions fitted a Joseph Hanlon.

I had no idea at the time who Hanlon was, but was told by the Detective Constable that he was certainly violent enough to perpetrate the crime, and this was borne out by his nickname which was 'Joe Bananas'. He told me Hanlon had sold 'jellies' (Temazepam) outside of Easterhouse Shopping Centre, but was now living in the Barlanark area, near to where the robbery occurred.

I had nothing else at that point so I decided to speak to Hanlon. I went to a flat in Sandaig Road and was allowed in. The flat was clean and new and in the hallway lay boxes of floor tiles still to be laid. Hanlon had an alibi for the time of the robbery but didn't strike me as being the type that would hold up a shop with junkies. He had black hair and eyes and thick eyebrows that made him look as if he was permanently frowning. He was small in height but had a stocky build. The interview went pleasantly enough, mainly because he knew he was on solid ground. I let the feeler dangle in the air regarding providing information in the future and left things at that.

Very shortly thereafter, a sergeant at Easterhouse and a cop at Shettleston both got the same two names for potential suspects which, in turn, got me a warrant to search a house where they were both staying. They didn't answer the door, so in I went and found one behind the lounge door with a needle and syringe plunged into his groin. He knew why we were at the door, and knowing he was going to jail wanted a 'going away fix'. Had that situation arisen now I would have been required to take him straight to a hospital, but as with the suicide on the railway line in 1981, a different set of guidelines (more specifically none) applied.

Both were taken to Shettleston for interview and an identification parade. One was identified and charged while I had to release the other as the shopkeeper still wasn't fit enough to view a parade. When he felt strong enough I arranged another identification parade, and he picked out the male I'd had to release earlier.

I then received a telephone call at Baillieston advising me of the identity of the third suspect. Who made the call? I thought then and do now that the voice on the phone was Hanlon's. Why would he do that? He had moved into Tam McGraw's circle of influence.

Thomas – or as he was known by the Scottish nickname for Thomas – Tam McGraw was another from a tough housing area. He was a thief who progressed to drug importation and like so many others grew very wealthy from the drug trade. He was the type who always seemed to evade prosecution. He possessed innate street cunning and was adept at manipulating police officers. He would be suspected of involvement in one of Scotland's worst mass murders. I'll elaborate on McGraw and those murders in chapter 23.

It may well have been that Hanlon, or on the instructions of McGraw, may have been trying to recruit his own tame police officer who would give him leeway in his criminal activities. If that had been the intention he, and possibly McGraw, had misjudged me badly.

I took the information at face value and obtained a search warrant for the house in Kildermorie Road in Easterhouse. When I searched it I found a section of broom handle with fresh saw markings at the end, a broken section of snooker cue and a saw. When I questioned the male who'd been in the flat he admitted his part in the robbery.

On the date of the High Court trial I was fortunate to have Gordon Jackson as the Advocate Depute. At that time, he was acting as the Crown Prosecutor. Having faced him subsequently when he was defending criminals I was glad he was on the side of the angels on this occasion.

After I had given my evidence, I remained in court to hear him present the chain of evidence in an expansive, demonstrative and almost inarguable fashion. He led the jury through the chain of events, including the matching, forensically, of the hair and pieces of snooker cue; like a primary school teacher with eager pupils.

Two of the three were found guilty and received sentences of four and three years, which I was delighted with considering I'd started with pretty much zero. I had persevered, got lucky, received good information from other officers, and great forensic support from the scientists.

When I got back to the office following the result I may well have been purposely over-jubilant in front of the supervisor who'd been so sarcastic when giving me the enquiry. It was probably a bit childish and needless, but I knew he'd never have closed that case. He wouldn't have gone to the scene, or walked the distances I did, or knocked on the doors I had. It was an act that, allied to another enquiry, almost lost me my promotion subsequently.

I endeared myself to him even less a couple of months later, when I basically hijacked an enquiry which other detectives had failed to progress, and which he as a supervisor should have addressed, given the nature of the incidents. They were sexual in nature and even someone suffering from ocular leprosy could see they were progressing in severity and, consequently, had the potential to escalate into a possible rape.

The first incident happened after 8 p.m. in late January, when two girls, aged sixteen and nineteen, were walking through the grounds of a local secondary school known as Bannerman High. The school gates were never closed and, although poorly illuminated, pedestrians frequently walked through the school, using it as a shortcut between two roads.

The girls saw a man walking towards them exposing himself and, making no attempt to cover himself, he reached out an arm as he drew level with them, and attempted to touch one of the girls. Naturally, they pulled away, ran off and contacted the police. The attending officers searched the area but couldn't find anyone.

In addition to his having just calmly walked on after the incident, the girls told the attending officers that the perpetrator had been accompanied by a golden Labrador.

Around the same time of night, but two weeks later, a twenty-two-year-old and a sixteen-year-old girl were seated on steps at playing fields at the rear of the same school when they were approached by a male who sat down beside them and placed his hand on the inside of one of the girl's thighs. He then did the same to the other girl. As the girls got up to run away he tried to put his hands up their skirts and touch them on the buttocks.

The girls saw a passing police car a short distance from the scene and flagged it down and told the officers what had happened. They both mentioned again seeing a golden Labrador which, they felt, had been in the care of the perpetrator. Again the search of the surrounding area failed to trace the suspect.

There was a third incident some five nights later, this time about 9.30 p.m., involving two fourteen-year-old girls. The girls were again within the grounds of the school when a male walking towards them put his hand between the legs of one of the girls and grabbed her private parts. Again he had the same type of dog with him.

Four nights later, a twenty-four-year-old woman, who was accompanied by her nine-year-old niece, was taking the same short cut through the school when they became aware of a man, who appeared to be shadowing them. He seemed to be veering to the left and right of them.

145

The woman quickened the pace to reach the roadway before she was seized from behind and a hand grabbed her breast and another hand went down between her legs at her private parts.

The perpetrator then started to pull the woman back but she managed to lash out with a pair of roller skates she'd been carrying. He clung on and increased the severity of his grip on the woman, but when the nine-year-old began to scream he let go of the woman and ran off.

Owing to the increase in severity of each incident, and allied to the fact that the descriptions of the perpetrator in each of the incidents was the same or very similar, and that on three of the occasions a dog had been seen, surveillance was mounted in and around the school. Nothing came of the surveillance.

Towards the end of February, an anonymous telephone call was received at the police office, to the effect that the person responsible for the indecencies had had his house windows broken by a further victim of an indecent act, but that this girl had not reported the matter to the police.

I'd been on annual leave for a period and on coming back in the second week in March updated myself on what had been happening within my area. When I looked through the various crime reports and saw the sexual incidents it was alarming. I also saw a note concerning the possible lead.

No one single detective had actually been tasked with the investigation of all of the crimes. Instead, the supervisor had passed them out ad hoc. One detective had inherited at least two of them, but no one had progressed the information about the vandalism to the windows of the alleged suspect.

I actually asked the officer who had inherited a couple of the incidents what they had done with the information, only to be met with, 'I've had a few things on so I haven't had a chance.' That was nonsense, but typical of the ennui among many of the CID in that division at that time.

Failing to address any series of crimes is bad enough, but these crimes involved sexual offences against females, some as young as fourteen. It was utterly beyond my comprehension. I always tried to adopt the attitude when investigating of, 'What if the victim was mine, or someone I knew?' Would I be happy with how it had been dealt with? I felt that personally, it kept me focused when investigating my inherited enquiries.

In this case, whether it upset people or not (which never really concerned me), I would not have forgiven myself had some woman been the victim of a very serious sexual crime because of police inefficiency. What the victims had endured, as it stood, was bad enough.

Given that the caller hadn't specified when the vandalism had occurred I sat down and began to trawl the paper crime reports since the beginning of the year. I didn't even know if the 'victim' of the vandalism would have been stupid enough to report the matter to the police, but I had to have a starting point.

I managed to find two possible crime reports, each related to broken house windows and, in one, the house lay not too far from the crime scenes. One had occurred on 26 January, the night of the first incident. That fact made my mind up to make the complainer for that vandalism my first interviewee. The other crime report concerning the broken windows was the backup.

I went to the house along with a young lad who was on his six-month secondment to the CID. The only person home was a woman who told me that her husband was at work. I didn't enlighten her as to why I was looking to speak to her husband. In the hallway of her home, when she'd opened the door, had been a golden Labrador, so I thought I might be at the right home ('Brilliant deduction, Watson. What gave you the first clue?').

I went back a second time and the householder still hadn't returned from work, but as we drove away we saw a male two streets away who fitted the general description and was wearing clothing similar to that of our suspect for the indecencies. When we stopped him and identified ourselves as police officers he turned out to be the householder we'd been looking to speak to.

We detained him, took him to a police office and interviewed him. Under tape-recorded conditions he indicated that he may have been responsible, but couldn't recall carrying out the attacks. He said that he'd been drinking and that if he had acted in that manner then he had a problem.

He was identified by most of the victims at a subsequent identification parade. I was pleased with the result. It hadn't been exactly astrophysics, but again I'd got off my backside and put shoe leather on concrete. Others hadn't.

Of course, the supervisor wasn't best please as he felt I'd shown him

147

and others up, but in my whole life I've never concerned myself with winning popularity contests. He'd had an opportunity to resolve the situation and so had others . . . but hadn't.

Women and children had been sexually assaulted. If the situation had escalated to where someone had been raped one could imagine the ramifications for the police. It wouldn't have made great reading if it had emerged that they had had an opportunity to apprehend the perpetrator and resolve the situation, but hadn't done so.

It wasn't in my nature, and offended my personal pride to sit and allow that situation to remain unaddressed. If others wanted to sit around drinking coffee and talking about holidays that was their decision. I got decent money to provide a decent return, and if they didn't like what I'd done, too bad.

I've never practised self-delusion, so I know many people found me difficult to work with. If there was a chance of closing an enquiry then I was totally focused on the task in hand. I could be abrupt, didn't play politics and, irrespective of rank, couldn't disguise it if I disagreed, or wasn't in favour of a particular course of action.

I don't mean I was disrespectful of authority, far from it. Given the upbringing by my parents and my time at seminary I had a healthy respect for elders and those in authority, but those same parents and my teachers at seminary had instilled in me a questioning nature. It was emphasised to me that if I thought something was wrong, or a situation was unjust then, if I failed to challenge it, the fault lay with me, and I couldn't later complain if I'd remained silent. Childhood teachings obviously have a bearing on an adult's nature. The Jesuits maintained if you gave them the boy until fourteen, they'd give you the man.

My commitment, I suspect, benefited the public, but was to the detriment of my career prospects. An Inspector once said to me that'd he would hate to work with me, but that if he, or any of his family, were a crime victim then mine would be the first name he'd want on the sheet as investigator.

Naturally, my inability to remain silent if I disagreed led to several confrontational situations in my police service, but confrontation wasn't something I shrank from. However, I was now in the supervisor's firing line. He prepared an appraisal which, although I never saw it, slaughtered me. It was apparently a real hatchet job. The reason I didn't see

PAUL FERRIS

Inseparable from Hanlon and Glover. Being in prison at the time of their murders may have saved his life. Ferris stood trial for the murder of Arthur Thompson Junior, his former childhood friend.

STEVEN/DEAN RYAN

Convicted of the slaughter of a Procurator Fiscal Depute. Remorseless. Their silence may have damned them at their subsequent trial.

COTTAGE BAR PUBLIC HOUSE Used as
a 'gang hut' by Paul Ferris, Joe Hanlon
and Bobby Glover. The murdered bodies
of Hanlon and Glover would be left
in a car near the pub in revenge for
the murder of Thompson Junior.

BOBBY GLOVER/JOE HANLON
Small time crooks who
stepped out of their
league. They underestimated
Thompson Senior and paid
with their lives.

WILLIAM LOBBAN

Sheltered by Glover while an
escaped prisoner and the
last known person to see
Hanlon and Glover alive.
Lobban's uncle was a very
close friend of Arthur
Thompson Senior.
Lobban disappeared after
the murders. Eventually
traced and arrested in
London.

JOHN PAUL McFADYEN/
RICARDO BLANCO
Both pitiless and
calculating. Executed a
Bristol drugs courier, then
buried the body on a
Scottish Moor. Convicted
of murder although the
body has never been
discovered.

THOMAS (TAM) McGRAW
Rarely seen photo of a very young
Tam McGraw. A thief then, but he
would later graduate to drug importer
and a manipulator of police officers.

MICKEY OATES MOTORCYCLE TOP

Limited edition issue and the key to solving the mystery of a newborn baby thrown into the Crinan Canal in Argyll.

– WONDERWEST WORLD

An Ayrshire holiday camp which was the scene of tragedy when a small boy wandered off. It sparked a huge search which resulted in the eventual discovery of his body.

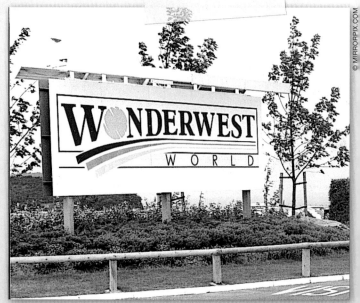

A YOUNG ARTHUR THOMPSON SNR
Family man, extortionist, killer and Security Services asset.

ARTHUR THOMPSON JNR
Junior was hapless and lacked his father's animal cunning (and luck). He was murdered just a few hours into his prison leave.

ARTHUR THOMPSON SNR
Relaxed at home. He survived almost as many attempts on his life as Fidel Castro.

© MIRRORPIX

FUNERAL OF TONY McGOVERN

Tony's coffin carried by two of his brothers, James and Thomas. All three would be gunshot victims, Tony fatally.

CROW ROAD CAR PARK

The spectacular scenery was in stark contrast to the discovery of a police officer's body.

MARK VASS

Self-styled businessman. In reality, an armed robber and suspected of at least two murders.

CADDER DEATH SCENE

Vass' propensity for violence would in turn result in his own murder.

HIGH RISE FLATS, MARYHILL
The high-rise building where an assassin using a rifle with a telescopic sight lay in wait to murder gangster Frank McPhie.

DRYING AREA
Reconstruction of the view the assassin would have had of his target area

SCENIC KELVIN WALKWAY
Remote inlet where Michael Hirrell raped a foreign national.

it was that when he showed it to a senior detective in rough draft, to let him know it was coming, he was told that it would be advisable to alter it drastically or it would in all probability backfire.

Grant Findlay was the Detective Superintendent at 'E' Division and was a fan. Grant had been a worker himself. When I'd joined the police he had been a sergeant in charge of a car crime and housebreaking unit, covering the north side of the city, and the unit's clear-up rate had been nothing short of phenomenal. Grant had ascended from sergeant to his current rank in nine years. He was aware of how I had been working since I'd arrived, and would have spotted the hatchet job immediately, and disapproved. Grant also knew that I'd left the Serious Crime Squad having been highly appraised by the Detective Superintendent there, Bob Arnott.

In addition to other work I'd been involved in while within the Squad, I'd played a role in a breakthrough in a murder Bob had been in overall charge of at Maryhill, and he'd been grateful for that as the enquiry had stalled.

The murder had begun incongruously with either vandalism to, or the theft of a hubcap from, a car. From there a tit-for-tat sequence of events began between two families, culminating in a man being attacked by three men wielding knives and a machete.

It had been a difficult enquiry and was a classic 'Who's lying?' 'Who's lying more?' 'Who's lying most?' scenario. Cops refer to these types of situations as having to 'burst' (break down) the witnesses.

A potential witness was the brother of one of the suspects, but he was proving highly elusive. I called my DSS contact and he gave me an address in high flats at the Glenavon area of Maryhill. The address was known as a 'giro drop'; i.e. just a convenience address. The witness didn't live there but would use that address to collect his social security cheque. I knew that his cheque would arrive in the post the following day and that guaranteed he'd be at that flat at some point.

The problem was that there was no set time that'd he appear so, along with another detective, Jim Duncan, I sat on the stairwell of the fourteenth floor waiting for him to arrive. In the films or television he'd arrive just as we got there. Unfortunately for us, we sat in that freezing stairwell with a Force 8 gale blowing through for three and a half hours.

I recall distinctly how we passed the time and that was down to Jim.

He was another who fitted the description 'burly detective' to a T. He was six feet tall and broadly built with a Sean Connery type moustache. Jim loved Western movies, and I loved films in general so, we ended up firing the dialogue to *The Magnificent Seven* and two John Wayne films, *The Man Who Shot Liberty Valance* and *Big Jake*, back and forth. I think we were word perfect on each film.

Our witness showed up eventually, and when we interviewed him he tried to take his brother out of the main picture by telling us that there was no way his brother had been responsible for the cause of death because he'd only struck the victim across the lower back. As he told us, he demonstrated where his brother had allegedly struck the victim, and he indicated that the blow had been over the kidney area. That just happened to be the fatal blow as it had split the victim open like a melon.

We eventually arrested three people for that murder, but Bob felt that the work that Jim and I had done had been instrumental in breathing oxygen into the enquiry. Consequently, he had shown his appreciation by giving me a very good exit appraisal before I headed east. As things transpired, the proposed 'hatchet job' appraisal at my new division was altered quietly to something more agreeable.

There is a phrase in an Ian Fleming novel, *Goldfinger*, which reads: 'Once is happenstance. Twice is coincidence. The third time it's enemy action.' I often think that could have referred to my dealings with Joe Hanlon.

My initial contact was total happenstance. The officer from Easterhouse couldn't have known what he had set off when he put his name forward as a possible suspect for the robbery at Garrowhill.

The next contact I had with Hanlon, while not exactly coincidence, was certainly not pre-planned. I'd brought him to the office at Baillieston, but can't recall exactly why I'd brought him there. It may even have been a random pull (stop), and I was looking to see what, if anything, he'd say. That sort of tactic isn't as easy nowadays, as there has to be a record kept of a person's presence at a police office, but back then it was easier to 'invite' a person to the office for a chat.

Either way, it turned acrimonious because, in Hanlon's words, I wasn't 'showing us any kind of respect'. By 'us' he meant Tam McGraw, Robert Glover and McGraw's other acolytes, who I stopped and harassed at every turn. In response, I practically snorted and literally spat at his feet. It wasn't a class thing to do, but I couldn't believe the balls of him. I told him that he'd overdosed on whatever McGraw was feeding him and that he and his 'crew' were trash; that my respect was for decent people who worked hard for a living, to provide for their families. It wasn't for shite-hawks who stabbed, threatened, sold drugs or shot people.

We weren't best friends at parting. The third meeting would definitely require enemy action.

23

MUZZLE HIM

There was a feud ongoing between Tam McGraw, Joe Hanlon, Robert Glover and Paul Ferris on one side and Arthur Thompson on the other. Shots had been fired by various factions. Arthur had been run over by a car and it had been necessary for army explosive experts to carry out a controlled explosion on a grenade which had been thrown into McGraw's pub, the Caravel, in Hallhill Road, Barlanark. The grenade hadn't detonated and, unbelievably, and perhaps ironically, had been taken from the pub and left in a nearby cemetery. Given the character of the participants, these incidents unsurprisingly hadn't been reported to the police.

On 25 May 1990, Thompson was run over in Provanmill Road. Efforts were made to trace the car that had struck him and then sped off.

On 26 May, the day after the hit and run, Paul Ferris walked into Arnold Clark Hire Drive, Hamilton Road, Mount Vernon, and signed a hire agreement to lease a Vauxhall Cavalier, registration G513 UGA, despite owning a White Ford Escort XR3i, registration F769 LGA.

The hire was supposed to terminate on 2 June 1990, but was extended by Ferris for a further week. Ferris had classed himself as a 'manager' on the hire agreement and given his Blackhill address. He'd also listed someone from Baillieston as a co-signer.

On 4 June 1990, Ferris was arrested and charged with attempting to pervert the course of justice after he failed to answer questions relating to the whereabouts of his white XR3i. The police suspected that car had been the one used to run Thompson over and had wanted to have it examined to eliminate it (or not) from enquiries. The white Escort was never recovered.

On 6 June, I happened to be driving in Sandaig Road, where Hanlon lived, when I saw him come out of the close mouth to his flat, enter the hired Vauxhall Cavalier and drive off. At that point I'd no idea Ferris had hired a car. When I checked the next day and found out that, with Ferris in jail, Hanlon had no right to drive the car, I viewed it as another opportunity to harass him.

He wasn't at home and he wasn't in the Caravel public house, where he was ostensibly employed as a manager, so I made arrangements for Arnold Clark to attend at Sandaig Road, where the car was parked, and remove it.

I later took a call from a car hire employee who told me that two men had shown up with the original key for the Vauxhall car. They were adamant that the hire had not been completed and demanded that the car be returned to them, or that they be allowed access to it. The staff member had told them that they would have to speak to the manageress who would not be available until 2 p.m. that afternoon.

My first thought was that given the determination to access the car there must be something in it that shouldn't have been there, and given the ongoing feud it may possibly have been a firearm. I headed down to the car hire complex, taking with me two young officers, a male and female, who were working in plain clothes.

When I examined the car closely, I noticed that a section of body work in front of the nearside wing mirror had been filled with cataloy (a putty used in car bodywork repair) and painted the same colour, in an attempt to conceal the damage. It had the appearance of a small hole. The manageress confirmed that when the vehicle had been hired by Ferris it had been undamaged.

Having looked at it I was convinced the hole had been made by a bullet. I contacted the Ballistics Department and arranged for someone to examine the car, especially around the damage. Just then, a car pulled into the forecourt of the complex, which contained McGraw, his son William, Joe Hanlon and Bobby Glover. This was obviously the team looking to access the car.

As I had seen Hanlon drive a vehicle which he had no right to be in, I detained him with a view to charging him, but he didn't have the original car key on him. Glover did and when I told him to hand it over he refused and decided to try and conceal it. That suited me just fine. I told him it would be a shame to break up a beautiful friendship so I arrested him and told him to cosy up with Hanlon in the back of the police car.

At this, McGraw decided to mouth off about how 'out of order' I was. I told him that if he uttered one more word he'd complete the (un)holy trinity. His reaction demonstrated to me how much leeway he'd been given by police officers, because there was a total look of disbelief on his face, and the astonishment in his voice was clear when he said, 'You'll give me the fuckin' jail?'

He'd uttered more than the one word I'd warned him about so I thought, 'Sod it. We'll squeeze him in somehow,' and began to walk from around the unmarked police car towards him. That was enough. He slipped the clutch and was off, but not before shouting, 'I'm complaining to your fuckin' boss. I'll have your fuckin' job.' I was quaking in my shoes, but there would be a surprise waiting when I eventually reached the office. However, before that I'd have an eventful car journey with two of the 'Three Amigos'.

To say they were blazing mad at being arrested on a car hire forecourt, and in front of the Queen Bee McGraw, wouldn't do them justice. I think they honestly believed they were far too big 'names' for that to happen. Again they were possibly overdosing on whatever distorted view McGraw had instilled in them on how to deal with cops. Either way, on the journey Hanlon blurted out, 'You're pushing us too far, and you might find yourself getting shot.'

I shouted out to the girl driving, 'Stop the car!' I think she thought something had happened because she braked hard. Hanlon and Glover, for their part, looked as if they thought the threat had been effective, and that they were about to be released. They couldn't have been more wrong.

Glover was next to me separating me from Hanlon. We'd stopped opposite waste ground so I said, 'Let's not fuckin' wait. There's a bit of ground over there. There's only a boy and lassie and you two tough gangsters. They'll drive off and the three of us'll go over there. Let's see if your heart is as big as your mouth, and we'll do it now.'

Glover turned to his left and looked at Hanlon for a good second or so. I thought (and was so pumped, hoped) they were about to take me up on the offer. Glover turned back towards me and said,

'You're mental. You're off your fuckin' head, do you know that?'

'Bear that in mind if you grow a set and want to come looking for me,' was my response.

I later apologised to the young officers for calling them a 'boy' and 'lassie', but there was no way I'd allow those two, or half a dozen like them, to intimidate me. The supposed 'most feared street fighter of his generation' Joe Hanlon, had remained silent throughout, although I'm sure with someone's back turned, or with a gun and up against an unarmed fat boy, he was a tough character.

When we got to Shettleston Police Office I charged Hanlon with stealing the hire car and having no insurance to drive it, and Glover with police obstruction. No sooner had I finished processing them when I was summoned to see a senior CID officer who informed me that McGraw had contacted him and told him that if he'd keep 'the pit bull on a leash' he'd ensure a sawn-off shotgun found its way to police hands.

When he told me this I actually laughed, and said, 'He's some hope, because I'm just about to go back out to get him.' However, the senior officer was clear in his instruction. 'Lay off.'

I was blazing and in an outburst said, 'This is unbelievable. A sawn-off shot gun? Big friggin' deal. He's got access to more hardware than Adnan Khashoggi. When is somebody going to accept he's the turn [target] and not the Sammies [dafties] he gives up?'

It didn't matter how much of a strop I threw, I was to lay off. Now bear in mind that even given my unscheduled stop with Hanlon and Glover, and in pre-mobile phone days, McGraw had managed to get to a phone, get through directly to a senior CID officer, and put up this deal before I'd driven back the short journey to Shettleston Police Office.

I'd first dealt with McGraw soon after I'd arrived at Baillieston when his bottom floor flat in Burnett Road, Barlanark, had been the subject of an attempted break-in. I'd gone up with a young cop who was on a six-month secondment to the CID. I knew of McGraw because of his being an integral part of the Barlanark Team, a group of organised thieves who specialised in attacking premises that carried large stocks of cigarettes and alcohol.

They violated the premises between 2 and 4 a.m. and if the premises were protected by an alarm they would cut the phoneline at, and in the vicinity of, the target. In those days, before alarms systems became more complex, this had a dual purpose. It isolated both the target premises and any surrounding houses, and that prevented any householders contacting the police.

After the 'turn', two of the gang would drive the stolen property back in a stolen car or van, so that if they were ever stopped by the police, it would be a maximum of two from the hit team of between four and eight who were caught. It had provided McGraw with a lucrative living.

Within the house he sat on a couch chain-smoking and drinking a mug of tea. He was about 5'8" tall and his build, colour of teeth and pallor suggested that his staple diet consisted largely of what he was puffing on, and what he was drinking. He was at pains to present himself as an ordinary guy and emphasised that anyone could see he had nothing worth stealing.

The flat was not ostentatiously furnished that's for sure, but he did decline my offer to look around and advise him where he could improve his home security. He was polite enough, but that may have been because he regarded me as another cop he could manipulate, and I think that is where the crux of the McGraw/police relationship lay.

When the noose became a little tight McGraw would give up something that was, to him, inconsequential, and too many officers were content to accept what he threw. However, in any dealings I had with informants I ran the show not them and there comes a time when it is apparent that the informant becomes the target, irrespective of how good the information is that they've been providing. That was something I never lost sight of. Too many times, however, when he dealt with cops, McGraw got more out of the deal than he gave up. That was a basic mistake on the part of the officers who dealt with him.

For my own part, I didn't like him from minute one. I certainly wouldn't have used him as an informant. I've used informants extensively throughout my service, and although you can never lose sight of the fact that you're dealing with criminals there has to be a basis, however tenuous, of trust. I would have trusted McGraw as much as I'd trust a scorpion I was holding in my hand not to sting me.

Intelligence suggested he'd been on the landing of the block of flats in Bankend Street in April 1984, when fire ignited the Doyle family home and resulted in the deaths of six members of the Doyle family. The Doyle family had run an ice cream van, and McGraw and his Barlanark Team members weren't happy about that as they wanted the lucrative 'runs' to themselves.

McGraw could maximise his profits because the cigarettes he'd stolen from the various premises were then sold through the ice cream vans. The vans also provided cover for selling heroin. The Doyle family were an inconvenience, so McGraw had a fire started at their home which became an inferno. There apparently wasn't enough evidence to charge him, but intelligence suggested McGraw was involved and a main protagonist.

Information and intelligence are the lifeblood of crime detection and consequently that means officers often have to deal with people who aren't exactly saintly. Almost 99% of the time the informants will have, at some point in their lives, been involved in criminal activity and officers understand that.

Intelligence also suggested McGraw had been involved in the deaths of six people, so would any officer want to deal with a reptile like that other than to turn the key on him? Undoubtedly, some did, but for my part, given the strong belief that he'd had involvement in mass murder, I felt he should have been 'jailed' at every opportunity. There's no doubt he was a self-preserver. I've already indicated how quickly he'd reacted when he felt I posed a threat and offered up a firearm to a senior CID officer to 'muzzle' me.

Having said that, I should make it clear that, to my knowledge, McGraw traded in information. Did any police officers take money from him? God, I hope not, because corruption like that taints every decent working officer, but anything is possible. I would never have thought cops would hand over heroin to informants, but there was a strong possibility that had occurred.

When you have a former Chief of Interpol, the head of the Australian Anti-Corruption Squad, a senior FBI figure and sundry other Law Enforcement members charged with corruption, the law of averages dictates that with 6,000–7,000 Strathclyde officers there will be rotten apples.

What I will say is that there have been reams of *Fantasy Island* nonsense, written purely to sell books and publications. If you notice, all the more sensationalist acts are attributed to dead people. Why? Because you can't libel the dead and they can't defend themselves.

Forget all this nonsense about McGraw being nicknamed 'The Licencee' because the police had given him a licence to commit crime with impunity. That nickname arose because the newspapers were initially very reticent (for fear of possible legal action) of actually naming McGraw in their articles. As a means of avoiding this they began to refer to him by that name because he had a public house.

Similarly, there was never any fight between Scottish Crime Squad Officers and Serious Crime Squad officers in the middle of a Barlanark street, over whether he was to be arrested. Do you think if that had happened people who'd worked in the Serious and Scottish Crime Squads wouldn't have known about it?

Back at Shettleston Office I had a final minor drama with Hanlon when it came to taking his photographs and fingerprints. I was with an older detective and was leaning against a worktop opposite where Hanlon had been told to wash his hands prior to being printed.

He said, 'You're no printing me,' and gestured towards me.

I uttered one word, 'Smashing', and pushed myself off the worktop towards him. Before I'd covered any distance he'd turned towards the other officer and said hastily, 'But I'll let you print me.' It was rather pathetic.

When the hire car was examined forensically Ballistics recovered a nine-millimetre bullet from the section of the car that had been disguised with cataloy It looked like someone had been out hunting old man Thompson again.

A few weeks later, I was in the office when I was told that Paul Ferris was in the foyer looking to speak to me. I had a good idea why. His driving licence had been in the sun visor when I'd searched the car, but I hadn't been prepared to trail about half the city to return it. I was sure he'd come looking for it, and was happy to give him his property back as I wouldn't have wanted him to claim that the driving licence had been found at a crime scene and he was the victim of (another) police conspiracy.

When I went out to the foyer I found Ferris, together with the conjoined twins Hanlon and Glover. As I was talking to Ferris I could see that the other two were almost giggling, and bore looks you see kids wear when they think their big brother is there to make everything all right. I hope I didn't disappoint them by not collapsing in a puddle on the floor, but I did ensure I was circumspect in what I said. Some five or six years previously Ferris had driven around the Balornock, Blackhill and Royston housing schemes in his red and black Vauxhall SRi with a microphone sewn into the fabric.

He would look to engage any police officers with whom he had contact in conversation, presumably in the hope that they would say something indiscreet, and provide him with evidence of how all the bad officers were out to get him. Ferris, for his part, was polite and quietly spoken, although that may have been because of an operating recording device, or perhaps he'd simply read Sun Tzu's *The Art of War*, or at least the section on knowing your enemy.

The next real interaction I had with Ferris, Glover and Hanlon was giving evidence at Ferris's trial when he'd been charged with murdering Arthur Thompson's son and, in the case of Hanlon and Glover, when I identified them at the scene of their body dump.

I have a rather stubborn nature and, despite what I'd been told, had absolutely no intention of ceasing to pursue McGraw and his cronies, but the opportunity to continue was taken out of my hands by my former Detective Inspector at the Squad, Pat Durkin, who recommended me for a further secondment at Force HQ.

24

MILITARY PRECISION

I'd enjoyed working for and with Pat Durkin. He was a worker throughout his police career and liked workers in return. He was of average height and always had that freshly barbered or just stepped out of a shower look. He had actually tried to manoeuvre my transfer to work for him at Easterhouse when he knew my secondment to the Squad was coming to a close, but hadn't managed it owing to the number of officers required to backfill the vacancies at the East.

He was aware that Pat Connor, a Detective Chief Superintendent, based at FHQ, wanted officers to staff an experimental robbery unit operating from the Criminal Intelligence Department at FHQ. Pat (Durkin) knew that I would work hard and try and make a success of the task, and told Mr Connor that.

In the late 1980s, there had been an alarming increase in the number of robberies involving the use of firearms throughout Scotland. Pat Connor wanted the robberies collated in an attempt to identify patterns and 'teams'. I worked with an officer who was trained in the input of data onto the HOLMES system and a Detective Sergeant. We received details of, and analysed, all the robberies involving firearms throughout Scotland.

We worked for a year and were successful in supplying information identifying six persons for robberies, and even provided suspects for a bank robbery in Sweden. We were also successful in linking robberies and teams where, previously, no connection had been made by the investigating officers. We preceded by a decade what the police now term 'Crime Pattern Analysis'. The police now utilise that system to examine serial and series crimes.

I mention this period for a particular reason. There was a robbery and a story – probably apocryphal – which intrigued me.

I worked with an officer who had served in the armed forces prior to his police career, and he told me that a story had circulated during his time in the military concerning Special Forces. The story circulating suggested that Special Forces officers – who like just about everyone – operated on a finite budget. Sometimes, that budget was so stretched that the units found themselves without desirable equipment. As a consequence, Special Forces units were encouraged to utilise their resourcefulness to overcome budget deficits.

There is extensive information available in the public domain nowadays concerning Special Forces selection processes and the operations undertaken by these officers, but I would treat many of the stories with a degree of scepticism. I don't believe that Special Forces officers are the supermen portrayed in some of the more lurid publications, but I do believe that, irrespective of height, build, body shape or social background, they will, in all probability, be innovative, courageous, resourceful and daring. That brings me to the robbery.

It involved four men and a bank in Edinburgh.

When a security firm delivered cash to a bank in the 1980s, there was often a delay in bank staff placing the delivery in the vault. The delay occurred from sourcing sufficient staff to carry the cash into the vault, and I suppose from lax practices.

On this particular day, three masked men entered the bank just after the delivery of the money. They were masked, gloved and fire-armed, and entered after the security staff had left and before the money had been placed in the vault.

One man covered the customers and staff, one vaulted the counter for the money, while the third covered the door and monitored his stopwatch. The fourth man waited outside with transport.

When two minutes had elapsed the only words spoken were by the man with the stopwatch. He said simply, 'Time, gentlemen,' and with that they were off, with tens upon tens of thousands of pounds.

Thanks and goodbye. Never a sniff of being solved. Precision-tooled.

Now, I would never cast aspersions on the reputation of the armed forces. It's a job I couldn't do. I only mention the story because of the manner in which the robbery was executed and the story I'd been told, which made for interesting speculation.

By the time we'd finished compiling the final report on our work and taken annual leave it had been a year since I'd left 'E' Division I found myself working from Shettleston on my return and little had changed.

Joe Hanlon had got himself shot under the arm and the bullet had exited his penile tube; a shot in a million. Detectives Kenny Simpson and Tommy Loan had been on duty and learned about the alleged shooting. They'd gone to the Caravel public house looking for Hanlon to try and confirm whether the intelligence had been correct. They spoke to Hanlon who was wearing canary yellow tracksuit bottoms and a t-shirt. When they put the allegation to him he pulled up his shirt and revealed an unmarked body, so the guys just took it that the story was untrue.

It later transpired that the information was absolutely true, but Hanlon, who'd signed himself out of hospital immediately after going there for treatment, had been wearing an absorbent type bandage when he'd been interviewed by the officers.

Kenny and Tommy would later joke about being unable to detect the smell of gas, given that they'd stood face to face with him and couldn't work out he'd been shot. In fairness, his pantomime would have fooled anyone, and to put the information in context, there were stories of car chases, threats and shots being exchanged on such a regular basis that it became a difficult task to separate fact from fiction.

25

TRIAD (AND TESTED)

Just after my return I was to experience some of the frustration felt by the detectives who had worked on the Philip Wong murder which had happened in Garnethill. Mr Wong had been a respected member of the Chinese community, but when investigating his murder the officers had found that information was unforthcoming. Their attempts to win over the reticent Chinese Community had been met with a Great Wall of Silence, but I suppose a Triad assassination ensured tongues remained tied.

On Monday, 29 July 1991, not long after I'd begun my shift, a uniform officer came through to tell me that the owner of a local Chinese take-away had come into the office, and was claiming to have been held hostage in his car the previous night. I spoke to him, and found that, although Vietnamese-born, he had lived most of his life in Hong Kong before arriving in Britain in 1979.

He told me he'd been working in his shop the previous evening when he'd been approached by two Vietnamese males, one of whom he knew. The men had asked him for work, but had been told by the shopkeeper that he had no vacancies. The three had then arranged to meet up for a meal at the close of business.

When the shopkeeper closed up he was met by the two men who, by this time, had been joined by two further Vietnamese. An amicable conversation followed during which the shopkeeper was asked to point out his car. As soon as he did all pretence of friendliness vanished, three of the men produced flick knives and he was bundled into the rear of his own car.

He was then forced to hand over his car keys and was driven to various quiet locations on the outskirts of the city. Throughout his time in the car he claimed that he had been punched, had knives held against his throat, and was threatened with having his fingers cut off if he didn't hand over £5,400. I'm not entirely sure, but I think that number may hold some significance in Triad culture.

He eventually agreed to go to his bank first thing in the morning. He was escorted by the man he knew, who accompanied him to the bank. He withdrew £4,000 in cash and handed it over and was given his car keys in return.

He described the men to me generally, but the only decent description he gave me was of the man he knew. He was about twenty-seven, 5'7" tall and obviously an Arnold Schwarzenegger fan because he had a *Terminator* flat-top hairstyle, and wore a black t-shirt and trousers. I was more interested in the fact that the bank video showed that he had tattoos of an eagle on both forearms.

I still needed more help and that was when the good relationship I'd cultivated with the Scenes of Crime and Forensic Laboratory staff paid off. I called Keith Eynon, who was the senior scientist at the Lab and he told me to bring the car in immediately and he'd assign people to work it.

I got the car parked in the loading bay at Pitt Street and Keith sent down Terry Randall and Andy Sweeney to sweep the car for hairs and fibres. Ronnie Downing and Ronnie McGeachie from Scenes of Crimes examined the touch/grab surfaces for prints. They managed to 'lift' several fingerprint impressions.

While the car was being examined I found a PNC terminal within the building. I hoped that by interrogating the computer's database using the information to hand I would be able to identify one of the suspects. I input the name given to me by the victim and the computer threw back several possibilities. Only one, however, had tattoos that matched those I'd seen on the bank CCTV.

I now had the name, alias, date of birth and last known address of the main suspect. I used another favour and spoke to the supervisor at the Office Systems centre who allocated me a typist and I dictated a case to the Procurator Fiscal, requesting a warrant.

With the hard copy in my possession I drove down to the Fiscal's Office and spoke to a Depute. They told me to come back in an hour and I'd have my warrant for my Vietnamese suspect. With the warrant in hand I had it uploaded onto the PNC, pleased that having inherited a Triad type enquiry at circa 9 a.m. that morning, I'd gathered video and forensic evidence and had a warrant for the arrest of one of the suspects by 4 p.m. that same day.

I circulated the suspect's details to all the Forces in the UK, but my victim was convinced that he would be found in London. I contacted a newly formed Triad gangs unit within the Metropolitan Police, and forwarded the photographs I'd had pulled from the bank security camera, along with the suspect's details. So far, so simple.

The following Sunday afternoon, the gangs unit in London saw my suspect entering a cinema in Chinatown, which specialised in showing undubbed Kung Fu films, and arrested him. I was delighted, and I flew down to London and collected my prisoner. However, all through the journey he had an unruffled air, as if he didn't have a care in the world, and that concerned me. I'd hardly booked him through at Shettleston Office before I found out why. The fix had already gone in.

My complainer was waiting for me and was desperate to point out that he was so sorry for the confusion. He hadn't actually been a victim. The money had been paid over voluntarily because, my 'victim' had displayed inappropriate behaviour towards my prisoner's sister, and the money was a gift of reparation; a sort of 'bond' to ensure he didn't transgress again. His only complaint was that he felt the sum of money he'd had to pay had been on the high side. Anything else I believed had occurred must have been the result of a misunderstanding in translation.

Chinese Nationals from their dealings with police officers in Hong Kong and China view police officers as a corrupt entity. I'd worked hard and called in favours in order to give him the best service I could, and hopefully improve, even if very slightly, his nation's view of police officers, so I was blazing with anger.

There'd been damn-all wrong with his English or understanding of the language when I first interviewed him. One thing is sure, after we'd finished speaking he had a damn sight better grasp of Anglo-Saxon oaths following the verbal volleys I fired into him. To top things off, he even had the brass balls to tell me to make sure to pop into his takeaway if I was passing, for a free meal.

It took what was left of my patience not to lock him up for bribery. Instead, I told him that if he saw me coming into his shop he'd best hide the aluminium containers he used for the food, as I'd be there looking to see how many would fit into his rectal passage.

I contacted the Procurator Fiscal's Office the following morning and the Triad was kicked when he appeared at court. I tried to pitch a case of wasting police time on the part of the victim, but the Fiscal felt it was best to cut our losses. After I'd calmed down to a frenzy, and was able to take a (sort of) dispassionate look at the situation I could understand, to a degree, why my victim had acted in that manner.

He would have had to go to court and give evidence against a Triad member, which was probably anathema to his cultural upbringing. There was no such thing as a protected witness programme in Strathclyde then and the police, with the best will in the world, couldn't provide him with round-the-clock protection. He had a business that he didn't wish to give up, and move elsewhere. Even if he had been prepared to do that he would naturally integrate into the local Chinese society, and would come to the attention of the Triads and be a potential victim of retaliation.

It was far easier to pay a 'tribute' and continue to earn a living and, when I dwelt on it, that burned me even more as I thought how impotent the police were in many ways. Sure I could identify and arrest his attacker(s) and, if fortunate, have a prison sentence imposed. If, however, the man had asked, looking into my eyes, whether I could have guaranteed his future safety I would have had to tell him I couldn't. Thankfully, all police services in the UK now operate a witness protection scheme, with some being more professional and better funded than others. Whether even that would have been sufficient to offset centuries' old tradition and persuade him to testify is debateable.

I suppose if one was to magnify the problem by a million you could appreciate how such situations have impacted throughout history on liberating/occupying (choose your own adjective) forces.

In Vietnam, Northern Ireland or Afghanistan, or any number of other conflicts, the indigenous people must have had to tread a fine line to survive. History will have taught them occupying forces can't/won't remain forever, and when they eventually leave then the 'opposition' will fill the vacuum, so it doesn't do to commit fully to the 'hearts and minds' policies.

26

BLOOD FEUD (THE WILD EAST)

The feud that had continued when I'd been seconded to FHQ climaxed with the murder of Arthur Thompson junior and the retaliatory murder of Joe Hanlon and Bobby Glover.

On 18 August, Arthur Thompson junior was on home leave from a prison sentence and a stone's throw from his family home in Provanmill Road, when he was gunned down. He hadn't inherited his father's DNA for cunning, toughness and ruthlessness but, more importantly and unluckily for him, he'd also missed out on his father's luck and nine lives.

A stolen car pulled up alongside him. Two of the occupants were Joe Hanlon and Bobby Glover. Thompson was shot several times and died of his wounds. Forget the utter nonsense about cool 'apprentices' and hit men from London as backup, and any other attempts to glamorise the murder; it was as sordid and cowardly as most murders are. After several attempts to take out the father they found the fat, gun-loving, drug-dealing 'would-be-dad-emulator' son a much easier target.

Three wounds from a .22 handgun proved fatal. He was taken to the Glasgow Royal Infirmary, but pronounced dead. The .22, although looking almost like the type of gun that a lady would carry, was the same calibre of weapon used in the assassination of the American Presidential Candidate Robert Kennedy in 1968 and the attempted assassination of the American President Ronald Reagan.

Naturally, the police were left with the twin headache of solving the murder and trying to anticipate how Arthur senior would exact his revenge. In the following weeks, the enquiry team worked hard and identified David Logue who claimed to have been instructed to steal a car. Ironically, the car which had been stolen from a railway station was owned by a police officer, who had parked it there to commute to work.

Logue had driven the car to round the corner from Glover's house in the Budhill scheme of Glasgow, and then went to Glover's house where he claimed to have seen Hanlon, Glover and Paul Ferris. Logue claimed that he told Glover where he'd parked the vehicle and how to start it. He was then told to disappear and keep his mouth shut. This was only hours before the murder.

The car was dumped in Ruchazie but, according to Logue, panicked that incriminating forensic evidence may have been left in the car, Hanlon and Glover ordered him to re-steal the car, lose it, and said he would be paid £1,000. Logue did as he was told but never received the promised money.

Thompson's revenge could have come straight from a Mario Puzo Mafia plotline. On the night before his son's funeral he had two of those he believed had murdered his son executed.

It's strange how fate throws people together and extending the hand of friendship may, subsequently, be a contributory factor in your death.

William Manson had been a robber and for one of his armed robberies he was caught and sentenced to eighteen years' imprisonment. He always maintained his innocence and served the full term of his sentence because he was never prepared to admit his involvement in the crime and rejected the opportunity of parole whenever it arose. While within the prison he had uttered numerous threats against the officers involved in his conviction.

When released, he was approached and warned by Strathclyde Police regarding his threats, but it appeared that prison had broken him. Arthur Thompson who had been close friends with Manson took him in for a period after his release and it was at Thompson's house the police went to speak to Manson. He wasn't home and Thompson apparently wasn't best pleased and told the officers what eighteen years in prison had done to Manson. In his photograph, taken at the time of his arrest, Manson had a goatee beard and a defiant look, but by the time of his sentence expiry he'd altered greatly.

Manson had a nephew, William Lobban, who when it suited him used his mother's maiden name of Manson. He had been sentenced to six years in prison for robbery, but had escaped while on home leave and managed to ingratiate himself with Bobby Glover. Glover and his wife had taken Lobban into their home and ensured he had a place to hide from the police.

While he was staying with the Glovers, he robbed a pub known as the Pipe Rack in Budhill. Wearing a blond wig and glasses he assaulted a barman. At the time, the robbery went unsolved and I have no doubt Bobby Glover knew Lobban had carried out the robbery.

A man by the name of William Gillen was shot and Ferris, Hanlon and Glover were arrested and charged with the crime. The evidence against Ferris was deemed stronger and he was remanded in custody – which meant that he was to remain in custody until the commencement of his trial for the shooting. Hanlon and Glover were allowed bail. They may have been delighted at having been granted bail but it probably cost them their lives.

It makes me laugh when I hear Ferris with his constant bleating about police conspiracies, 'fit ups' and corruption, because if the police hadn't sought his remand in custody he may not have presently found himself in the land of the living. I wonder if he ever reflects on that in quieter moments.

I have no doubt whatsoever that had he been loose on the streets he would have been lifeless along with the others in Hanlon's Ford Orion, which was parked near the Cottage Bar on 18 September 1991. Irrespective of how devious, suspicious or streetwise he is or perceives himself to be I believe he would have fallen for the deception just as his friends did.

Technically, the murders of Hanlon and Glover remain open or, using the euphemism adopted by Strathclyde Police, 'unresolved'. I suppose it sounds better than 'unsolved'. Consequently, I'll be careful in what I say as I wouldn't wish to jeopardise any potential new lines of enquiry that may emerge, although I doubt any significant police work has gone into the enquiry since 1992.

William Manson was a very good friend of Arthur Thompson senior and was grateful that throughout his time in prison Thompson maintained contact.

William Lobban was the nephew of Manson and looked up to (and may have been frightened of) his uncle's reputation. Lobban was very close to and trusted by Hanlon and Glover.

Lobban phoned Glover at his house the night before Arthur Thompson junior's funeral and asked to meet him. Lobban, Hanlon and Glover got into Hanlon's Ford Orion car. It has been suggested that at some point Hanlon and Glover thought they were en route to access an automatic weapon.

Hanlon and Glover were never seen alive after they left with Lobban. They were found dead in Hanlon's car the following day by Alan Cross who was the manager of the Cottage Bar, which was Hanlon and Glover's 'gang hut'.

Somewhere near what is now the location of a large supermarket and motorway they were clinically executed but NOT by Frank McPhie and Paul Hamilton: the former a ruthless gangster, the latter a drug dealer. Both have previously been named in the more sensational books as having carried out the executions. In such books everyone named as responsible for shocking acts of violence, drug distribution or murder have one thing in common ... they're all dead. That, in turn, makes them convenient patsies for the woven tales of fantasy because you can't libel a dead person. Consequently, any aspiring writer can insert whichever dead villain is most suitable for their tale without possessing a single grain of fact.

Neither were Hanlon and Glover executed in the manner that's been portrayed, nor did they try to make a getaway. I don't believe they had time to react at all. Speaking to people who have Special Forces training it was made clear to me that, unlike in the cinema, you don't produce a gun and hold conversations with people while covering them.

Everything is designed to be carried out in the shortest time possible. In a firefight they want to break off the engagement within thirty seconds. If the shooting is pre-planned there is no conversation. Any elongated conversation or delay lessens the advantage of surprise, and advantage and surprise are everything.

A person is also most vulnerable within a confined space because their opportunity of escape is proportionate to the confined possible movement, and there is nowhere more confined than a car. That was why so many of the executions in Northern Ireland and Mafia hits in the USA and Italy took place when the victims were within motor vehicles. If the vehicle is stationary you're basically trapped and a perfect target. You've no room to manoeuvre.

The bodies weren't disabled to allow Thompson a chance to deliver a dying valediction, or tell Hanlon that he'd murdered his father (which he hadn't), and the corpses weren't laid out in the Caravel for some kind of sick funereal viewing. Do you think Thompson put all that planning into the murder to then chauffeur the corpses through Glasgow and proportionately increase the risk of detection?

I believe they were stored at business premises near to the Cottage Bar and a son of a London gangster who was in Glasgow for Thompson junior's funeral drove the Ford Orion to Darleith Street and parked it fifty yards from the Cottage Bar.

It's so strange how people's paths are interlinked by fate. I first encountered Hanlon by chance; I was the only police officer to arrest him and Glover jointly and, although I shouldn't have been, I was the first detective on the scene of their body dump.

When in the CID I was always in the habit of starting work about 7.30 a.m. although the official time was 8.30 a.m. I liked to get in early and see what crimes had taken place in the previous sixteen hours or so since I'd last been on. It also afforded me the chance to plan out my day, or if I was looking to interview someone I could be in and out of the office and catch them before they went to work, or catch up on paperwork when the office was quiet.

On that particular day, I'd come in and checked what enquiries I'd been allocated. I'd caught a couple of housebreakings and a break-in to a car. I contacted the victims of these crimes and let them know I'd be up to see them. I established where I wanted the Scenes of Crime officers to concentrate their examination and asked the victims to draw up a list of stolen items. Following that, I drove back to Shettleston office.

There were two older uniform cops who worked within the CID office at Shettleston, Jimmy Urquhart and Alex Scott. They were the initial contact for members of the public looking to speak to the CID. They would note details for crime reports and also took charge of any productions (exhibits) seized from crime scenes. Both were top guys and would do anything for you. They were funny and played up their Statler and Waldorf image from *The Muppets*.

I came into the office and asked Jimmy if there was anything doing. Jimmy told me that a call had come in that there were allegedly two bodies in a car near the Cottage Bar. I looked closely at Jimmy to see if there was a punchline as he had a dry comic delivery, but he was absolutely serious.

There were at least five or six other detectives in the room, but no one had stirred and, puzzled, I asked Jimmy if anyone was on their way to the scene, but he told me there wasn't. I gave him an 'Eh?' and, in response, he looked around the room, resumed eye contact with me, shook his head and gave me a look that said it all.

I asked Jim to let the control room know I was en route and drove down to the Cottage Bar. The uniformed officers who'd attended the scene initially had stretched police crime scene tape across the entrance to Darleith Street, at the junction with Shettleston Road. The Cottage Bar was sited just at that junction.

I asked the uniformed officer what we had and was told 'two bodies in that car', and he pointed towards a Ford Orion parked about fifty yards further up Darleith Street. From where I was I could see that another officer had taped off the top end of the street in a similar manner to where I stood.

For an incongruous moment I actually wondered if it was some kind of elaborate practical joke, given that no other detective had responded to the call, but I immediately dismissed the thought. If Jimmy Urquhart and the cop at the scene had been pulling my leg then they'd missed their vocation. Their performances would have had Al Pacino looking over his shoulder.

I walked to the metallic blue Ford Orion. I knew it as Joe Hanlon's car, but I didn't look in immediately. I knew there would be nothing I could do for whoever occupied it now. I wanted, firstly, to visually inspect the outside of the vehicle, surrounding pavement and roadway area, to make sure there was no obvious physical evidence that might be lost through careless crime scene management. I was certain that irrespective of who was in that car that this location was the body dump and a secondary crime scene, but not the murder or primary scene.

After I'd made sure that my size elevens weren't going to trample any physical evidence I noticed that an exterior door handle was missing. I looked inside the car without opening the doors or touching anything. Two bodies: one I could see immediately was Joe Hanlon, and the other I was 95% certain was Bobby Glover.

I couldn't be absolutely certain at that stage that it was Glover because of the position in which the body lay. They hadn't exactly been care-fully positioned, but more to ensure that they wouldn't have aroused the suspicion of any police cars the driver may have encountered en route to where they now lay.

They'd been dumped almost outside of their gang hut, the Cottage Bar, and near where Arthur junior's cortege would pass by later that morning. You didn't need to be a cryptographer to decipher that message. It was loud and clear.

I contacted the control room and arranged for Scenes of Crime Officers to attend and advised them to supplement their photographic cameras with video equipment. This was an unusual crime scene, and it would require visual documentation because the car would have to be removed with the bodies inside, to be examined forensically at Paisley Police Office, who had special facilities for that. I also requested that officers from the forensic science laboratory attend and check for any chemical or biological items that might be relevant to the upcoming enquiry.

I requested Ballistics too, although realistically both Ballistics and the lab officers' work would begin later when they could access the inside of the car, and it would be the same for the pathologist. Their work would be of more relevance subsequently, but they would still wish to attend the scene of the body dump. I also arranged for uniformed officers to begin knocking on doors of the flats that over-looked the scene.

That meant that when Pat Connor, the Detective Chief Superintendent (who would eventually oversee both the Thompson and Hanlon and Glover murders), Jim Orr, Detective Superintendent (who was in charge of the Arthur junior murder enquiry) and Jimmy Johnstone, Detective Superintendent (who would inherit this enquiry) arrived I had every-thing up and running.

A couple of Divisional Detectives arrived and proffered their opinion as to who the second body was, but I told the bosses that it was Bobby Glover. Pat Connor asked me to attend the Royal Infirmary later to confirm absolutely that it was Glover, but overall they were content that I knew Glover well enough to have correctly identified him at the scene.

Apparently, it has been indicated that McGraw went to Eileen Glover's house and told her that Bobby was dead prior to the police knowing, and much has been made of how sinister that was. I don't find it sinister in the slightest. I'm the last person to pitch up as an apologist for that reptile, but logic tells you that given the manager of the Cottage Bar found the car and saw the bodies within, then the police would not necessarily have been the first, or the only people to be made aware of the find.

It was obviously Joe Hanlon's car and he was easily recognisable, plus he and Glover were well-nigh inseparable. Staff from the Cottage Bar would, if they'd looked in the car, have also been able to recognise the clothing worn, so it wouldn't have taken a genius to make the identifications. From there, a phone call probably alerted McGraw to what they suspected and, armed with the information, he made his way to the Glover home.

After I'd overseen the management of the crime scene I was contacted late afternoon by control room staff, and advised that the bodies had been removed from the Ford Orion, and were currently at Glasgow Royal Infirmary, to facilitate X-raying.

Pathologists like to have corpses that have died as a result of gunshot wounds X-rayed. This provides them with a better idea of bullet tracts before they commence the post-mortem examination. I confirmed the identities of both and returned to London Road and updated the bosses.

Before the thought crosses anyone's mind – no, I did not derive any kind of satisfaction from the deaths. That isn't the way I live my life and thank God I'm not that sick an individual. Both of them were the architects of their own demise. One was a small-time drug dealer who never appeared to possess the sharpest intellect, and the other was a small-time resetter (fence) and 'Jack the Lad' type. It was their misfortune to fall under the influence of the likes of McGraw.

Neither of them had any real grudge against Thompson senior or junior, but found themselves, among other crimes, involved in several shootings and a murder. The shootings and murder involved pre-planning, stealing cars and carrying firearms. They wanted to be gangsters and perhaps had believed those who thought old man Thompson was past it or over the hill.

Maybe, in some ways he was, but if you have a Philippine Cobra trapped under a forked stick it is still a Philippine Cobra, and they'd have done well to remember that. Joe Hanlon and Bobby Glover had chosen to live their lives in a certain manner, but with that choice came the risk of the violent and premature end they suffered.

Given the interconnection between the initial Thompson murder and the retributive murders that followed, both enquiries were run from London Road, and there was an overlap of intelligence and enquiries.

I really liked those types of enquiries because, given the characters of the victims, the people you were pushing for information were generally high-grade criminals, and that afforded the teams of police officers opportunities to disrupt their criminal activities. The officers were freed from the day-to-day enquiries that engulfed much of their time and could make their presence felt. Many criminals found that their 'businesses' couldn't operate as freely because of the police activity.

It was on this enquiry that I managed to recruit a first-class informant and also found out that Arthur Thompson had himself been recruited by the Security Services as an asset.

As part of the enquiry, officers from the Fraud Squad had been drafted in to look at Thompson's income. The Senior Investigating Officers were hoping to try and get some kind of leverage on him. One of the Fraud Squad Officers was someone I'd worked closely with in the past, and had a friend who was highly placed within the Inland Revenue. He pulled me to the side one afternoon and told me that he'd just come back from Edinburgh where he'd decided he'd speak to his Inland Revenue friend and back-door things.

In his words:

He punched Arthur's details into the computer and within a minute the head of the Inland Revenue came bursting through like an Exocet missile demanding to know who had accessed Thompson's file.

My friend told me that reaction meant only one thing; Arthur's touting [informing] to the Intelligence Services.

I found that information very interesting but not earth-shaking as informant recruitment is a 'food chain' business. The higher you are up the chain the greater the pressure you can exert to recruit higher grade informants. It made perfect sense for the members of the intelligence community to make their pitch to the highest profile Glasgow gangster.

The informant I recruited on this enquiry was a by-product of my searching for one of three escaped prisoners. In addition to William

Lobban, who had disappeared from sight following his meeting with Joe Hanlon and Bobby Glover, there were two other high-profile escapees that Pat Connor wished traced, to ensure they had no involvement in the murders.

Michael Healy had escaped from Shotts Prison after being sentenced to ten years at Paisley High Court for an armed robbery. He'd concealed himself in a butcher's van which delivered meat to the prisoner kitchens and burst out of the rear of the van once it was within Glasgow city centre. He was six feet tall, slim built and had blond hair. It had been suggested he'd disguised himself as a woman in the past, although at six feet tall I hope he'd had the decency to wear flat shoes, unless he was looking to pass himself off as Claudia Schiffer.

The other escapee was John Daly who was 5'9" tall and had a stocky build. He'd escaped from the High Court when appearing for trial following a robbery at Saltmarket in which he levelled a shotgun at a pursuing police officer.

Lobban was another who liked to dress as a woman (some of these people must have been very popular in prison). He used the alias 'Gary McMillan' and was 5'7" and muscular through lifting weights. Bizarrely, Lobban had fled Dungavel semi-open prison in March 1991, just three months shy of the end of a six-year robbery sentence.

I was at a house in the East End of Glasgow searching for Healy. The householder looked painfully thin. Additionally, a severe childhood bout of chickenpox had left him with a pitted complexion. There was nothing wrong with his thought processes though. He'd had a decent prison sentence some years previously and hadn't enjoyed it. He had been fortunate that the girl he was with had stayed the course so, when he was released, he decided he was going to sober up and fly straight.

He now earned his living legitimately but his prison sentence still enhanced his credibility factor with other villains. I think he was resentful that he worked hard to earn for his family while others earned their money by other means. He was amenable to an approach and proved to be a valuable source of information after that. He actually provided information concerning a model of handgun he'd seen Arthur senior with that was of interest to the enquiry.

Several weeks after the murders, I was dispatched to see Arthur Thompson and issue a 'threat to life warning'. I felt like an idiot conveying that message, given all that had happened previously, but at least he listened before saying, 'You don't really need to tell me that, son.' But I'd been instructed to and did.

27

CAPITAL COWBOYS

For several reasons Pat Connor decided to send me and 'B' then a Detective Sergeant, down to London. There were people there who had been friendly with Hanlon and Glover, and he wanted them spoken to. Although there was speculation that he was dead, Pat either had an inkling that Lobban had fled to London, or had raw intelligence that he was there, and hoped we would be able to flesh out the bones of the intelligence.

So I found myself on a BA flight to 'The London' with B.

We picked up our hire car and reported to King's Cross Police Office where, after introducing ourselves to the Detective Superintendent there, we were allocated a liaison. He was in the CID and held a supervisory rank. He is no longer with the police, but I've seen him on *Sky News* several times as he is one of the 'former police officers' used by news channels to provide comment on topical police issues.

It was late afternoon or early evening when we'd arrived, so at the close of business, some of the CID officers suggested we may like to go for a drink at a nearby pub. Our liaison officer had had a couple of drinks when one of his colleagues decided he would play with this guy's head. Our liaison had been asking a few questions about what our intentions were for our first port of call in the morning, which involved a visit to flats in the Haringey area.

His colleague, claiming to have insider knowledge of our 'mission', began to lay out scenarios that involved masks, shotguns, kidnapping, boots of cars and 'back up North'. It would have been outrageous even for the 1970s television programme *The Sweeney*, but I could see our Met contact swallowing not only the bait but also the rod and reel into the bargain. I whispered to the story spinner to ease it back as our liaison's eyes had widened to the size of saucers, but he was enjoying himself too much.

The following morning when we turned up at Kings Cross office we were told that our liaison had called in sick and not surprisingly the Detective Superintendent couldn't spare anyone else to assist us so we were on our own.

We managed (thanks to the London A–Z) to find the area and flat in Haringey. We were looking for a fraudster who had been in business with both Hanlon and Glover. He'd been a regular at the Cottage Bar which they'd used as a base for their business dealings, and we hoped he may possibly have information on Lobban. We rang the buzzer for the specific flat, and noticed that each tenant had a security camera built into their mailboxes, allowing them to monitor any callers.

'What is it?' Scots voice; Glasgow accent.

'We're police officers down from Glasgow. We're looking to speak to so and so.'

'Okay. Hold on a minute.'

A minute turned into five minutes and we looked at each other, pressed the buzzer and got no answer.

'I'll check round the back. He's done a runner.'

I'd never in my career lost a prisoner out of the rear of premises, because the likes of Eric Young and Bob Harvey had instilled in me from my first days as a uniform cop that it was basic to cover the back when looking for someone. Here though we didn't have a photograph of the guy we were looking for, weren't even sure we were at the correct flat or the geography of the area, and had no means of communication. And being just the two didn't want to split up in the off-chance Lobban was within and burst past.

Now, however, we had to take a chance, and I told B I was going round the back to see if there were any entrances. As I walked along the driveway that led to the rear of the flats a dark-coloured car driven by a bespectacled male drove past me and onto the road. I only managed a quick glimpse of the car and occupant.

I shouted to B that we may just have lost our target but that I intended checking the rear in case it was a ploy to draw us away and let someone in the flat escape. The windows of the flat were of the sash type (opening vertically) and I could see that one had been partially raised. I let B know that I was going to check the inside of the flat, and to be ready in case anyone came rushing out the front.

I levered myself up and into the flat and noticed correspondence addressed to the man we wanted to interview. I cleared the flat, went back out the way I'd entered and told B I was sure we'd lost our guy. Even given I'd only managed a quick glance in profile I was convinced it was our prospective interviewee. We decided to head back to the police office to lick our wounds and drove back on the main route we'd taken to get there. By this time, some twenty minutes had elapsed since I'd seen the male in the car.

We were in a city we didn't know, in a population of several million, had been given the slip by someone we had never met, had no authority, no jurisdiction and had entered a flat illegally . . . The car emerged from a junction on our left forty yards ahead. If you'd written that scenario into a film script I would have convulsed with laughter, but that's exactly what happened.

'That's him there on the left,' I shouted. B hadn't seen him or the car at the flats, but he trusted me enough not to even ask was I sure, and took off after the car. Our target had obviously spotted us because he started to drive like a maniac, jumping red lights and cutting up cars. B decided to take a few chances too as he took me on 'Mr Toad's Wild Ride'. At one point, he overtook on the blind crest of what was (in keeping with the nature of the enquiry) appropriately named 'Shooters Hill'. Thank God the approaching milk float swerved. I turned around just in time to see several gallons of milk whitewashing the pavement and road.

We almost wrote off two more cars at a roundabout before our target pulled up outside Tottenham Police Office, bailed out of his car and ran into the foyer of the office. Incongruously, he was wearing slippers. I was right behind him, and literally dragged him from the foyer of the office where there were other members of the public, back to our car. All the while he was screaming for help.

Cops loathe and love vehicle pursuits in equal measure. They love the adrenalin, but loathe that they aren't really in control of the situation, and cops do like to feel that they have control. We were content that in this case we were after someone intent on getting away, whereas in most pursuits cops don't know if the vehicle they're pursuing contains kilos of drugs, armed or dangerous criminals, or simply someone who has a £30 warrant for their arrest. Consequently, through a combination of fear, adrenalin and relief Rodney King type situations can arise.

In the rear of the car we both began shouting at him at once, asking what the hell he was playing at.

'Who ur youse?' Through fear his voice was higher than ours by a couple of octaves.

'What the fuck do you mean who are we? We told you, we're the polis from Glasgow.'

'Where's yur warrant cards?'

We produced the cards and after he'd viewed them he slumped down in the back seat and said, 'Thank fuck!'

'What's the deal wi' you getting off your mark?'

'The deal? I saw that shaven-headed nasty looking bastard (that would be me) and thought Arthur had sent two hit men down fae Glasgow to do me in.'

It certainly broke the tension, and the formalities over we took him back into the office I'd dragged him from. We introduced ourselves to the duty officer and he gave us a room to carry out our interview. Our capture was so relieved that we were cops that we got the statement we wanted, and more.

Unbelievably, not one person (police or member of the public) came out to investigate a man being dragged from the foyer of a police office. We also found out that the route he'd taken when he first drove off had been a circuitous tour of the back streets to make sure he'd lost us. He'd almost had a fit when he found himself only fifty yards ahead when he'd driven back onto the main route.

I think some of the Met troops thought all we were missing were spurs and Stetsons as we were a couple of cowboys. Given B had just about broken every other road traffic regulation in existence bar drunk driving, and I'd illegally entered a flat through the rear window and kidnapped someone from a police foyer, I can understand why we were perceived as suicide bombers without the vests.

We spent a week down in London and managed to trace and interview enough people to make us think that Lobban was still alive and definitely in London. We told Pat Connor as much when we returned and reported back to him. He told us that we were trying to work another trip back down to do our Christmas shopping.

He must, however, have been sufficiently convinced by what we told him and satisfied with the work we'd done because we found ourselves back on a plane within the week, to see if we could glean anything further. I'm sure Pat was privy to information from various other sources and had the 'big picture', and used what we brought back as a supplementary source of confirmation.

He'd tasked us with locating and 'charming' our way into a house in south London which was supposedly occupied by a Possilpark boy who was friendly with Lobban. That was well out of the area covered by our King's Cross contact who had, by this time, returned to work following his brief bout of illness and been convinced that we really weren't part of a Wild West show. He contacted the police office nearest to the house we wanted to visit and arranged for a Detective Constable to meet us at the police station, to direct and accompany us to the house.

We arrived at the police office and out came our contact in his dark Crombie coat, fashionably styled long hair, and a striped shirt and tie so loud we needed polarised Ray Bans to look at them.

'Orl right, boys. U dahn the Big Smoke from the Jockland wiv a little enquiry? Ah'll get u up there and we'll see wot's wot. We got a few bad boys on this manor so we cahn't 'av' ya getting inta bovver.'

He'd managed to piss us off in the space of four sentences but we were guests so we played nice. We got to the house and knocked politely, letting our guide take the lead. A male aged about twenty answered the door.

London accent. 'Yeah wot?'

'Ow ya doin? These gents is police dahn from Scotland and looking for so and so. Ju know the bloke?'

'Never eard of him, Guv.'

'Orl right, mate. Sorry to bovva ya.'

Door closed and our guide turned to us with a, 'Sorry, lads. No luck,' expression. B and I looked at each and gave the door a slightly less polite knock. It was opened by the same male.

'Wot the fack's the problem? I told ju the geezer don't live here. Fack off.'

With that he made to slam the door in our faces. That was something that had been done to us in our combined police careers – never.

When he pushed the door closed he'd released his grip on the door facing. That facing collided with the back of his head when it careered back off the wall of the hallway. He let out a yell and shouted,

'Whit the fuck ur ye playin at?' in a broad Glasgow accent.

Would you believe it? It seemed the bump on the head had made him bilingual. As we accepted his unspoken invitation to come in our Met contact bid Sayonara with, 'See u got in, gents. Ah'll wait in the jam jar.' And with that he almost choked us to death in heel-dust, such was his desperation to be out of there.

Once inside, we asked, 'What's with the fake London accent?'

'Easier when you're dealing with the polis down here. They buy it.'

We then proceeded to confirm that Lobban wasn't in the house and got the information we needed. Based on that and other people we spoke to in London we flew back on 23 December, now totally convinced that not only was he alive but hiding out in London.

That was confirmed on New Year's night when Pat Connor called me at home and asked could I be at London Road within the hour. I got there and was told that Lobban had been indiscreet in contacting someone in Scotland. He'd been trying to confirm who it was that had been looking for him. I don't think he was convinced we were actually police officers. In making the contact, he'd indicated where he'd be at a certain time and had been arrested by Met officers.

Together with B and Jimmy Johnstone, the Detective Superintendent, and some other officers I was booked onto the last flight to London. The airline was prepared to delay departure for fifteen minutes which left us little time to spare if we were to make that flight. We had a Traffic Officer to taxi us to the airport.

The Volvo T5 was rocketing down the outside lane of the M8 at 120 miles an hour, with me in the front passenger seat when, for some inexplicable reason, an old woman driving along in the centre lane with nothing in front of her decided she would deviate into the lane that we were in. We were dead. Simple as that. There wasn't any space to avoid her.

The Traffic Cop didn't even blink. Simultaneously, he braked and steered into the inside lane, avoiding the collision by a hairbreadth. Thank God for the Traffic Department's intense training because he knew his surroundings, knew there was no traffic travelling behind in the inside lane and hadn't diluted his concentration by chatting.

No one in that car spoke for the next few hundred yards. Actually, I don't think anyone had even exhaled. They couldn't. Everyone was too busy untangling their fingernails from the roof upholstery. With a coolness that would have shamed Steve McQueen, the Traffic Officer uttered the only words he spoke on the whole journey:

'The Advanced Braking System on these is reputed to be excellent. I'd been looking for a situation to test them.'

In London, Jimmy Johnstone and B took Lobban back to Scotland for what would be an unhelpful interview and left me with a mortice key that Lobban had in his possession when arrested; a key, plus a photograph of him bare-chested, wearing a leather waistcoat, leather cap, with a snake draped around his shoulders. We had no idea where he'd been living in London.

He'd been arrested in the Earls Court area so it was a question of walking, knocking, asking and hoping. We showed the photograph to shopkeepers, waiters, bar staff and the various companies who rented property in the area. An impossible task given that it was a key, a photo and a metropolis.

Jimmy Johnstone lectured on major crime investigation at subsequent Detective Training Courses using the Hanlon/Glover enquiry as his reference point. He would tell the officers that he'd left me and other officers in London with a key and nothing else and, in return, he'd been given the door it fitted. A good story, but we put in long frustrating hours to get that result, and it wouldn't have happened if the people involved had treated the trip as a holiday and adopted a 'this is impossible' mindset. Instead, it was a case of the more you apply yourself the luckier you get.

At one of the scores of rental property companies dotted along Earl's Court Road and the surrounding area, we'd got lucky with someone who recognised Lobban from the photo and gave us the address of the property. We'd held onto the hope that if we located where he'd been living it would reveal some gold nuggets that would advance the enquiry, but we didn't get as much as a grain, far less a nugget.

It was sickening after so much determination and hard work, but unfortunately that often happens in police work. The effort isn't always in synch with the end result. Sometimes, you can be very lucky and sometimes you don't get what you think you deserve.

We'd expended a great deal of time and effort and located and arrested Lobban who would be returned to prison and receive a further six-year sentence for robbing the Pipe Rack pub. In interview he'd denied all knowledge of the murders. Given that it was his phone call that had enticed the victims to meet him the night they were murdered, plus he was the last known person to see them alive, that was doubly frustrating.

While on the run from prison, he had carried out another armed robbery. He was desperate and didn't want to go back to prison. His uncle was very good friends with Arthur senior and Lobban was very fond of (and afraid of) his uncle. I'm sure he was also afraid of Arthur's retribution. Arthur needed someone who could convince Hanlon and Glover to be at a specific spot. His uncle was able to contact Lobban. Hanlon and Glover trusted Lobban, and would have met him and followed him to wherever Lobban suggested quite happily.

All just a horrible coincidence it would appear.

Three weeks after I returned from London, I was promoted to uniform sergeant at the former 'B' Division, based at Partick Police Office, but I hadn't finished with the enquiry just yet.

28

TRIAL AND ERROR

Paul Ferris had been charged with murdering Arthur Thompson junior and I was called to give evidence at the trial at the High Court in Glasgow, and presumed my evidence would have been confined to my involvement on the day I'd seized the bullet-holed hire car. Presumably, the prosecution wished to highlight previous bad blood between Ferris, who had hired the car initially, and Thompson, with the inference being that Arthur had fired the 9mm round into the car wing.

After I'd presented my evidence to the court, outlining the circumstances in which, I'd first become aware of the car hired by Ferris, his Counsel Donald Findlay QC began his cross-examination.

He tried to suggest that I could not have realised that the repair job on the wing had been an attempt to disguise a bullet hole. In reply, I responded that I felt it was self-evident, given that was specifically the reason I'd requested a ballistics examination.

Mr Findlay persisted, however, and said that I had jumped to a conclusion as the damage could have been caused by any number of items including a ski pole, which he lifted up to display to the jury. Don't ask me where the ski pole fitted into the grand scheme of things, but I responded to that suggestion by telling Mr Findlay that I would pay good money to see him try and drive a ski pole into a car wing and create a single round hole.

'Perhaps not the best analogy I've ever used,' was how he replied.

Then, however, to my utter astonishment he shifted his line of questioning onto the Hanlon and Glover murders. It hadn't been mentioned, but he knew I was part of the enquiry team. I'd been photographed by a newspaper photographer's long-lens camera at the crime scene so someone from the Ferris side may have recognised me, but I couldn't believe it when Mr Findlay asked me how they'd been killed.

These were crimes that were still under investigation and I could see no relevance to this case as it stood. The Thompson murder had happened four weeks before the deaths of Hanlon and Glover. Perhaps Ferris was trying to insinuate that Hanlon and Glover alone had been responsible for shooting Arthur junior, hence the reason they were killed in revenge. Then again I don't possess Mr Findlay's legal astuteness.

I looked at the prosecuting Advocate Depute waiting for an objection to the question, but it never came. The papers had been full of the fact that firearms had been used, but I kept the answer as vague as possible.

'Firearm death,' I believe was my response.

'Where were they shot?' persisted Mr Findlay.

I again looked for the objection that never came, so I took matters into my own hands. As politely as I could I addressed his Lordship directly.

'Milord, these murders are still under investigation and I'm being asked to reveal what could be classed as specialist knowledge in open court.'

His Lordship, however, directed me to answer the question, but forbade any reporting of my answer by the journalists thronging the court. It wasn't the journalists who concerned me. It was the public gallery, which was thronged with villains, some of whom could have been potential suspects in the murders of Hanlon and Glover.

I'd been directed to answer, but I took a few precious moments to compose my answer. When I did answer the question it was in terms picked up in my forensic medicine course.

I've wondered since whether the manner in which I phrased my answer was the basis for wildly inaccurate speculation on the manner of their deaths. I think quite a few heard and misinterpreted a couple of words used, and when they performed their addition, warped two plus two into five. If so, that suited me fine.

The jury returned a verdict of 'Not Guilty' against Ferris, and he walked free, acquitted of the murder of Arthur Thompson junior. It had been Scotland's longest running trial. Two pieces of evidence introduced at the trial had, in my opinion, a huge influence on how the jury arrived at their verdict. One was paper and one human.

The paper evidence was introduced at the beginning of the trial, and the human evidence near the conclusion, and both benefited the defence rather than the prosecution. Given, the length of the trial and regardless of how sensational some of the evidence may have been, juries are human beings, and like all human beings there is a limit to their levels of concentration.

Sitting through six hours of evidence, five days a week for eight weeks on end would tax the concentration (and perhaps boredom) threshold of most people. Is it possible that jurors' minds could start to wander to what was for tea that night? The football match the night before? The attractive fellow juror? A family special occasion? If that were to occur, would it be stretching speculation too far to assume that evidence heard at the beginning and towards the conclusion of a trial would resonate more clearly in the memory?

Hypothetically, if you were constantly trumpeting that the police were out to get you, by whatever means possible, that you were an innocent victim, that it was a case of giving a dog a bad name and hanging a very tight collar around it . . . are you then formulating your defence pre-trial? If you shout loudly and often enough then if or when, the hammer does fall and you're apprehended, you've already sown the seeds of doubt in people's mind.

'You see what I mean? I told you they were out to get me. I'm innocent.' It is quite a clever strategy.

At the beginning of Ferris' trial the matter of a letter was addressed, which had been circulating, purporting to have emanated from Mr Alf Vannet, a Crown agent. The letter alleged that Ferris had been a Serious Crime Squad informant and had been paid for providing information.

The poor grammar and spelling mistakes made it rather obvious that it was a fake, and it was ably demonstrated as such by Donald Findlay when he placed Alf Vannet, the alleged author of the document, in the witness box. Mr Vannet confirmed the document as fake. Could that confirmation have influenced the light in which the jury viewed the person on trial?

I'll make reference to how devastatingly effective a fake document can be in the following chapter.

Towards the end of the trial, the Crown introduced a supposed star witness, Denis Woodman. Prior to Woodman's appearance, David Logue had given his evidence and had reiterated what he'd told the police regarding his links to the car used in the murder, who he'd seen at

Glover's house, and how he'd disposed of the vehicle after the murder. The defence could not shake him on his evidence.

Enter Woodman. How the senior police management and Crown Office had failed to research Woodman's background thoroughly before utilising him as a prosecution witness is beyond astonishing. They appear to have accepted at face value that Ferris, on sharing a cell with someone of whom he had no previous knowledge or relationship, would simply babble to this cellmate about a murder he was alleged to have committed.

Yes, it has occurred in the past, but Ferris by his own admission, felt betrayed by his former mentor Arthur senior, his boyhood friend Arthur junior, and another former friend, McGraw. I'm no psychologist, but surely even the most superficial personality assessment of the person on trial should have caused the prosecution team to be especially wary of Woodman's story.

Given the feelings of betrayal Ferris harboured, would that not cause him to be wary, distrustful, paranoid even and, therefore, extremely unlikely to 'confess' to a complete stranger. When those possible personality traits are factored into the equation then they should have caused the prosecution to examine Woodman's credibility much more closely. Utilising him as a prosecution witness was strategically (in my opinion) a major error.

Armed with the knowledge the defence team were privy to concerning Woodman's past history, they could have tasked a two-week police probationer with dismantling his credibility . . . far less a legal practitioner of Donald Findlay's quality.

I would hazard a guess that Mr Findlay didn't sleep the night before he was to cross-examine Woodman. He was about to experience the Holy Grail for lawyers – his Perry Mason moment – because it is really only in the realms of television or cinema that a witness breaks down and is exposed. Here, however, Mr Findlay had been presented with the perfect opportunity to demonstrate his cross-examination skills.

In a media-thronged Glasgow High Court, at the most high-profile trial in a decade and the longest-running in Scottish history, he'd been given an opportunity to gut, fillet and dice an obvious liar like a sushi chef with a tuna. A scenario he could only have dreamt about when he graduated from university had been laid in his lap. I'll bet he bounded into the High Court that morning like Tigger.

Woodman was a professional liar who'd previously given evidence for the prosecution in trials against cellmates, alleging confessions had been made while they shared cells. He swore on oath that his children were dead, which was utter nonsense as they were alive, and any case the prosecution may have built gurgled around the plug hole and followed Woodman's credibility swiftly down the drain. Having listened to all the evidence the jury returned a 'Not Guilty' verdict and Ferris walked free.

29

TRADECRAFT, TRADESMEN AND APPRENTICES

It is strange how Woodman found his way to a cell with Ferris and had his credibility exposed so easily and conveniently by Ferris' defence team. Very skilled practitioners no doubt, but were the defence team more experienced and skilled than those on the prosecution side, or was there something more serpentine being played out in the shadows?

'Tradecraft' is a term used by the Intelligence Communities, and it refers to techniques or skills which are tried and tested. What I know of the Security Services would fit on a pinhead, but from my very limited knowledge they appear to operate on the principle that if a method is tried and tested it will work again and again. All that is required is a little tweaking.

Eric Young, who tutored me when I first joined the police, told me of an incident from his days in the Scottish Crime Squad, in the 1970s. He and other team members found themselves part of the recruitment training of a prospective Security Services candidate. The officers were informed that the 'agent' was within a hotel room, within a certain Glasgow hotel and, unknown to him, there was a hidden firearm within that room.

The candidate had in his possession a phone number which equated to a 'get out of jail card'. If he found himself in trouble he could provide the phone number to, say, the police and the matter would be resolved. However, in a classic 'Catch 22', he'd been told that if he used the phone number he would no longer be considered suitable for recruitment.

Eric and others went to the room and found the firearm where they'd been told it would be, and duly arrested the room occupant. He was subsequently provided with a lawyer, paraded in front of a Sheriff in a specially convened court and prosecuted by a Procurator Fiscal Depute, all of whom were aware of the nature of the test.

The prospective agent was found guilty, sentenced to imprisonment and found himself sandwiched between two detectives in the back seat of a car en route to HMP Barlinnie. Up to the gates they drove, and he never opened his mouth from arrest to arrival at the prison, far less mention any phone number. It was only at the gates that the cops turned him loose and enlightened him, but he'd been prepared to undertake his sentence.

Fast forward two decades and I find myself within Maryhill Police Office one afternoon, heading to the control room which was located within the office prior to the introduction of modern call centres. There had been a broadcast that I hadn't heard properly so I wanted to clarify what had been said.

Then, you had to walk through the charge bar in order to access the control room, which lay behind the duty officer's desk area. As I reached the charge bar there was a fair-haired male between two suited officers with another three similar 'suits' hovering around. I didn't recognise any of the faces, but I did recognise that the duty officer was having trouble with the fair-haired man's name and details. He was mispronouncing what I knew to be a Scandinavian name and address. Having lived in Sweden for two years I could speak, read and write Swedish and to a lesser extent Norwegian.

I spelled the name and address phonetically for the duty officer who also had to explain to him his rights as an accused person so he innocently asked me to convey those rights in translation. When I began to speak to him in his own language I saw the confusion in his face and the colour begin to drain from the faces of the 'suits' on either side of him.

They were from Special Branch and their prisoner was a prospective candidate for one of the Scandinavian Security Services. They were running a similar ploy as the British security services, only this time he'd been arrested for allegedly beating up a prostitute. Same principle, just tweaked slightly from twenty years previously.

The only problem was that these geniuses hadn't carried out any forward planning. They'd brought their prisoner to the only office in the whole of Strathclyde that had a Swedish-speaking cop. Not only that, but he was on duty when they brought their prisoner to that office, and he happened to walk through at the exact moment they were playing out the pantomime. What were the odds?

The candidate, for his part, looked as if the three cherries had dropped into place, and something was amiss because my showing up at just that point and speaking an obscure language was just too much of a coincidence. I left them debating who was to have the job of phoning their Special Branch bosses and relay the good news. So, the same trick decades apart, which leads me to the subject of fake letters.

The Zinoviev Letter was one of the greatest political scandals of the twentieth century, and triggered the fall of the Labour Government in 1924.

The letter which was leaked to *The Mail* purported to have been written by Gregori Zinoviev, a leading Russian Communist. It called on British Communists to mobilise 'sympathetic forces' within the Labour Party to support an Anglo-Soviet treaty and encourage 'agitation and propaganda' in the armed forces.

As a consequence, *The Mail* bannered the front page with 'Civil War plot by Socialist Masters' and 'Moscow Orders to Our Reds'. Labour lost the election by a landslide.

The letter was a total fake, but influenced enough people to believe that voting for a Labour Government would be tantamount to voting for a Communist Government. The letter had been sent to *The Mail* by Stewart Menzies, a future head of MI6, and had been written by an MI6 asset. It was generally believed that MI6 and MI5 officers, if not directly behind the construction or leaking of the forged letter, did nothing to dissuade the belief that the letter was anything other than genuine.

A forged letter which has the potential to influence opinions? An interesting concept.

So, if you accept the principle that the more things change the more they remain the same, would that influence the Security Services' recruitment of assets? I've already spoken of how it had been confirmed to me that Thompson was a Security Service asset.

Hypothetically, if I had as an asset a top gangster (we'll call him 'The Tradesman'), but he was starting to become long in the tooth and not be as productive as in the past, what would be a potential course of action? One course could be to recruit an up-and-coming gangster, because that way I would continue to have a similar source of information, but also this asset is younger and more vibrant. An 'apprentice' if you like.

Would the best way to make an approach be when someone was riding the crest of a wave, or, when they were in a vulnerable position, such as awaiting trial on a serious charge with the prospect of lengthy imprisonment? Personally, I have always found it easier to recruit informants from a position of (their) vulnerability. You remember the analogy of the house catching fire?

Say a talent spotter leaked an obviously fake letter and, in addition, led an unknowing and uninvolved talented defence team to a prosecution witness, who just happens to be a known perjurer. Would that be sufficient to sow the seeds of doubt and influence a trial outcome? And if it did, would the recipient of that good fortune be expected to show their gratitude?

Of course, it is all just fantasy and nonsense, but is it any less so than the other sensationalist conspiracy theories the more lurid books proffer?

Bear that in mind when those shocking stories appear in newspapers and gangster biographies, with journalists citing the usual suspects as sources. The thing with conspiracy theories is that they can be warped to fit any scenario. If you take some fact and weave it together with the correct dose of fiction, you've got a winning recipe. I suppose the trick would be to have just enough fact to act as the glue that holds the whole nonsense together. So don't believe everything you read.

30

GOOD CAREER MOVE

My year as a uniform sergeant passed off quickly and largely uneventfully, owing to the fact that I had a top group of officers who formed the shift. They weren't a perfect shift. You'll never get that, but they were pretty damn good. There was a great blend of experience and youth, with the latter benefiting from the mentoring of the experienced officers. I relished being able to organise and task them. I'd also forgotten how much fun it was operating among a hard-working, motivated shift.

The one downside during my year came when I had to charge a police officer, but it gave me an insight into how certain types within the police view the path to progress. It also reiterated a theory I'd long held, that the police service consists of two types: there are real police and those who are *in* the police.

Two days after Christmas 1992, various members of a family were contacted by a man purporting to be from Clydebank CID. He claimed that one of the family had been reported missing and, although he had an address for the alleged missing person, he didn't have a phone number for her.

The female in question had been married previously to a police officer but had divorced him. It didn't take the family members long to realise that the person making the calls was the inebriated, police officer ex-husband, trying to pass himself off as a fictitious Detective Constable, and they contacted the police to complain.

I inherited the enquiry and it transpired that the cop had married a second time, but his second wife had moved out shortly before Christmas. As happens to so many over-holiday periods he'd got drunk, was lonely, and looking to rake over old coals.

It happens all the time during the festive season. People are bombarded through the mass media with images of happy families, and when people feel that they're not sharing in the hyped domestic bliss they drink too much, become morose and do foolish things. It's one of the reasons the suicide rates are so high at that time of the year and cops, despite some views, are as human as the next person.

The officer worked in another Division on the south side of the river so I had to interview him at his work and charge him with three instances of Breach of the Peace. It wasn't the happiest I've ever been in my police career, but it needed done and I did it. When I returned to my own office, an officer senior in rank, who knew where I'd been, asked how I'd got on. When I told him he said, 'That can do your career a lot of good. They'll note that at HQ.'

I looked at him in disdain and told him that if that was how you progressed, he could stick it. What the cop did was wrong and he paid for it, but to view his misery as a career opportunity was anathema to me. The senior officer reached Chief Superintendent. I stayed at Sergeant rank.

The other instance that stuck with me from that period was being taught a lesson in how criminals perceive uniform and CID officers differently. I tried to interview a thief who was in custody, to gain information and failed miserably. It was something that as a detective officer I was used to doing, and prided myself on being reasonably good at; establishing a rapport and gleaning criminal intelligence.

Surely now, it would be even easier as I held a rank. I couldn't have been more wrong. The captive audience wasn't the least interested in playing. I was a uniformed officer and just one of several hundred uniforms. A 'suit' was an individual and the perception was that they could assert more influence on the prisoner's situation.

What confirmed my belief in that theory was that several months later, and having transferred to the CID at Saracen Police Office, I interviewed the same male. Similar set of circumstances; he'd been caught committing a crime and was in jail. Only this time, when I spoke to him, he couldn't shut up. He didn't even recognise me from a few months previously.

31

DETECTIVE AGAIN

I'd been a uniform sergeant for a year, which was the minimum period that the police personnel department liked detectives who'd been promoted to spend in uniform. Pat Connor came into the office one evening when I was on late shift and asked if I would be interested in returning to the CID as a Detective Sergeant, working from 'C' Division which, among other housing areas, encompassed Maryhill, Possilpark, Ruchill, Saracen and Milton.

Although violence and drugs hindered the quality of life for the many decent people who lived in these areas, they nevertheless provided opportunities for great police work. I'd loved my time at Partick, supervising an excellent group, but Mr Connor didn't have to ask twice.

I had my usual first-day greeting problem; it seemed to follow me like a sheepdog follows a farmer. I arrived at work at 8.20 a.m. which was ten minutes before my official commencement, but I'd been a year in uniform where you arrived ten minutes before muster. I'd got out of my habit of being in the office for 7.15 a.m.

When I walked into the CID general office, which was located on the first floor, a senior CID officer was there with a group of Detective Constables and a CID clerk. There was a snide comment about the time of my arrival and the fact that they were already at work.

Well 'at work' was a misnomer because it was coffee-drinking, golf-talking time, but I was never in after him nor away before him following the comment. It had nothing, however, to do with him making the remark as, within a day or so, I would have been back to my previous routine of being first in. Subsequently when he did come in after me and leave before me I made sure I looked exaggeratedly at the wall clock.

Saracen was a great office to work as it covered Possilpark, Parkhouse,

Milton and Saracen itself, and there was always something happening. It was an unusual morning if you came on duty and you weren't greeted by the 'brown bag trail', which referred to the brown paper bags used to hold bloodstained clothing.

Each item of clothing was 'bagged' separately to prevent cross-contamination. If the locals had been indulging in their usual jousting tournaments there would be a trail of brown bags longer than a queue for free beer.

Fortunately, I have to say that not many of the victims were innocents abroad. Much of the violence stemmed from drug fallouts, and consequently, when you interviewed the 'victim' at the hospital they invariably trotted out more fairy tales than Hans Christian Andersen. In fact, his were probably slightly more factual.

It got so that before they turned the key in the ignition of the bull-shit tractor, you would pre-empt things by saying:

Let me take a wild guess at what happened . . .
    You were walking along the street when for no reason you know, you were punched/kicked/headbutted/stabbed/slashed [whichever combination fitted the injuries] by one or more, who you can't describe and wouldn't be able to recognise, and who never uttered a word throughout the attack, and you've no idea why this should have happened to you. Is that about right?

The victims seldom wished the police to investigate the matter further, and that was fine with most of the detectives because they had enough on their plates, trying to provide a service for the decent people who'd been crime victims through no fault of their own.

That doesn't mean that if there was a chance of clearing a crime and locking someone up that you ignored the opportunity, simply because the victim was not prepared to assist or was pond life. Far from it. Even if you knew that the victim wouldn't identify the assailant(s) then, provided you could gather enough evidence to put a case to bed, you'd do it. What you had to become adept at was not flogging a dead horse with no chance of a clearance.

If I'm being truthful, I also have to confess that there were occasions I didn't close a case if it meant my sole witness was some decent member of society or a young child. I took the view that if the victim wasn't prepared to assist me or identify whoever was responsible then why should some decent man, woman or child have their lives potentially made a misery.

With no witness protection, was a decent person to be accosted in the street, and told to tell the police they'd seen nothing, or be threatened just so I could clear a crime stat that wouldn't reach a court given the victim's non-participation? I'm not talking about an enquiry where I had supplementary evidence. That was a different matter. I'm talking about impacting upon a decent person's personal life by floating through, clearing a crime in which the victim was basically being obstructive, and then disappearing into the sunset.

I never, though, applied those rules in my personal life or brought my children up that way. I couldn't ask other people to provide a statement or have their children do it and then be a hypocrite if it happened to involve mine.

Indeed, when my son was only eight years old he witnessed suspects for a housebreaking and went through the ordeal of being interviewed, attending an identification parade and a subsequent trial.

Fortunately, he didn't have to give evidence because after the Procurator Fiscal Depute had spoken to him in the witness waiting room on trial day he returned to the defence agent. He emphasised that the boy was a solid witness, and if he didn't get a plea he'd make sure the Sheriff crucified his client.

Similarly, I never magically morphed into 'Tommy' – the deaf, dumb and blind kid from the song by The Who – the minute I'd concluded duty, although many cops did. That only confirmed my long-held view of there being two distinct types; 'real Police' (who are sadly in the minority) and those simply 'in the police'.

I held the belief that if you were a cop you could never really regard yourself as being 'off duty'. So much so, that I even found myself rolling around a street with three guys in front of my wife and kids.

We'd come out of a video store about 7 p.m. near where we lived and a decent working-man type was waiting on a bus to go home, being baited and hassled by three thugs. The man had told them that he didn't want any trouble and was minding his own business. One of them punched him.

That's when you're dumb and 'police', or, 'whoops didn't see that let's get out of here, *in* the police'. I grabbed the one who'd thrown the punch and identified myself as a cop. We were 200 yards away from a police station and the only way I could get him there was to manhandle him physically. It was pre-mobile phone days. I'd got him about thirty yards when the two with him decided they weren't having it.

The four of us ended up on the ground with me telling my wife to get to the police station for help, and my kids in the car with their eyes the size of saucers. The guy I'd originally grabbed managed to get away owing to my trying to ensure his friends couldn't soften my ribs too much. I did, however, keep hold of the other two, mostly because of a passing member of the public who asked my wife what was happening. He believed her that I was a cop and assisted me in restraining the two of them, until some uniforms came along.

The original victim who'd been punched grabbed the first bus home but, thankfully, called the cops when he got home, which meant that like all good tales we had a beginning, a middle and an end. There was an unfortunate postscript to the incident though.

Three hours after my rolling around the street, uniform cops attended a report of a noisy party. The door was opened by the male who'd punched the man at the bus stop and had squirmed from my grasp. Without a word and without warning he headbutted one of the attending officers and fractured the cop's skull.

The following day a senior officer took a call from the Commander of the division in which the incident had occurred, thanking me for my actions. On passing on the thanks on behalf of that Divisional Commander he must have felt compelled to tell me his war story as a means of bonding. He told me that he'd been in a Chinese takeaway with his wife once when two boys had started a shoving match and he'd told them they should take that outside.

Brave as a lion and 'in the police'.

32

SILENCE ISN'T ALWAYS GOLDEN

CID officers when working late shift and night shift are, by tradition, required to leave what are known as 'operationals' for the Detective Chief Inspector. These are synopses of the various reported crimes and they highlight what, if any, input detectives have had into these incidents. This ensures that the Detective Chief Inspector is briefed should he be asked any awkward questions by a Divisional Commander or his Deputy.

The notes were also for the benefit of whichever detective inherited the relevant investigations. The notes could include which witnesses to an incident had still to be traced and interviewed, whether Scenes of Crime examiners were required etc.

In bygone days just about every crime, from an attempted break-in to a car to an attempted murder, and all points in between, required an explanatory note of sorts. Nowadays, the notes are more selective as uniform officers are now allocated the investigation of crimes which were once the domain of detective officers.

When I'd been at 'D' and 'E' Divisions most detectives would try and insert a funny comment or two, in an attempt to brighten up the following morning's readings for the day shift officers. Having just arrived at the Division, I presumed that 'C' Division would be the same. My attempt at humour earned me a rebuke from Jimmy Lindsay, the Detective Chief Inspector.

I would work for Jimmy on several murders and incidents and enjoyed it as he ran a good major enquiry. He was thorough and not only did he have a good clearance rate in respect of the murders he ran, but he also had good conviction rates too. The Procurator Fiscal Service liked him because he brought them evidence which they could prosecute. That may sound strange, but I can assure you it wasn't always the case when people were charged with serious crimes.

The view held by some at the Procurator Fiscal's Office was that, on occasions, a case lacked a sufficiency of evidence, and it appeared that the sole purpose for the submission was so the police could claim that a murder had been detected. Jimmy was very much down the line and didn't relish any deviations from professionalism.

The Milton area had a car theft problem. Kids would steal cars and then rally them, trying to attract police attention and entice them into 'a chase'. Being kids, they were utterly reckless and had no regard for the consequences.

Their manner of driving to evade capture was heart-stopping and the potential threat to public safety meant that police pursuits were banned in densely populated urban areas, unless the pursuit involved a specialised Traffic Driver. Stealing the car often wasn't enough though. The thieves, as a final act of nastiness, would set fire to the car, or 'torch' it.

Many times the operational would read, 'stolen car recovered, burned-out or torched'. One simple line, but it really didn't begin to address the inconvenience, distress or rage felt by people who'd worked hard to purchase their car, only to have it taken and destroyed by these little bastards. Unfortunately, detectives (and cops in general) can become too blasé through dealing with such instances day in day out, with me, on occasion, being head of the guilty list.

A report had been taken of the theft of a motor vehicle. When noting details for a crime report an officer will try and establish whether the stolen vehicle contained any items of value, such as golf clubs etc. In this case, the item of value was an urn containing a loved one's ashes.

When I came to type the relevant note for that crime I typed that I hoped the thieves just dumped the car and didn't torch it, as the poor bastard had endured one burning already and a second would really be adding insult to injury. A crass throwaway line in retrospect and Jimmy sent me a note saying so.

It wasn't too long, however, before I was close to the top of his hit parade and it followed the murder of a Procurator Fiscal Depute, Marshall John Stormonth.

Following a report of a fire within a flat in the Botanic Gardens in the West End, the Fire Service found a body bound, gagged and dead. Not long after the fire crew were making their grisly discovery a phone call was received by a newspaper. A voice, subsequently described by one witness as belonging to a young boy, announced that he wanted to tell them about a murder.

He said the body in the flat was Marshall John Stormonth from the Fiscal's Office and claimed that Stormonth had picked up and murdered a boy and tried to burn the body. The caller called himself 'Mr Tomkins'. Talk about subconsciously wishing to be caught, as will become clearer subsequently.

I was called out early that morning and found Grant Findlay was the 'on call' senior CID boss. He was dealing with the incident initially although Jimmy Lindsay would inherit it. Once it had been established that the deceased was in fact Mr Stormonth, I was tasked by Grant with breaking the bad news to a male with whom he was in a relationship, although they'd recently quarrelled.

Since vast percentages of murders are committed between intimates, Grant naturally wanted me to gauge the reaction when I broke the news of the death to his former partner. His reaction to the bad news and my instincts would dictate my line of questioning.

When I broke the news to him his grief was as genuine as a penitent's prayers. I told him I was sorry for his loss and left him to compose himself and went to tell Grant that the ex-partner wasn't our murderer. Grant had been joined by a very senior uniform officer from the Division. When I told him the ex-partner wasn't good for the murder Grant, with a smile, said, 'I'm disappointed in you, Gerry. I was sure you'd get a burst (admission).' I gave him the stock detective's answer when faced with that jibe.

'The hardest man to burst is an innocent man.'

I knew Grant was happy enough with my judgement call but the uniformed senior officer decided to make his *Columbo* pitch.

'But the phone caller said the dead man was Marshall John Stormonth so he must have been very close to him to know his full name. He must be a suspect.'

I told him: 'If I'd killed my wife I wouldn't refer to her on the phone by her full name. That isn't the rhythm of speech an intimate would use. It wouldn't surprise me to find the caller was reading from something he'd taken from the house, like a bill or card.'

When we eventually put it together I would be proved correct.

We began to timeline, and found that Mr Stormonth had been out socialising with two other members of the legal fraternity at The Tron Bar, near the Saltmarket, in Glasgow. He left at about 11.30 p.m. telling them that he was heading home as he needed to do some work on a legal appeal. Unfortunately, he didn't go home. Instead, he detoured and it cost him his life.

Marshall was gay, although not openly, and when he detoured it took him to Kelvin Way in the West End of the city. It was risky of him to use that area to try and pick someone up as, from working in the Procurator Fiscal's office, he would have known that the area was subject to periodic sweeps by officers working from nearby Partick Police Office. Lust, however, is a far more powerful force than circumspection.

When we interviewed members of the gay community they recalled seeing him in Kelvin Way in his blue Renault 5 car, in the company of two men. That was the last positive sighting of him alive. It appeared we were looking for two perpetrators.

The post-mortem revealed that Mr Stormonth had been strangled, but although a tie and a belt were on the body, the pathologists were unable to state definitively whether strangulation had been by ligature or manually, owing largely to the damage that the fire had wrought on the body.

It is increasingly common nowadays for indoor murder scenes to be set alight, as the perpetrator(s) (who all watch *CSI*) try to obliterate, potential DNA evidence on the victim and in the house through fire. Though DNA was unheard of then, the perpetrators were working to the same principle, only they were trying to destroy any fingerprint or trace evidence.

In an attempt to mask their presence at the scene, they'd set fire to pillows and clothing in the bedroom near the victim's head. By setting fire to an area of Mr Stormonth's flat no consideration had been given to the potential threat to life of the other occupants who lived in the building.

Mr Stormonth had an active social life as a result of being a talented Gaelic singer who sang tenor in a choir, and he was popular with work colleagues. In fact, he'd had a party in his flat a week or so before his murder, which made things a little more difficult. When the scenes of crime officers managed to pull various fingerprints from the inside of the flat it meant that we had to try and obtain elimination fingerprints from people who'd had access to the flat.

We needed to account for the outstanding 'scene marks'. That way, should we charge someone, it would close off an avenue in the defence strategy. At any trial proceedings, the defence could try to use any unidentified fingerprints to suggest that, although their client had been shown to have been on scene, the unidentified prints belonged to the real murderer.

That meant that we had to trace and take elimination fingerprints from people who had been within Mr Stormonth's flat at any one time. This led to some interesting situations with lawyers and members of the gay community.

Murder is grisly, and none more so than that particular one. It is the ultimate taboo to take another human life and it falls to police officers to investigate the crime. Although cops understand the grave nature of the crime under investigation, nevertheless situations occur in murder enquiries that lighten the bleakness for the investigating officers. Cops often display a very dark sense of humour as a defence mechanism which helps ensure that through humour they remain detached and objective.

I'd been asked to catch up with a female Depute at one of the minor courts to obtain her elimination fingerprints as she'd been in the murder flat. I was with another officer. We spoke to her between her prosecuting cases and asked for ten minutes of her time. She was a tall, willowy blonde with green eyes and a Kristin Scott Thomas proper accent. Her name was Barbara.

We had the usual mechanics required for capturing elimination fingerprints, namely, a brass pad, ink and elimination print forms and wipes to remove the ink. We set the pad up on a desktop, and asked Barbara to remove her jacket as the cuffs were tight-fitting. Barbara was extremely reluctant, but we explained that the ink, when we rolled the digits of her fingers, would get on her mint-green jacket.

Barbara then uttered the immortal words, 'I don't have anything underneath the jacket' and flushed the colour of a Chelsea Pensioner's jacket. In an instant she became 'No bra Barbara'. We naturally couldn't take the 'elims' at that time, but made arrangements for a time when she was wearing more suitable attire. Before we left we gave her our absolute assurance that not a word would pass our lips, which as cops, meant we restricted relating the story to the first fifty guys we met.

Some weeks after we closed the enquiry I took a phone call at work.

When I identified myself the Edinburgh private school for girls' accent hissed, 'You bastard. NBB, is it? I can't look at anyone from your effing Division when they appear at cases I'm prosecuting.' There was a hint of levity in the voice.

Mmmnh. It seemed someone had let the nickname cat out of the bag.

'Morning ma'am. I'm not quite sure what you're referring to. Could you be more specific?'

'Sergeant, if you are even five minutes late for a court case I'm prosecuting, I'll make sure the Sheriff issues a warrant for you, and you'll be in a cell overnight with three of the ugliest, nastiest creatures down for court that day. I'm sure you'll all have fun playing houses.'

There was a chuckle as she terminated the call. I knew she was joking (wasn't she?), but just in case, I made sure I was ahead of the cleaners waiting for the court doors to open when there was even a hint of her involvement.

Two sources of information were crucial to advancing the murder enquiry. One was David Morrison, a Detective Constable at 'A' Division, which covers the city centre, and the other source was two kids. Both sources possessed dynamite information.

David had an informant, to whom he'd given the pseudonym 'Tomkins' to use whenever he contacted David at work. 'Tomkins' was seventeen-year-old Dean Ryan and he'd given David several 'turns' (information). Dean had a twenty-one-year-old brother Steven, who'd worked as a security officer for Tomkins' car garage in Springboig on the outskirts of Glasgow. Dean had chosen the code name himself, probably out of brotherly hero worship.

When David Morrison heard that the caller to the newspaper had used the name 'Mr Tomkins' he contacted Jimmy Lindsay and told him about Ryan. When Ryan's fingerprints were compared against crime scene marks they were found to match 'lifts' from a chair within the flat and the hallway outside the scene. Amateur psychologists may interpret his using the code name Tomkins as a subconscious desire to be caught and punished for his crime, but that would have required a degree of remorse, and that was something neither he nor his brother possessed.

I have my own less esoteric view. He was comfortable using the pseudonym Tomkins when calling the police office for David Morrison.

When he called the newspaper and was asked his name, he was so taken by surprise that he automatically defaulted to the name he used to disguise his informant identity.

The two kids were to prove every bit as vital if not more. They were a couple of harum-scarum characters. He was nineteen; tall, lean and blond. She was sixteen; short, blond-streaked and pretty. They'd somehow fallen in with the Ryan brothers through a friend of a friend of a friend. They'd confided in this friend that they had information about the lawyer's murder, and the 'friend' passed that on to the enquiry team.

I was sent to where they were staying in Lanarkshire to scoop them up, and took them to Motherwell police office for interview. They were both as nervous as kittens, given that they felt they'd been implicated by proxy in the murder of a Procurator Fiscal Depute, so getting them to tell their tale wasn't too difficult.

They'd been staying in a house in Allison Street on the south side of the city when, the night after the murder, Steven Ryan knocked on their door. According to them he was buzzing with excitement, and eventually told them he'd been responsible for the lawyer's death. He not only told the couple, but proceeded to act out what had occurred within the murder house. He told them that he and Dean had met Stormonth in Kelvin Way and pretended to be gay in order to rob him. In what was a foolhardy decision, for which he paid a terrible price, Stormonth invited two strangers, of whose background he knew nothing, back to his house.

Their intention once within the house may, initially, have been to rob him, but somehow it escalated. Steven Ryan told them that once within the flat Dean had struck Strormonth across the head with a champagne bottle, and they bound his wrists and ankles. Steven Ryan then demonstrated for the benefit of the captive audience how he'd strangled his victim. He pantomimed wrapping a tie around the neck and putting his knee into the victim's back and pulling the neck back with the tie so hard that the tie snapped.

According to the witnesses, Steven Ryan told them that Dean had appeared to be in a trance watching the strangulation, but the spell broke along with the tie, and Dean got a belt, which was used as the ligature to butcher the victim. It was a murder confession by proxy, because these kids demonstrated to me what Steven Ryan had shown them. Both were upset as they repeated what Ryan had said and mimed in the flat. They'd breathed a huge sigh of relief when Steven Ryan had left.

On 26 November, along with other officers, I went to a flat on the south side of the city and detained Dean Ryan for the murder. I showed him a photo of Marshall Stormonth, and asked him if he knew the man in the photo, or whether he'd ever been in his flat. He denied knowing him or having been in the flat. That was a hopeful start because his fingerprints belied that.

Among other items I took from the flat was a pair of red jeans, and they provided valuable evidence in the case against Dean Ryan when compared with tapings from the crime scene. Forensic analysis matched fibres from the jeans with those found on the pillow case at Stormonth's head, on his trousers and within his Renault car.

I was hopeful, given his age and the fact that he'd dealt with the police as an informant, that I could induce him to talk at the interview. I tried to ensure there were no physical or psychological barriers in the interview room, so I removed the table which sits in the interview room, and left just the three chairs and the tape running on a smaller table. I also made sure he faced me and the bare wall behind me.

It didn't make a bit of difference, because he blanked every question I put to him. He refused to answer any questions and asked for a lawyer. I didn't give up though and put all the allegations to him, giving him every opportunity to dispute the horrendous sequence of events. He wouldn't respond to any of the questions, and I felt frustrated and slightly deflated when I concluded the interview. I prided myself on being a fairly good interrogator and always believed that engaging an interviewee in conversation was half the battle towards a positive interview result.

If I managed to induce conversation I could always subsequently reroute the topic of the conversation, by circuitous means, towards the crime they were suspected of. However, someone who sat and 'no commented', or worse said nothing at all made things very difficult indeed. I got the impression that he and his brother had already discussed their strategy should they be detained and interviewed by the police.

There was still enough to arrest and charge him, which I did. Even when charged he continued to keep his counsel and made no reply to the charge. He was seventeen years of age, and charged with what amounted to the slaughter of another human being, but there wasn't a flicker of regret or remorse. Unlike Marshall Stormonth's ex-partner I knew this was the right one, or at least, one of two.

Two days later, I detained the elder brother Steven Ryan in a flat in Wilton Street, in the West End of Glasgow. He'd described so graphically how he'd carried out the murder to the boy and the girl I'd interviewed, and both felt that when he'd been boasting about the sequence of events he'd especially enjoyed miming the strangulation.

I showed him a photograph of Marshall Stormonth and asked him the same questions, but he wouldn't speak then and continued to maintain that silence, both within the flat and throughout the interview that followed. He was arrested and charged with the murder, and he mirrored his brother's lack of contrition.

It was a pretty good case, but with precognition time came problems. The two kids involved failed to show up for their precognitions and had disappeared. I felt that they'd probably panicked and rabbited. I managed to track them down to Blackpool and the Procurator Fiscal for Glasgow, Mr Docherty, who was preparing the case for trial issued warrants for their arrest.

I arranged for Blackpool officers to execute the warrants and drove down and collected them and brought them back to Glasgow. It was as I thought; the case was very high-profile, involving the death of a Procurator Fiscal Depute, and that, allied to their genuine fear of the Ryans, had induced the panic flight. The problem was that it was a Friday, and that meant they would be held custody until appearing at court on the Monday.

They were scheduled to be held at Maryhill Police Office over the weekend, but I felt that given their only 'crime' had been to make themselves temporarily scarce I would try and make their weekend a little less stressful. They'd fled to Blackpool not Brazil, and it had only taken me a phone call to locate them.

We had a room at Saracen Police Office which had served as a locker room but had been cleared, pending a decision as to how best to utilise it. I spoke to Jimmy Lindsay and took responsibility for them over the weekend. I arranged for a couple of chairs, a radio and a portable television to be put in the room and I collected them from Maryhill each morning.

They were provided with showering facilities in the respective locker rooms and then spent the day in the room. I also got them takeaway food and come 7 p.m. they were returned to their cells at Maryhill. Before they appeared at court I spoke to Mr Docherty on the Monday morning. I told him that I'd dealt with them over the weekend and was happy that their disappearance was an aberration and gave him my assurance that they would be there for the trial.

They were released from the court, and when it was time for the trial I arranged for other officers to pick them up and convey them to court when they were scheduled to give evidence. I was a witness so I wanted to ensure there was no potential guilt by association. They both reiterated in court what they'd told me in their statements.

In their choice of prosecutor the Crown Office had ensured that they were giving themselves the very best chance of a conviction. Kevin Drummond, QC, was the choice. Mr Drummond was *the* leading light among his Advocate peers. I'm not sure of the machinations that were involved to secure him as the Advocate Depute in this case, because as far as I was aware Mr Drummond, at that particular time, was operating as Defence Counsel. However it had been achieved I was delighted, as he had also been the Advocate Depute who secured convictions in the no body/Fenwick Moors case.

I was provided with a first-hand demonstration of his considerable courtroom skills when it came time for me to give evidence. Both brothers had refused to answer any questions, which as I've indicated frustrated me, but I hadn't simply accepted their 'no comment' and wound up the interviews. I'd tried everything to get them to comment, put all the allegations to them, appealed to their better nature (some hope) and stated that if they'd had no involvement in Mr Stormonth's death then surely, as human beings, they would wish to assist the police enquiry.

The Roman philosopher and scholar Cicero maintained: 'Though silence is not necessarily an admission, it is not a denial, either.' I was an eager participant as Mr Drummond exploited this maxim to the fullest.

Mr Drummond had me read out the transcript of the questions posed. After each allegation, he would stop me and dramatically say, in his best Shakespearian voice, for the benefit of the jury:

'He was asked whether he'd smashed a bottle over a man's head, strangled him, and set fire to him and he refused to answer and kept silent?' He would then add the caveat, 'As he was entitled to do.'

By the time I'd read the questions and the 'no comment' answers and Mr Drummond had expressed his incredulity that both had remained silent, he had more than made his point to the members of the jury. Any decent person faced with such allegations would, if they'd been innocent, surely have tried to assist the police. Their silence damned them.

Both were convicted and Dean Ryan was sentenced by Lord Osborne to be detained without limit of time, while Steven Ryan was sentenced to life imprisonment. I was really pleased for several reasons. I'd been part of a real collective enquiry. Members of the public had done the right thing, Jimmy Lindsay had run his usual tight enquiry, the forensic scientists and scenes of crime officers had come up trumps, and the members of the prosecution had capitalised on the evidence brought to them.

On the day the verdicts were returned Mr Docherty wrote person-ally to Leslie Sharp, then Chief Constable, offering his gratitude to the police team led by Jimmy Lindsay. He wrote that it would be invid-ious to single out any individual, but it would be inappropriate not to commend myself as I had been of immense assistance during the inves-tigation and throughout the trial. It was a very nice touch.

The Ryans were to attract headlines over a decade or so later when they failed to return from work placements on a 'Training for Freedom' programme. The public were never alerted to the fact that two ruth-less, unrepentant killers had gone walkabout, until after they'd been returned to prison, a fact which the newspapers made great play of.

33

FRANKENSTEIN SUTURES

Various books and programmes glamorise police work by short-circuiting and concising police procedures, and I can appreciate that may be necessary in order to drive a plotline, or fit into an hour's television schedule. Others, in an effort to appear as 'authentic' representations of police work, are at great pains to emphasise how boring police procedures and normal police duties can be.

I have to say that, at the risk of appearing sanctimonious, I never found it boring. Of course, some areas aren't as 'sexy' as others. Standing at a crime scene for hours in the pouring rain isn't fun, but while on patrol or working as a detective if you were complaining of boredom then you only had yourself to blame. If I wasn't actively working an enquiry I used downtime to reappraise enquiries I hadn't closed, or cleared paperwork, or, even better, used the opportunity to get out and about and chase up informants, or 'noise up' criminals and stop cars and suspect persons.

What is perhaps a more accurate assessment is how you could be involved in the most mundane aspect of your police duties when suddenly your adrenalin needle rocketed from zero to red in a heartbeat. It may be that aspect that is, for many, the attraction of the job.

May 1994, and it was a warm spring night about 11.30 p.m. I was on night shift and just returning to Maryhill Office. I'd been over at a satellite office collecting a statement left for me by an officer, relating to an enquiry I had. I was in the car with a girl who was on her six-month secondment with the CID, with not a care in the world until a car emerged from a junction just in front of us and almost took the nose off our car.

It fishtailed along the road, and it certainly appeared from the manner of driving as if the sole occupant knew we were police in an unmarked car and was determined to evade us. The car chase ended in a nearby housing scheme called Summerston, when he leapt from the still-moving car and allowed it to crash into the garden wall and garden of a house.

I jumped out of our car in pursuit, but I knew the minute it began that it was trouble. The driver had one of those old style wooden-handled screwdrivers in his hand, with an eight or nine-inch steel bit.

He was about 5'10" and I knew him to be a horrible bastard who fought with the police at every turn, and habitually carried weapons.

He had convictions for robbery, reset and almost every variation on crimes of dishonesty and had served several custodial sentences. Although it probably wasn't going to end well, I had to make sure that it wasn't me, a member of the public or another police colleague who had no chair to sit on when the music stopped.

I had the measure of him speedwise and he realised that. Several times he turned and threatened me with the screwdriver, but I made sure I kept as much of a reaction space as possible, while hoping for an opportunity that was advantageous to me.

I ran him down to the rear of a group of pensioners' flats, and as we were approaching the flats I caught a glimpse of a uniform in my peripheral vision. The girl I was working with, although not able to keep up owing to wearing a skirt and heels, had broadcast the route of the foot chase. The attending cop was responding to the assistance request.

He was a young lad, and I didn't recognise him which as it turned out wasn't surprising as this was his first night on duty, but he wasn't slow to produce his baton. I shouted to him to circle to the right and keep out of the arc of the weapon. Our villain now had two targets which lowered his advantage.

He turned and tried to run through the rear entrance of one of the flats, but because the flats were pensioner-occupied the rear entrances were always kept locked to stop people using them as a shortcut or gathering area. He realised his mistake, spun around and tried to run through the gap between the young cop and me.

He started to lose his footing on the wet grass, and as he did so I grabbed the wrist holding the screwdriver and kicked his legs from under him as the young cop hit him about the collar bone area with his baton. As he pitched forward I think his face caught my knee, and that knocked any fight out of him.

By this time, we'd been caught up by my colleague and an older uniform officer who was the young cop's tutor. I told my partner and the young cop to wait by the stolen car, arrange for its removal, and ascertain what damage had been caused to the property the car had run into. Along with the older cop who was driving, I conveyed the prisoner to Maryhill office.

The following night I encountered a uniform Superintendent who was on duty and who had recently finished checking the welfare of the prisoners in custody within the Division. He was typical of so many senior officers inasmuch as in police parlance, 'he'd never seen an angry man'.

He began with the concerned introduction, 'Are you okay, Gerry? That must have been frightening.'

Quickly followed by: 'I've just come from visiting him in the cell. He's got some face on him.'

I think he must have expected me to attempt to fudge or flannel, but there was no chance of that happening. I said to him: 'Yeah, and it was me who gave him that face. Did you see the screwdriver he was trying to ventilate me with? I'm not in the job to be some bastard's dartboard. Maybe next time it'll make him think twice about fighting with the cops.'

He stammered and spluttered and said: 'Oh, eh, quite right; quite right,' and then found that he had other pressing engagements and made a hasty exit, no doubt worried he may have been tainted by guilt through association.

The prisoner was in custody over a weekend and was scheduled to appear at court on the Monday. On the Saturday he complained that he'd suffered a broken jaw during arrest, needed to have the injury X-rayed, and was sent to the Western Infirmary from where he escaped on foot during treatment.

The police helicopter was scrambled to assist in the search which ended in a park a mile or so from the hospital. He was seen trying to conceal himself in some bushes and, as an older cop approached the bushes, the villain shouted out that he had a blade. That, in turn, prompted the cop, without further ado, to give him a centre parting with his baton. He really wasn't encountering the caring/sharing side of the police, was he?

He was taken back to the hospital and the doctor who had been examining him when he'd bolted was given the job of treating the head wound. He was happy to oblige and did what cops call a 'Frankenstein number' on him.

Generally, doctors will try and insert many small sutures to try and make a wound less noticeable and more aesthetically pleasing. However, when doctors or nurses are themselves subjected to physical or verbal abuse then a doctor may use about three sutures to close a six- or seven-inch laceration. The end result is never too bonny to say the least and hence the Frankenstein reference.

He pled guilty to ten charges prior to trial and was given several years in prison.

Several months later, while in America, I was on patrol duties with detectives from Las Vegas Metro, and they asked me what I carried. I knew they were referring to what firearm I carried in the course of my duties. I explained to them that we didn't carry firearms, and that all we had was a pair of handcuffs and a short piece of wood. They looked at me in total bemusement, and asked what we did in confrontational situations. As an example, I told them about the situation those few months previously and that only made them snort with laughter and shake their heads. One of the veteran detectives, Pat Franks, said:

Ger, our cops get a nightstick and spray to use if skels [perpetra-tors] want to wrestle. If they produce a knife, that's a lethal weapon every bit as much as a gun, so your cops over there must be Bruce Lee or Obi Wan Kenobi. If what you've just described happened here then he'd have been told, 'Put that down, asshole, or the next voice you hear will be St Peter telling you you're at the wrong gate, and the down escalator is over there.'

The other detectives gave him an 'Amen'. It may have sounded like a Clint Eastwood line, but he wasn't exaggerating, nor was it bravado either. Some years later, a Las Vegas officer was involved in his third fatal shooting in the line of duty. In each situation he had been alone, as had been the villain he'd confronted. Each time the villain had pulled a knife and wound up dead.

Law enforcement agencies in the USA have always placed a high value on officer safety and, thankfully, since my episode officers in the

UK have seen an improvement in their equipment. Protective vests, extended batons and CS spray ensure that they are better placed to protect both themselves and members of the public. Firearms? I really don't know. Is it better to have a piece of equipment and not need to use it, or need it but not have access to it?

There is a huge responsibility in carrying and producing a firearm and I wonder what would have been the outcome if I'd been armed and, instead of keeping my distance until I could try and manoeuvre the situation to my advantage, I'd simply had to produce a gun. Situation resolved immediately and safely, or a life lost? I'm thankful I've never been placed in the situation where I was forced to make the choice.

34

DOG RUNS

I'd had a good arrest record working with the girl – we'll call her 'J' – who was on her six-month secondment, but I was also starting to view her as a not-so-lucky charm. I'd just come back from that Stateside holiday when I found myself in another confrontational situation. This time, however, the aggressor was man's best friend.

'J' and I were late shift and had just taken a report of a mugging when Jim Duncan who I'd worked with previously in the Serious Crime Squad and another detective we'll call 'S' began their night shift. The victim was a female Provident collector and she'd been mugged while collecting in an area that was known as 'Robbery Row'. It had happened in Liddesdale Road in the Milton area of Glasgow. Liddesdale Road consisted then of rows of four-storey flats, all of which had verandas and close mouths. The close mouths were poorly lit and were ideal areas of concealment for prospective muggers or ambushers.

Provident collectors were representatives of The Provident, a financial organisation. One area of their business related to loans, and these loans were generally to people on lower incomes. There was no actual money advanced. Instead, the person borrowing was provided with cheques which were accepted at various shops and stores throughout the country.

Many of these low-income families would use the cheques to purchase school uniforms or clothes for kids at birthdays and Christmas. They paid back the loans weekly to a collector or representative of the Provident. Given that the collectors carried several hundreds of pounds in cash they were ideal targets for mugging.

We had interviewed the victim and, given the location of the incident and her description, thought we may have a possible suspect. We had no other witnesses so were unlikely to be granted a search warrant, but I'd had dealings with this particular suspect previously (we'll call him 'Merry'), so decided to wing it and pay him a visit.

The four of us went to his flat in Liddesdale Road which was very near the mugging location. He lived there with his girlfriend and new baby. That much I knew, but what none of us was aware of was that he'd another recent addition to the 'family' – a pit bull terrier.

We didn't know it was a pit bull at that point because whenever cops knocked on a door in our area and heard an aggressive bark and growl they adopted a set procedure. This was as a result of the amount of criminals in our division who were keeping dogs that reacted to cops like athletes to a starting gun. The procedure was that as the house-holder began to open the door one of the attending cops would hold the door from the outside and instruct the householder to secure the dog in a room before the door was fully opened.

Consequently, when 'Merry' came to the door he was told to lock the dog away. We were on a fishing expedition, and money was the only thing that had been stolen so nothing was to be lost by the delay in, hopefully, gaining entrance.

I managed to talk my way into the house, and after explaining why we were there he let us have a look in the living room and, finding nothing there, went to the main bedroom to continue the search. With the baby being so young the cot also occupied the main bedroom and with four detectives, 'Merry', his girlfriend, the baby, a double bed and bedroom furniture, you could barely draw breath, far less manoeuvre.

We needed to evacuate a few people, but before we could make the smart move, enter 'the Terminator'; fifty-five pounds of snuffling, snorting, snot-trailing, solid muscle. Oh you bastard – a fucking pit bull terrier. They'd been outlawed as dangerous dogs in 1991 owing to the amount of savage attacks they'd been involved in, some of which had resulted in deaths. Many people had either ignored the legislation, or bought dogs which were so borderline legal that it took an experi-enced vet to tell the difference.

Now, don't ask me why anyone with a newborn baby or any kids at all would want one of these things in the house, and please don't try and tell me there is no such thing as a bad dog only a bad owner. Certain types of dogs are bred to fight and, consequently, are aggres-sive and combative by nature. I don't care how many times you show me a prohibited dog rolling over and wanting its tummy rubbed, the potential is always there for tragedy.

There were two world famous illusionists who worked in Las Vegas named Siegfried and Roy. They utilised lions and white tigers as part of their act. They were the only people to have bred the unique white tigers outwith captivity. At their huge house in Vegas they had a glass floor, and under that a swimming pool where the tigers swam and roamed. They swam with the tigers, played with them, and had raised and interacted with them since birth. They'd performed literally thousands of times. The tigers were just like pussy cats to them ... until one night in the show one of the tigers grabbed Roy by the neck and finished his performing career right there.

In our case, I don't know how this thing had got loose, but the second it entered the room the hackles were up and it decided it was time to spread the fear. It took one look at Jim Duncan, and whether it thought there was most meat on Jim, who was a big guy, I don't know, but it launched at him and the chaos began. Jim flat-footed the dog away and then performed a standing jump onto the bed. Maybe he thought the owners had taught the dog not to go up on the bed, and that might discourage it, or maybe he was hoping to use the bed as a launch pad to reach the top of the wardrobe, but it mirrored his leap and drove towards his face.

I was screaming at 'Merry' to get 'a hold of the fuckin' dog'. His partner was screaming and trying to shield the baby. Jim was just screaming, and 'J' had gone into the lotus position and was chanting Buddhist-type mantras: 'I am a tree. I am not here in this room'.

I saw Jim adopt the classic 'footballer in a wall facing a free kick' pose; i.e. one arm covering the face and the other his balls and, to this day, I would swear I saw 'the Terminator' get his arm, but perhaps 'S' caught it just before it locked. He launched a flying kick at the dog and knocked it (very) temporarily off balance. That really pissed it off, and it then locked onto 'S' as the threat and proceeded to turn him into its personal piñata.

I began to sink my size elevens into its ribs, and by that I mean I was putting in full-force kicks, but it simply shook its head and shot a look which I interpreted as, 'If that's your best, nancy boy, then wait till your turn'. It readied itself for me and I was wishing I had the consistency of mercury and could slip between the floorboards. It was only 'Merry' grabbing the collar with two hands and heaving and dragging it, claws tearing the carpet, snot and blood dripping, into a room that saved me.

'Merry' was later charged with the robbery. I drove 'S' to the hospital for treatment and then home. I had to pull his night shift and, from memory, Jimmy Lindsay never paid me the overtime. I arranged for a police dog handler to capture 'the Terminator', and I had it examined by a vet who confirmed that it was a prohibited breed. Ultimately, that meant the big kennel in the sky and definitely no 'I'll be back' for that bad boy. I actually like dogs, but having that dog's contract cancelled didn't bother me in the slightest. It was bad seed, and I viewed it as potentially saving the owners' child from a future mauling.

They say things come in threes, and that was the case with my dog encounters over the next few months; my second being a German Shepherd while chasing John Lyons who came from the Milton housing scheme. Again the chase and encounter arose when things were quiet, and I was out and about midmorning looking to see what mischief I could get myself involved in.

I was driving in an area of Milton when I saw Lyons and knew there was an arrest warrant in force for him. I can't recall what the warrant was for. There'd been warrants issued previously for him for armed robbery and the discharge of a firearm. He'd gone on the run when those warrants had been in existence and had been cocky with it, calling cops at the police office to taunt them.

When he saw me he ran and I chased him until he ran through the front door of what I knew was his aunt's house. I didn't follow him in the door because I knew he would make straight for the back door, hoping that any pursuing cops would waste time looking for him in the house. I ran down the side path and opened the back door to be greeted by him followed closely by the household German Shepherd.

There was a metal dustbin at the back door and I decided to get my retaliation in first and grabbed the lid and gave the Alsatian a bang on the bridge of the nose to concentrate its mind. It turned tail and Lyons gave himself up. I drove him to Maryhill where, after booking him through, I took him up to a cell. As he was going in to the cell he burst into tears at being banged up.

So much for armed robberies, loosing off a gun and taunting the police, but it was completely in character with my experience of so many of the so-called Glasgow gangsters.

My third canine encounter proved to be an absolute topper.

I took a phone call one afternoon from Alex Sharkey who was then a Detective Constable at Maryhill. He had an enquiry and the suspect was staying in an area covered by Saracen where I was stationed. The area was known as 'The Jungle', and wouldn't have been out of place in the Projects in Baltimore. It has since been demolished and rebuilt, but at that time consisted of tenement flats which housed more than their fair share of thieves, resetters and drug dealers. It also housed quite a few decent families too.

Sharkey was about 5'9" with a battleship-type build, and back then had black wavy hair, black eyes and a booming laugh. He was looking to speak to the suspect and was hoping to hook up with me when he went to the house, as I'd had previous dealings with the occupant. He told me that Drug Squad Officers also had a visit planned and that they had a search warrant already.

All this was well and good but I knew that the suspect kept a Japanese Akita called Taz (I think short for Tasmanian devil. Cute, eh?), and Taz was a bastard of a dog. The drug cops knew Taz as well. It put the fear of God into quite a few hardy cops. I gave Sharkey a, 'Sure, no worries', through gritted teeth.

The following morning, off we trotted up to the flat. We got to the door and the Drug Squad boys were in front with a cop, who we'll call CJ, first in line. CJ looked like a drug addict himself. His complexion was almost grey, he had lank hair and was painfully thin. In fact, he was so skinny that if he'd another two bellybuttons he would have looked like a flute.

Generally, when they had a warrant and were in warpath mode they knocked quietly, as if they'd used a marshmallow hammer. They then crashed the door and were in the house before anything could be discarded and the occupants knew what was happening. This time seemed different.

They banged loudly on the door and declared that they were the police, had a search warrant, and demanded the door be opened. That set off the deep booming bark that gave me a shiver. I looked at Sharkey and thought about getting behind him because there was more meat on him for Taz to chew. From the look he shot me on hearing the bark he thought the same, only he probably formed the view that, with me being tall, Taz would have a bigger bone to gnaw.

It's strange how dogs can generate such fear when they have only one method of causing you harm – their mouth – and that is generally small. I mean they can't headbutt or elbow or kick or punch you or, like other animals, inject you with venom, or tear you to pieces with their claws . . . but they still put the fear out.

I really wasn't looking forward to this and couldn't understand why they hadn't brought along a dog handler. They banged again and shouted for the door to be opened and I silently thought, 'Fuck don't antagonise it further.' CJ, who was looking through the letterbox, passed back that the living room door was closed and that the dog wasn't in the hallway. They began to crash the door.

As the main door capitulated the living room door opened and Taz came charging down the long hallway. Our suspect had a well-furnished house from his drug dealings, and that included the expensive-looking, cream-coloured, deep pile carpet in the hallway.

Strangely, when the door had gone in the troops hadn't rushed into the house the way they normally did. In fact, they stood back and Alex and I looked at each other wondering whether they were waiting for us. Neither of us moved. I was fixated on this monster heading towards CJ who was wearing a long parka type jacket, into which he was reaching.

It was the kind of long jacket/coat from which you see robbers produce a shotgun. He wasn't showing any sign of panic and for a crazy nanosecond I thought, 'He's got a gun and he's going to blast the dog'. As it transpired I wasn't too far wrong, and it became obvious why they weren't charging into the house. This was an ambush and revenge mission.

CJ produced a red metal cylindrical object with a black plastic nozzle and as Taz reached him, all balls and snarling, intent on demonstrating exactly who was (literally) top dog – *Doosh!* CJ depressed the plunger of a portable fire extinguisher and gave Taz a mouthwash of carbon dioxide.

Splat! Taz shat on the cream shagpile and shook his head trying to clear the senses and trying to figure out how he wasn't enjoying his past-time of terrifying cops.

Doosh! The plunger depressed again.

Splat! Taz dropped another load on the shagpile and turned tail.

CJ pursued Taz along the hallway. *Doosh!* CJ hit Taz in the ass giving him a carbon dioxide enema. This was payback time, and there was no mercy.

Taz now dropped what was left of his bowels, as he was running along the hallway. You can often read crime scenes from the blood splattering. Here, it was a shit trail that told the story.

Doosh! Another shot in the ass. Taz pissed on the carpet as he reached the living room.

CJ ran the dog into the corner of the room where Taz, in abject surrender, lay on his back with his legs up in the air.

CJ, who'd probably shat his own pants previously because of Taz, wasn't in any kind of forgiving mood. *Doosh!* Taz got a last blast and suffered the final indignation of pissing on his own belly. Taz's humiliation was complete.

The last I heard was what Sharkey told me. Taz's owner had sold him to someone in Fife who operated in similar circles to himself. He convinced the buyer that Taz was ferocious, but Taz had been well and truly tamed by what the drug unit called their 'canine converter'.

I would imagine he would have become 'gun shy' and crapped on the spot at the sight of anyone in a longish coat, which in Fife in midwinter probably meant Taz became incontinent.

The unit thought that they'd found the perfect solution to the 'devil dogs' they were facing with increasing regularity. Word, however, quickly seeped down from the highest police levels that, 'any use of what was being euphemistically referred to by officers as a "canine converter" would result in disciplinary action'. There's always a killjoy at every party.

35

TWO CHOICES

Many crimes are the result of a combination of motive and opportunity, and when desperation is your motive, you'll seize on any opportunity, and that includes breaking into a police office, which is what happened in late June 1995.

I came in at my normal time of around 7 a.m. to find that during the night someone had entered the Inspector's room. They'd certainly stolen personal items, but what hadn't yet been established was whether they'd also taken anything of a confidential nature.

There was, naturally, a panic on because someone was going to have to break the news to Mr Douglas Kelly who was the Divisional Commander and be prepared for the volcanic reaction. Mr Kelly was a tall, white-haired imposing figure.

The likely bearer of the bad tidings was Jimmy Lindsay, and he didn't relish having to tell him that someone had left the ground-floor windows to the room open because it had been a warm night ... in the middle of the dishonesty capital of the West of Scotland!

Possilpark and Saracen thieves were legendary. Compared to them Ali Baba's forty couldn't have stolen ice in the Arctic. They once stole a wall-mounted television from a busy bookmaker's shop in the middle of the day. I watched the CCTV footage and still can't work out how they did it.

They were like Vikings inasmuch as they ranged far and wide in their plundering. They particularly liked working Glasgow city centre and football matches. They would pick pockets at football matches after 'marking' someone who'd had too much to drink. In the city centre, they would indulge in what they called 'tack lifting'.

They would follow vans delivering to stores in the city centre and time how long the driver was in the store with the various parcels.

Using a short crowbar, which they concealed up the sleeve of a jacket, they would jemmy open the rear door between deliveries, help themselves to a few parcels and be in the pub for opening time to sell the goods.

While in the Serious Crime Squad I was out one morning about 9 a.m. with Gerry Boyle. Gerry was my Detective Sergeant and like me was always looking to self-generate work when we had downtime. Gerry had worked Maryhill, Possilpark and Saracen before transferring to the Squad. Rather than malinger at Ralph Slater's or one of the other stores, or sit in a shop drinking coffee and wasting time, we were out prowling.

We were in Renfield Street when Gerry recognised two of a well-known 'tack lifting' team eyeing up the vans. We'd only watched them for a few minutes when they made their move. I ended up running down the middle of a busy Renfield Street chasing one of them before he ran into a large Boots department store which at that time was on the corner of Renfield Street and Argyle Street.

I thought I'd lost him as he'd disappeared from sight before finding the cheeky bastard had tucked himself under the leg space of one of the checkout tills, still with the crowbar up the sleeve. Apprehension was by far the exception rather than the rule, and because it was so rare he simply accepted it as an occupational hazard.

Before anyone gets the idea I'm lauding these people I can assure you I'm not. They are/were lazy bastards who look(ed) for an easy life and had no interest in a hard day's work. If they had taken on a job and applied the same thought and commitment to that as they did their thieving they'd have rivalled Richard Branson.

I was told about the break-in to the office when I walked through to collect the reports of crimes that had occurred within the previous fourteen hours or so. The cop working indoors was of the older type, and didn't like the supervisors who'd been on duty when it had happened and was revelling in their panic.

The supervisors had remained on duty because they were in the middle of compiling a report as to why they'd left a police office vulnerable to the break-in. They were probably looking to source a London *Yellow Pages* directory to put down the arse of their trousers to lessen the spanking they were facing.

I didn't share the Bar Officer's enthusiasm. For 'neds' to come into the office through a hopper window left on the latch and pillage was something I took as a giant 'fuck you', and that couldn't be allowed. As the Bar Officer was regaling me with the story I happened to notice a message scribbled on a writing pad on his desk.

He'd been told by the night shift who'd he'd replaced, to pass a message on to a plain clothes cop called John McCall. John had an informant who was a degenerate drug addict, and he'd walked into the office during the night demanding that John be contacted as he had some information. John was off duty and the informant had been told he'd have to wait until the morning. Apparently, he'd then tried desperately to convince the cops in the bar to advance him £10 against the information he had for John. He claimed the information would net him far more than the £10, but he hadn't a hope of persuading those cops to part with any money and was thrown out of the office unceremoniously.

I knew him, and knew that although not in the same class as the other thieves within the area he was still good by any other standards. The informant was also the type that if he was hurting for money for heroin, he would risk breaking into the office. It wasn't much, but as there wasn't any other line of enquiry leaping out I decided he was as good a starting point as any.

I contacted a local Justice of the Peace and pitched my case and he issued a warrant to search the suspect's house. By this time it was about 7.20 a.m. and 'S' had come on duty. He was fully recovered from his dog wrestling bout and I gave him a quick update as we walked out of the door, but not before he warned, 'If he's keeping anything bigger than a fucking hamster in there, you can forget it.'

We went to a block of tenement flats which were only a couple of minutes from the office and knocked on the door. I had an officer cover the rear of the building to ensure nothing or no one came out of there without us knowing. I shouted through the letterbox that I had a warrant and banged on the door. For good measure I gave the door a couple of heavy thumps.

They weren't sufficient to force the door and weren't intended to. I only wanted whoever inside to believe it would be forced if he didn't answer. He shouted, 'Don't put it in, Mr Gallacher. It's too much hassle to get it repaired. I'll open it.' The minute he did he was pushed into the living room and onto the couch. This needed to be quick and painless if we were to get the right outcome.

You tanned [cop-speak for 'broke into'] the office so I don't want to hear any denials. You've got two choices and a five-second count-down to make the right choice. Either you get us back what you knocked and go to the Sheriff Summary [Court], or I'll have it round Possil all the people you've stuck in [informed on]. The clock's ticking.

Junkies are such an enigma. They know no loyalty or truth when they're fully hooked. It could be their eighty-year-old grandmother who had only £5 to last her for food and heating for the rest of the week, and they'd steal it in a heartbeat. When you have to investigate that aftermath you detest them. However, they are pathetic creatures too. Their addictions, dependencies and total lack of self-pride or self-respect render them almost helpless.

I didn't relish putting the hard word to him, but if we had an unre-solved break-in to the office we would be a laughing stock within the area we policed and would lose respect. That really wasn't an option. His choice took him only a heartbeat. He wasn't so befuddled that he didn't realise the consequences of being 'outed'. He took us to the only bedroom where there was a sports bag with clothing inside. I radioed for one of the night shift sergeants to attend, and he identified the bag and clothing as his. The sergeant also told me that he was missing various other items, among them a ring.

I turned to our suspect and he summoned his girlfriend and told her to go and get the ring he'd obviously traded for drugs. She was back within ten minutes with the ring. I told him I wasn't doing this in stops and starts and wanted everything back so he led me to nearby Closeburn Street where he'd hidden a briefcase containing confiden-tial papers. Thereafter, to a drain in Barloch Street, adjacent to the office, where he'd tossed a set of keys. We had a full recovery of everything stolen and an arrest by 8.15 a.m.

As predicted, the Commander was set for stratospheric launch when he learned of the break-in, but the launch was aborted when he was told that I'd got the stolen items back and had bagged someone for it. It saved some supervisory officers from potential disciplinary action. Years later one of those officers was in a position to assist my career advancement. I had never sought thanks for nor mentioned the inci-dent but hoped that the favour might be returned. It wasn't.

36

ONE VIOLENT ACT TOO MANY

The end of September 1995 brought a murder in the Cadder district of our policing area, and not a police officer who had dealings with, or had even the slightest knowledge of the victim, mourned his passing. He was a Class-One, Grade-A sociopath called Mark Vass.

He had the nickname 'Basil' after the character Basil Fawlty from the television series *Fawlty Towers*. I think the nickname had arisen from schooldays when he was much younger, and tall and lanky in the manner of John Cleese who played Basil Fawlty. I often wondered if he'd been bullied as a boy as well.

As he grew he filled out and was actually a good-looking lad; tall, dark eyes and hair. He became part of a four-man robbery team whose method of operating was as honed as any London team. He was friendly with people such as John Lyons, Paul Docherty and Peter Hetherington. All three had at one point or another either been charged with or convicted of armed robberies. Lyons, I've mentioned. Hetherington would stand trial with Vass for the murder of a security guard during a robbery and Docherty and Vass would have a fateful (and fatal) falling out. I'll cover both incidents later in the chapter.

The team went equipped with firearms which they were prepared to use in the commission of the robberies. They would begin by stealing two high performance cars. The first car was used in the robbery and getaway, but was ditched within a half mile or so of the robbery scene when they would switch to the second car. Their reasoning behind this was simple.

By the time details of the getaway car had been broadcast over a police communication system and the helicopter had been scrambled, everyone would still be busy looking for the first car. In the confusion that invariably follows these type of crimes, they would have already switched to the second vehicle and be long gone before details of the subsequent car had been obtained and circulated.

Like all good plans their robbery methods were also simple, but effective. They drove the getaway car up to the bank. One remained in the car while the other three entered the bank just as the cash had been delivered, and before it had been placed in the vault. One controlled door entry, and pity help any officer who chanced on the robbery and ran in hastily. The second forced the customers to the ground and ensured there was no one prepared to try any heroics. The third vaulted the counter and grabbed the bags. They torched the second car and the clothing worn during the commission of the robberies to ensure there was no trace evidence available to police investigators.

I first encountered Vass when I was in the Serious Crime Squad when he was suspected of a robbery which had occurred on the south side of Glasgow. I got him in a bar in the Bishopbriggs area on the outskirts of Glasgow. He was seated at a table in the lounge, dressed in designer clothing and with his current girlfriend, a good-looking blonde. He was dragged out separately from her, and I interviewed him at Govan Police Office. There was no substantial evidence against him and he knew it and was consequently cocky with it.

He enjoyed a lucrative six or seven years of robberies not only in Glasgow, but throughout other parts of the UK. I'm sure for someone who'd possibly been bullied he loved the taste of power that wielding a firearm brought him, which was to have tragic consequences for others.

In 1991, while I was still at 'E' Division, he committed his first murder. Andrew Smith was on the Cadder towpath of the Forth and Clyde Canal with a couple of friends, and had been drinking. They passed Vaila Street where Vass lived in a flat in a block of maisonettes. These maisonettes all had verandas and Vass was on the veranda when he became involved in a verbal slanging with Smith.

He followed Smith to a bridge on the canal path where Tresta Road meets Balmore Road and brutally stabbed him to death. I can't recall whether he'd waited until Smith was alone, or whether the two Smith had been with were too afraid of Vass to speak up, but either way he was never charged, although he was the murderer.

In March 1992, he was part of a three-man robbery team who held up a security van behind Boots in Greenock on the Clyde coast. Derek Ure, a twenty-one-year-old security guard, was shot dead during the robbery. Vass went on trial at the High Court with Peter Hetherington for the murder after he left a fingerprint on the licence plate of the getaway car.

Midway through the trial Hetherington walked free owing to an insufficiency of evidence against him. Vass produced a witness – his then girlfriend, who was a nurse – who gave evidence that, at the time of the robbery, Vass was with her in England. The jury at the conclusion of the evidence took two hours to return a 'Not Proven' verdict.

He ran from the court smiling, proclaiming he was 'glad to be free'. Two murders and numerous armed robberies, where he'd no doubt gleefully stuck a loaded firearm in the faces of terror-filled victims, and he'd escaped punishment every time. I'll just bet he was glad.

On 21 July 1995, I was working when a report came in of an incident in the Cadder area involving Paul Docherty, who had been friendly with Vass. I'd had previous dealings with Docherty too. While in the Robbery Unit working from FHQ, I'd viewed bank footage of a robbery and had identified Docherty as one of the perpetrators. It had resulted in his arrest and appearance at the High Court, but he hadn't been convicted.

In May 1995, I'd seen Docherty urinating in Maybury Street in Ruchill, in the north of Glasgow, and when I stopped to speak he threw away a paper bag which contained brown powder. I charged him with urinating and obstructing me under Section 23 of the Misuse of Drugs Act 1971, and sent the brown powder for forensic analysis. Docherty was about 5'8", with dark, lank hair and was thin as a rake.

The incident in July was the result of a falling out between Vass and Docherty and, in the confrontation, Vass had almost amputated Docherty's arm with a machete. Tendons in Docherty's arm had been severed and at the hospital I was informed by medical staff that Docherty had sustained irreversible damage to the injured arm which would in turn impact on his future mobility.

Initially, Docherty had been taken to Stobhill Hospital, but was then transferred to the Glasgow Royal Infirmary for emergency surgery on the arm. I spoke to Docherty, but he wasn't interested in naming his assailant, or giving me a statement. What he did tell me, prophetically, was that, 'it would be sorted out'.

I had the crime scene examined forensically and several blood 'lifts' taken, in the hope that there might be something to tie Vass to the scene, but the blood was Docherty's. With no other witnesses that I could trace, allied to Docherty's lack of cooperation, I had nothing to charge Vass with. I was desperately frustrated as I knew that given this latest incident, combined with what had gone before, he probably now perceived himself as being well-nigh untouchable.

On 27 September 1995, I was at Glasgow Sheriff Court as a witness for a trial. As I entered the foyer Vass was crossing the other side of the foyer. In cop parlance he 'eye-fucked' me, which meant he basically gave me the long hard, 'I'm a tough guy. Who the fuck are you looking at?' stare. I was blazing, but the middle of the Sheriff Court foyer wasn't the time or the place, but that wasn't going unanswered.

The accused in my case pled guilty early so I left the court along with a young cop who had been at the same case. As we turned the corner from the court into Norfolk Street Vass was standing alone, and on seeing me stuffed what appeared to be a piece of resin into his mouth and swallowed.

He knew what was coming, and I don't know if he intended to call a legal representative, but he moved towards his jacket coat pocket, which was enough for him to find himself flat on his back on the ground. His mobile phone was accidentally stood upon in the course of things.

He was arrested and driven, bleating that he had done nothing, to nearby Aitkenhead Road Police Office, where I charged him with an obstruction under the Misuse of Drugs Act. He was moaning that he was due to appear back at court at 2 p.m. that afternoon, so I told him that he was in the right place to ensure he wouldn't miss his appearance.

Having him as a captive audience, I decided to try and quiz him about the Docherty assault, and his words were, 'He stole something from me.' I asked him whether it had been drugs, but he wouldn't answer. I told him I interpreted his silence as being a confirmation that it had been a fall out over drugs, but he still wouldn't respond.

Finally I asked whether he was concerned about retribution coming his way. He must have been drinking from the same Prophecy Well as Paul Docherty because he said, 'Not from Doc, but his brother's fuckin' mad.'

Paul Docherty had a brother Eamonn, who until the attack on Paul had been living, if memory serves me correctly, in England. I actually made a note of Vass' comments in my police notebook and, as things transpired, they proved not just prescient but tantamount to an accusation from the grave.

In 1995, a sunbed tan was as much a fashion requirement as now. Possibly with the proceeds of robberies, Vass began a small sunbed-for-hire business. He purchased several sunbeds and a van, and would deliver them to people for a set period of use.

On 29 September, his van, which was parked outside his house in Cadder, was smashed up and Vass, incandescent with rage, went out armed with a baseball bat and a Krooklok (a solid metal steering wheel clamp) to sort out whoever was responsible. That was exactly what Paul and Eamonn Docherty hoped for. For once it was Vass who found himself staring down the gun barrel.

Eamonn had a sawn-off shotgun which he loosed at Vass' legs. It was a reducer, but didn't put him down, and he ran to a hedge leading to a garden which he tried to clear. But Eamonn Docherty caught up with him and opened his head up like a canoe with another blast from the gun. Vass died there.

I've spoken about how, as a uniform cop, I've stood freezing at crime scenes, and things never change. Given that the van, the initial scene of shooting, and the scene of the fatal blast all had to be protected until we were satisfied that all available evidence had been gathered, several cops were given a cold stand.

They were very fortunate though as an elderly woman who lived in a flat nearby was more than kind. She kept the cops plied with hot tea and biscuits throughout the night. One of the females Vass had had a relationship with wanted to put flowers at the scene, but as it was still under examination they were left, supposedly to be placed at the scene after it had been released.

There's a story that a detective who couldn't stand him and who had had a recent run-in with him took the flowers and gave them to the woman who had supplied the tea and biscuits to the cops. She was very touched that the police would show their appreciation that way. Who knows? The story might be apocryphal.

Irrespective of how Vass was viewed, he'd been murdered in a residential street and you can't just pick and choose whose case is worthy of diligent investigation and whose isn't. If you start down that route it is the beginning of officers believing themselves to be judge and jury, and sole arbitrator of right and wrong. It wasn't the most difficult to solve and wasn't so much a 'whodunit?' as 'how to prove it'.

We knew who had the likeliest motive, and we had civilian witnesses, so it was a question of speaking to them and ensuring they were prepared to do the right thing. I spoke to a couple at Saracen office and got eyewitness statements and, on Monday, 2 October, I went looking for Eamonn Docherty and found him at the parental house in Skirsa Street, in Cadder.

I searched the house, detained him initially and then removed him to Maryhill Police Office where I interviewed him under tape-recorded conditions. Docherty spoke initially, but then decided he'd said too much and refused to answer any further questions. He'd said enough and I arrested him.

Another Detective Sergeant had interviewed Paul Docherty while I was interviewing Eamonn. After he arrested Paul we charged both of the brothers with the vandalism to the van, the murder and various firearm offences.

At the High Court in January 1996, Eamonn's plea of 'Guilty' was accepted to the murder of Vass, and Paul walked free.

37

UNLUCKY IN LOVE

April 1996 found me standing in the bedroom of a first-floor flat in Lyndale Road, in the Summerston area of Glasgow, staring at the deceased occupant of the bed. He had on a Republic of Ireland football top which bore only the slightest bloodstaining at the chest section. He had died from a single penetrating wound to the upper torso at the sternum, and again there was a distinct absence of blood.

The only other occupant was a small, slightly built woman of thirty-four whose face belied her years. She'd had a seventeen-year on/off relationship with the man now lying dead. She told us initially that there'd been a knock at the door, and he'd gone to answer it and there'd been a disturbance, and he'd come back in with the fatal injury.

We knocked on a few doors within the flats, and no one had heard anything so that story didn't really ring true. Alex Sharkey and I took her down to Maryhill for interview. The story that she eventually related may seem bizarre in the extreme to many, but to any cops who have ever worked socially deprived inner-city areas it was as commonplace as sand in a desert.

The deceased could have been classed as her common-law husband, given that she'd been in a volatile relationship with him for some seventeen years. Several years previously, she'd ended the relationship and begun seeing someone else. I don't think that relationship could have been viewed as a success either, given that in November 1995, her new beau drew a five-year prison sentence for assaulting her, to her severe injury and permanent disfigurement.

It's difficult to believe, but despite his attack on her they'd reconciled, and had arranged to marry in August 1996. However, in the interim, she had recommenced her relationship with the man now lying dead in her bedroom, and he'd moved back into her home. That hadn't

234

interfered with the wedding plans though as she still intended marrying her jailed attacker. Scarlett O'Hara and Rhett Butler it wasn't.

I'd dealt with a few cases of women having been assaulted by their partners and always regarded it as the height of cowardice. Despite, however, having been used as a punchbag it didn't seem to deter the victims from resuming, or wanting to resume, the relationship. That, in turn, obviously impacted on the case preparation. You would put in quite a few resource hours compiling the evidence against the partner only for the female to contact the Procurator Fiscal and beg for the case to be dropped as it would ruin the relationship.

Ruin the relationship?

On more than one occasion, I'd revisited the victims with one of the specially trained girls from what was then known as the Female and Child Unit. We emphasised to the victims that assistance was available if they wanted to break free of the abusive relationship. The reply was usually along the lines of, 'But he loves me really.'

Here were women so starved of affection and whose self-esteem had been holed so badly beneath the waterline that they equated any kind of physical contact, even assault, as a demonstration of love.

On the night of the murder, her partner of seventeen years had come back home after having been out for a drink. An argument began over her plans to wed the man currently serving the five-year prison sentence. She'd stabbed him once in the heart which was all that was required to produce the small wound whose fatal outcome never ceased to fascinate me.

Alex and I arrested her and charged her with murder. In reply she said, 'Ah didnae mean tae dae it. It wisnae meant. It wisnae premeditated.'

At subsequent judicial proceedings, the Crown took what she said at face value because they accepted a plea of 'Guilty' to the lesser charge of culpable homicide, for which she received a three-year custodial sentence. She served eighteen months before release.

I attended the post-mortem examination and, a few days later, a second post-mortem examination, this time conducted by a pathologist acting on behalf of the defence. A post-mortem examination, irrespective of how respectfully the pathologist conducts it, is quite frankly the clinical destruction of the human remains. You wonder how a pathologist could find anything to dissect during a second autopsy, but they can be requested by defence lawyers to ensure that there is no dispute over the cause of death presented by the prosecution.

I mention this because I found myself basically having to act as a mortuary attendant for the pathologist conducting this second dissection, and it wasn't to be the last time it happened. When an initial autopsy is conducted, the mortuary attendant wheels the remains out on a stainless-steel gurney and will lift and turn the remains as the pathologist requires.

I presumed that the same courtesy would be extended to the pathologist conducting the defence autopsy, but whether it was to do with contracts or payment the attendant presented the remains on the gurney and disappeared.

That eventually left me with two choices: wait for ages while the pathologist tried to manoeuvre the corpse, or assist him and get out of there a lot quicker. I pulled on the scrubs and plumped for option two. I would imagine that, nowadays, that would be absolutely forbidden given the strict adherence to health and safety regulations.

There may have been a case for the prosecution to imply that the deceased had gone to bed, fallen asleep and then been stabbed in a premeditated manner. Given, however, that there were only two people in the flat, and one of them would never be able to give his version in this life, then that theory would have been difficult to prove. Either way, there was nothing in either post-mortem which contradicted the woman's version of events.

That would be that ... you would think.

Released in October 1997, she began a relationship with another male, but not the one she'd intended to marry. This was another male entirely, and barely a year after release she was in another drinking session, which was swiftly followed by another argument. When the police arrived they found the male with two penetrating wounds to his back, and the knife used to inflict the wounds in the sink with the water running.

This time, the victim claimed that her boyfriend had attacked her with the knife, and that she'd successfully wrestled the knife from him, and while he was on top of her and assaulting her she'd stabbed him in the back. When she was examined subsequently by a Police Casualty

Surgeon he reported that her injuries were consistent with her version of events.

Hopefully, she managed to eventually settle on a happier, less volatile relationship.

38

TIMING

They say the opportunity to progress can hinge on timing. You can be in the right place at the right time, or factors combine in concert to your benefit.

I was highly rated by my Divisional Commander, Douglas Kelly, and his deputy, Campbell O'Connell, and they viewed me as worth further advancement. Jimmy Lindsay had transferred to another unit and had been replaced as Detective Chief Inspector by Stevie O'Brien, who was in agreement with the other senior officers. I'd known Stevie before I joined the police. I'd been working with British Rail and been granted day-release to undertake an HND in Business Studies. Stevie, who wasn't in the police then either, was on the same course.

I was only eighteen and had been signed with East Fife FC at the time, and for me the course was an excuse to skive off work one day a week. It's a weak defence, but I can only say I was very young, and immature in many ways. Stevie was a good amateur footballer, and so we would talk a lot about football. Stevie, however, was dedicated enough to complete the course.

He always wore an expression as if he had the worries of the world on his shoulders, but actually could deliver a humorous line in a deadpan manner that Jack Dee would have envied. He was a first-class detective, a really good boss and strong. He was secure enough that he wasn't afraid to ask opinions, but ultimately made the final decision.

I was always a hard worker and had cleared umpteen attempted murders, serious assaults and robbery enquiries. In those days, in that division, every other day seemed a 'brown bag day'. Two particular enquiries didn't harm the regard those bosses held me in. One was a murder and the other a shooting. It sounds crass when a human is dead and someone has killed him, but the murder was rather run of the mill albeit, as with so many of the enquiries I was on, there was a slightly unique twist. It was the first one Stevie inherited as Detective Chief Inspector.

A man had been stabbed to death outside flats at St George's Road. I knew there were CCTV cameras, located at a nearby caretaker's office, which might cover the scene. I went there and sat for several hours until I managed to catch a group of youngsters and the deceased. I'd had dealings with the deceased and he wasn't a particularly nice person and, in fact, had numerous convictions for violent acts.

As I've indicated with Mark Vass, cops can't allow a victim's reputation to impact on how they investigate. If they did they'd soon find that slipshod practices would start to creep in and that would, in turn, impact on their ability to operate effectively when the victim is someone deemed 'decent'.

I recognised a couple of the younger ones in the victim's company and traced them and they gave up the perpetrator. Stevie sent Mike Johnston and me to look for him, and we eventually traced him to a holiday home park near Dunoon, on the west coast of Scotland, and we brought him back to Maryhill for interview.

Despite the CCTV placing him in the victim's company as well as other witness statements, he continued to deny being responsible, and after exhausting our avenues of questioning we arrested him. He may have thought we were bluffing and that if he denied the obvious he would walk out of there, but he quickly realised that wasn't the case when we charged him.

He put his head in his hands and began to cry and ask himself what he'd done. He then asked for a chance to tell his side of things. That placed Mike and me in unusual territory because he had been charged, and anything he said subsequently would have to be at his own volition, and under Scots Law would be classed as a voluntary statement.

Under Scots Law, to ensure accused persons haven't been pressurised or coerced into saying something detrimental, a voluntary statement has to be taken by officers who are impartial and unconnected with the case. Our accused, however, wasn't having that, even when we painstakingly explained the procedure to him. He wanted us to hear what he had to say, and no one else.

We went out to Stevie and told him what we were faced with. He told us to go back in, note the voluntary statement, and if it came down to a legal judgement we'd see where the dice fell. As it transpired, our actions were never contested by legal challenge as the boy pled 'Guilty'.

In football, coaches are at pains to emphasise that you should be on the move, especially in the penalty box area, but they also teach that there is an art in standing still, letting the play develop and being ready to exploit the opportunity when it presents itself. The opportunity to return a nasty vicious bastard to prison for good presented itself in 1996, and all I had to do was stand still and have it served on a plate.

I know I've mentioned before about affording villains too much credit, but it still amazes me how stupid they can be sometimes, and how they are often the main contributors to their own downfall.

Take James Daniels, for example. James, or as he is more widely known and referred to, Jamie, in a similar vein to Tony McGovern, was regarded as the primary force within his family of brothers Norman, David and Ronnie, all of whom were well known to the police. Another brother had died while trying to swim a river to escape police apprehension. The remaining siblings were collectively referred to by the police and media as 'The Daniels' but Jamie had a higher profile than the other three.

They began in the late 1970s with a scrapyard in Lochburn Road, Maryhill, about a mile from Maryhill police office. I was told by a reliable informant that they concluded that particular business deal by appearing one day at the yard, where they informed the then owner/occupant that he'd just retired. They subsequently 'acquired' several other scrapyards which they used as a base to store and alter the appearance of stolen cars.

They once had a suspect stolen vehicle seized from them and removed to a police office in the North of the city to await forensic examination. The secure area of the office where suspect cars were stored was full, and as it would be several hours before a space would be available the vehicle was parked within a semi-secure area of the office. Four hours later it had disappeared. Believed re-stolen.

As with so many criminals in Glasgow they progressed to the drugs trade, given the vast potential profits, but kept the lucrative scrapyards and an interest in cars. They were also careful not to flaunt their millions.

Nice house here, expensive piece of jewellery there but strove to remain under the radar. None of the four brothers has ever served a significant jail sentence and various newspapers credit them with being Scotland's richest crime family.

In an effort to obtain evidence of criminality scores of police operations have been mounted against James Daniels and tens of thousands of pounds expended, all unsuccessfully, and what happened?

In October 2009 he became involved in a road rage incident that his inflated ego wouldn't allow him to walk (or drive) away from. A jail sentence followed simply because the victim stepped up and told the truth. Mind you, from the self-preening adopted by numerous members of Strathclyde Police senior management when in front of the media, you could have been forgiven for assuming that it had all been the result of a 'cunning plan'.

William McMillan Bennett finished what remained of his life breathing prison air because of similar arrogance. Bennett was another horrible nasty bastard. He was a murderer like Vass, but additionally he was a rapist too. He'd received a five-year sentence for rape in 1962, a fifteen-year sentence in 1968 for robbery and attempted murder, and then, when out on appeal in 1970, he'd committed a murder and been given a life sentence. In 1996, he was out and in society, albeit on a life licence, which meant basically that should he involve himself in criminality he could be recalled to prison immediately.

I was late shift one evening at Maryhill when I took a call from someone I'd known growing up in Balornock. He'd lived near to me and, like my parents, his folks had stayed in the scheme since the houses had been built. His dad had been the postman for the area and my elder brothers were of an age with his. He was desperately frightened and looking to see me right away. I met him, and once he had recounted his story I fully understood why he was so worried.

He had inherited the parental house when his parents had died, and had been living there with his wife and son and daughter. Subsequently, he'd bought a house in Bishopbriggs and the house in Balornock had lain empty. He'd contemplated buying the house which was owned by Scottish Homes.

Given the length of time he and his family had lived there he would have been able to purchase a large three-bedroom home with front and rear garden for about £15,000. If he held onto the house for the obligatory three years that was required when someone purchased a local authority house he'd have stood to make a decent profit.

He bought and sold cars as a sideline, and at about the beginning of 1996, he'd encountered Bennett who, out on licence and tasting freedom, wanted to buy a car. Bennett had bought a car and a relationship of sorts developed to the extent that the victim had allowed Bennett to move into the house in Balornock as a tenant. Bennett was supposed to pay rent, but being the gangster he was very quickly decided that the accommodation should be of the rent-free variety.

In the last couple of days in April 1996, he told me he'd gone to the Balornock house to ask Bennett about the rent. He was with his daughter although he left her to wait in the car while he went in. He was let into the house by a young girl and went into the living room area while the girl went to find Bennett.

A short time later Bennett barged into the room and with no warning stabbed him and shot him once in the leg area. The victim told me he'd managed to stagger out to the car and his daughter had driven him to hospital for treatment.

Terrified that worse may follow if he told the truth, he invented an imaginary location and assailants for the cops who interviewed him, after they'd been alerted by the hospital that they were treating a gunshot victim.

He'd been prepared to maintain the charade until his daughter, on arriving home at Bishopbriggs, found Bennett waiting outside in a car and panicking she drove off. Bennett pursued her through various streets before she finally lost him. That was the final straw. Knowing the ruthlessness and capability of Bennett, and in genuine fear for his life and the wellbeing of his family, he decided it was time he told the truth and called me.

He had a place he and his family could safely stay that night, but as extra security I arranged for uniformed personnel to be stationed in a car outside, to buy time until we could set things in motion the following morning.

I spoke to Stevie O'Brien first thing the next day and together with another Detective Sergeant, John Duffy, we obtained full statements from the victim and his family and had Bennett's licence revoked. Stevie, John and me went to the house in Balornock and searched it under warrant and had a full forensic examination carried out.

It was quite some time after the shooting had taken place, but we had to ensure that it closed off an avenue for the defence at any subsequent judicial proceedings. We'd have looked dumb at best standing in the High Court and being asked why, when given a potential crime scene, we hadn't had it examined properly.

Stevie decided – rightly so – that given my personal knowledge of the victim that we needed to limit any potential inference of collusion and, consequently, John was detailed to continue any further enquiries and submit the report. There wasn't really a great deal more we had to do other than await judicial proceedings.

We found ourselves sitting at Kilmarnock High Court several months later, but we weren't even required to give evidence. Once the victim and his family testified the Crown prosecution were content to let the jury judge credibility. It didn't take long.

Bennett was given eight years for the shooting and stabbing, seven years for possessing a firearm while a prohibited person (banned from possessing a firearm owing to his prison record), and three months for placing the daughter and her boyfriend in a state of fear and alarm. The sentences were to run consecutively; over fifteen years in total.

He died a few years later in prison, and I wondered whether the bitterness, frustration and rage he must have felt were contributory factors in his death. There he was, back in prison for the rest of his life because in his arrogance he believed that his violent history would prevent anyone speaking up against him.

As I've indicated I was well-regarded by Douglas Kelly, Campbell O'Connell and Stevie and the former two had already submitted a report to personnel seeking to advance me, but you need luck and timing. Mr Kelly retired, Mr O'Connell and Stevie were promoted, and that meant a whole new management team. The new Divisional Commander decided he wouldn't be pushing anyone he didn't have personal knowledge of. That meant any chances of advancement were on hold. Some timing's good; some not so.

39

A BODY IN THE BOOT

I was eventually interviewed by the incumbent Divisional Commander and must have impressed him to a degree because I found myself appointed to the role of uniform Acting Inspector. The Divisional Commander, in his pre-appointment pep talk, had told me that the shift personnel I was inheriting were not particularly productive. I knew he was letting me know I had a challenge.

In the end it wasn't a challenge as they turned out to be a good group who worked well for me. I spoke to them individually, listened to what they had to say and to any moans they may have had, told them what I was looking for and arranged for a bit of off-duty bonding.

I was also fortunate in 'acquiring' an officer who had finished his secondment with the CID and was returning to uniform. I'd worked with him and spoke to him when he was finishing. With a bit of sleight of hand, I managed to have him transferred to the shift until his appointment as a detective. He was a natural leader and developed less experienced colleagues and motivated other less productive officers and in turn made my job that much easier.

Things actually ran so well that I found myself out walking, almost as a beat officer, to fill in my time, which was mostly taken up with complaints against the police and interviewing candidates for the police. I enjoyed interacting with the public again in a manner not always afforded in the CID. There you can become so intent on solving the crime, and so focused on obtaining statements and gathering evidence, that you can often overlook the impact the crime has on the victim.

Walking and being visible encouraged people to approach and speak to me and, of course, I'd get complaints and moans, but they were about issues that affected quality of life. The advantage I had being in charge of the shift was that I could allocate officers to address the concerns. As a detective, I derived a great deal of satisfaction from clearing a difficult enquiry, but there was a different, but equally satisfying feeling, from resolving small situations as a uniform officer.

On one of my walks through Maryhill, I was stopped by an elderly lady who had lost her wedding ring in what could only be described as a jungle of a front garden. She lived in a four-storey block of flats which shared a common close, and that meant two front gardens. Her side was well-kept, but the other side hadn't been maintained. She'd gone out to try and tidy up the mess and lost the ring.

I looked at the garden and thought that a pride of lions could have concealed themselves there, so finding the ring wouldn't be easy. I don't get too many bright ideas, but it hit me that the Support Unit kept metal detectors, so I went up to their office at Springburn to pitch my case. It took two minutes to find the ring, and the satisfaction gained was certainly different from that derived from spending hours trying to 'burst' lying suspects to eventually get at the truth.

If truth be told, I found the role of Shift Inspector a piece of cake. The shift was working well, I had decent sergeants, and after all the experience I'd gained previously, it was simply a case of keeping a light hand on the rudder. I thought I'd left detective work and criminal arrests behind for a period, but I'd forgotten how unpredictable police work can be.

They say that lessons learned in childhood remain clearest in the memory, and I'm eternally grateful to an impromptu lesson taught to me while a child and living in the USA. If the following seems improbable, or smacks of name-dropping, I make no apologies, because it is all absolutely true.

My two eldest sisters had immigrated to America, initially to New York, and subsequently to Los Angeles. They'd persuaded my parents to give it a try, and as a result, for a year, we lived there before my father decided he preferred Scotland and we came back home. I was naturally enrolled in school for the period we spent there. I was ten years old.

The school was in Hollywood, was called the Blessed Sacrament, and was (and still is) located on Sunset Boulevard. Then, it occupied one point of a triangular courtyard with a church of the same name and a convent taking up the other points. The convent is no longer there and the area has gone downhill in the interim years. We lived on

Formosa Avenue, and I would walk every morning along Sunset Boulevard to get to school.

I suppose, like any kid at a new school, I found it difficult initially, and my settling-in period wasn't aided by my speaking in a totally different accent from the others. I'd also been placed in a class that was the equivalent of my years, but not my learning. The class were doing fractions and basic maths which I hadn't been taught yet at my primary school in Scotland.

I wasn't stupid, but with being new, my accent, and not being up-to-date with the work I found myself having problems with some classmates. I've never been bullied in my life, so it meant I was in frequent fights, and yes, they do indeed send you to the Principal. Among the staff were nuns from the convent who taught at the school, and they loved my accent, so I was as the Americans say, 'cut some slack'. Outwith school hours was another matter, and I did find myself often having to take on more than one assailant.

One of my sisters was friendly with a man who had fought in the Korean War and was now involved in ophthalmics. Then, martial arts were uncommon disciplines, but this guy had reached black belt status in both karate and judo. His teacher, or *Sensei*, was a man named Bruce Tegner.

Bruce Lee began in Hollywood teaching martial arts, but prior to him Bruce Tegner taught the pampered stars. He choreographed the fight scene between Frank Sinatra and Henry Silva in the film *The Manchurian Candidate*. His gym, or *dojo*, was located on Sunset just a couple of minutes from my school. On the two occasions I went along with my sister's friend, Tegner's tuition with him was one-on-one, and not the larger classes being taught nowadays.

Whether that was Tegner's preferred method of teaching, or my sister's friend paid extra for that, or martial arts hadn't yet grown in popularity I really don't know, but I went there to wait because my sister's friend had told me that among the people Tegner taught were George Reeves, who was Superman on television, and Ricky Nelson who was a pop star.

I do recall him telling me – possibly to cure my bug-eyed look – that both were poor martial artists. One thing was certain, my sister's friend certainly wasn't. Three men armed with a metal pipe and a knife tried to mug him one night. He hospitalised two and the third ran off. The story made the *LA Times*.

I sat at the side and watched the lesson and after it was over my sister's boyfriend was practising some moves, and Tegner spoke to me. When I started speaking it was obvious I 'weren't from around these parts', and he said to my sister's friend something like 'Where is that accent from?' He in turn explained that my accent was getting me into a few fights which in itself was no big thing, but that sometimes I'd find myself outnumbered.

I'm not sure whether it was *dojo* protocol, but he asked Tegner's permission to show me how to fall. Not only was he allowed to show me how to break a fall, but Tegner himself supervised two moves that have helped me avoid injury in several confrontational situations during my time in the police.

One was a basic leg sweep, and it was simply a case of when grabbed, or in close quarters, you hook your leg or heel behind your opponent's and remove their balance so that they fall back. Someone falling back will release their hold on you because when someone is falling backwards their first thought is to put their hands out behind them to break the fall.

The other move shown was in response to a headbutt. The natural reaction of someone who realises they are the target of a headbutt is to pull their face away, but that opens up soft bone target areas to the hard bone of the attacker's forehead. I was shown instead to drop my head down towards the attacker. I've twice had people try to headbutt me, and as a result of those lessons, the people trying it have ended up with a split eye because their soft bone has collided with the hard bone at the top of my forehead.

All well and good, but how did we get from Hollywood to Maryhill?

Very late at night at the beginning of October 1997, two girls in their early twenties, walking in Clarendon Street, were confronted by a man with a knife. They were near the Bank of Scotland ATM. He put a knife against the face of one of the girls, demanded money and grabbed her wallet. He pushed the other girl into a doorway and the girl was so terrified she threw her wallet onto the ground for him to pick up. One of the girls had a slight cut to the side of the face, but she didn't need any treatment for the injury.

The following night – after 8 p.m. – a man in his late twenties was grabbed as he carried out a transaction at the same Bank of Scotland ATM. He was struck on the face with a knife and a demand was made for money. He'd struggled briefly with his assailant before dropping his wallet and telling the assailant to take it. He had his wallet, bank card and £100 stolen.

The two crimes were linked, and it was obvious the perpetrator was a dangerous and desperate individual, which was borne out a couple of nights later, when a thirty-year-old woman using the same ATM, was grabbed by the throat. An object was pressed into her throat and money demanded. She handed over her purse which contained cards and £20.

The next night – a twenty-three-year-old man, who was with his girlfriend and using the same ATM, was grabbed from behind and a knife pushed against his neck. Again, money was demanded. The perpetrator made the man put his card into the machine. The victim sustained cuts to his hands after grabbing the knife blade to prevent being slashed.

Everything pointed to it being the work of the same individual. There was absolutely nothing to indicate who he was, but it appeared that if he wasn't apprehended soon a potential tragedy might not be too far away. The CID were also under pressure to apprehend whoever was responsible, especially when a senior detective officer commented that 'the police were looking far from competent', and 'the plan of action in place up to that point required to be redrafted'.

Surveillance was set up on the ATM and a covert camera installed behind the cash dispenser, but not another incident occurred over the following week and eventually the surveillance was withdrawn.

As if on cue, at about 7.15 p.m. on 18 October, a twenty-year-old woman using the ATM had a knife placed at her neck and money was demanded. The camera caught the moment with the knife against the woman's throat, as well as her clearly and understandably terrified expression. It also caught the face of the perpetrator, but although the image was circulated no one was able to match a name to the image.

Stevie O'Brien wasn't too thrilled to say the least. He arranged to have an undercover van placed in a position to monitor the ATM. Surveillance was placed 24/7 on the bank and ran for a full week, but there wasn't as much as the hint of a crime. The robberies were both worrying and slightly embarrassing for the police, but even so, given the resource drain and cost involved, that level of surveillance could only be sustained for so long, and after a week it was withdrawn. They were no closer to identifying who was responsible.

I was a uniform Shift Inspector throughout this, and hadn't been on duty when any of the previous robberies had taken place. My main task as a Shift Inspector was to ensure my shift afforded the ATM and surrounding area extra attention, that my officers were familiar with the image obtained from the bank security camera, and had knowledge of the suspect's description. I hadn't had any input into the investigation. As a Shift Inspector I had other priorities and, besides, it was CID territory and there were numerous detective officers working the enquiry.

I was working late shift on 1 November when he struck again; same ATM and same MO. A twenty-three-year-old man was grabbed from behind and a knife held at his throat and money demanded. The victim had his wallet, which only had cards in it, snatched from him. The suspect was territorial that's for sure, and he showed no signs of stopping. In fact, the only sign he seemed intent on displaying was a two-fingered one to the police trying to apprehend him.

He hadn't got anything. I was convinced that he was a desperado and probably needed the money for drugs. He'd lain low for a spell and now, on his first effort back, he'd failed to get any cash. He'd try again that night. I was sure of it; call it a hunch or gut instinct.

Any cop, who hasn't hidden in administration roles or personnel and actually carried out proper police work for a period, will tell you that hunches aren't simply the realm of script writers. Cops do get them and should heed them.

There were several detectives working late shift and I spoke to them about the recent attempt, to ascertain how they intended to respond to it. Their view was that it had happened and he had got away, and therefore wouldn't be so stupid as to push his luck again that night. I told them why I held the opposite view and urged them to put a watch on the ATM. They responded by telling me that they had several things ongoing so couldn't devote time to that. I'd tutored a couple of them and was disappointed that they hadn't more faith in my instincts.

I was convinced he'd be back, although don't ask me how I was so sure. I felt that desperation would draw him to an area he felt comfortable operating in. Out of courtesy, I asked the detectives for an unmarked car and in full uniform headed down to a spot where I could take observations on the ATM.

I parked the car on a cobblestoned street approximately fifty yards from the bank. It was an unmarked car, but I should qualify that by declaring that just about every four-year-old in Maryhill, Possilpark, Saracen and surrounding areas knew a CID car as well as they knew the ice cream van. Additionally, I was in uniform, so deep undercover I most certainly wasn't.

I'd been sitting for some fifteen minutes when the suspect appeared and stood immediately opposite the car. I recognised him from the security image immediately. He was so transfixed on the ATM and his next potential victim that he failed to recognise the car, or notice me, despite having been smart enough not to commit any robberies during the period the bank had been under surveillance. Well, maybe not so smart! But as I mentioned earlier in the book, it's better to be lucky than good.

I jumped from the car and told him I was detaining him. My intention was to handcuff him and call for a station to come down and assist me. The best laid plans . . .

Firstly, I'd made a stupid error that I'd have flayed a probationer for. After a while sitting in the car the portable radio cops use to receive and transmit broadcasts had begun cutting into my side. When positioned on a belt and when sitting in a car for a period they were awkward and uncomfortable, and I'd unhooked it from my belt and laid it on the passenger seat. When I jumped out of the car I left the radio behind. As it transpired, it wouldn't have made much difference either way.

I told him to put his hands on the boot of the car, and then told him to reach an arm behind him, with the intention of handcuffing his hands behind his back. He swung the arm, caught me on the face, and spun towards me with his hand reaching for his trouser waistband.

Anyone who has been in a ruckus knows it is nothing like the films or television. The fights aren't choreographed. Unless you are a puncher, and can put someone away with a clean shot or with a blow to the throat, or some other similar debilitating area, then fights are clumsy, flailing, untidy efforts. Additionally, even if you're fit, you can find yourself running out of steam, so you want to end them as quickly as possible.

I knew this person carried a bladed weapon and had threatened, terrified and cowed his victims with it, so I believed he was going to use that if he could. Protective vests hadn't been introduced then so I was very vulnerable. I grabbed his right hand as we struggled before

I instinctively defaulted to the leg sweep I'd been shown so many years previously. I swear I never executed that move more smoothly or efficiently. As he fell back I was aware of the sound of metal on cobblestone, and I knew it was the knife skittering away.

I followed him down, and there was another spell of grappling before I managed to put a choke hold on him. A choke hold is a very dangerous move to implement as it restricts the oxygen supply to the brain, but as far as I was concerned I wasn't prepared to afford him the opportunity to break free, reach that knife and threaten my safety.

The adrenalin that was whooshing through me caused me to hiss in his ear, 'That's the oxygen to your brain shutting down. You keep struggling, you'll either be dead or a vegetable.'

Thank God he saw the light and gave up completely and I managed to cuff him. As soon as I'd gotten the cuffs on him my anger subsided as quickly as it had erupted. I was breathing hard from the struggle when I reached for the radio and shouted to the control staff that I had an apprehension and was looking for a unit to assist with transport.

I hadn't had time to broadcast a request for assistance so perhaps they thought it was a run of the mill lock-up, but the reply was that all units were engaged. That left me with a dangerous prisoner to transport to the office.

I got him to Maryhill, but for some reason a story grew up that officers who were in the back yard at Maryhill saw me remove the prisoner from the boot of the car. Now I'd just arrested a man suspected of having been involved in numerous robberies and attempted robberies in which he'd held a knife at his victims' throats. A man that I'd struggled to subdue and who had a knife when arrested; a very dangerous individual. Do you think that being on my own and wanting to ensure my safety would have caused me to transport him to the office in that manner? Mmmm? Interesting concept.

I presented him at the charge bar and word quickly spread about the apprehension. Then followed one of the most pathetic situations I've witnessed in the police. One of the detectives who'd been so busy previously, and had so much other work on that he hadn't the time to watch the ATM (but still hadn't left the office in the interim), came scurrying through. He asked me if I wanted him to corroborate the prisoner's processing.

That meant his name would be recorded against the arrest, and the bosses would see it, despite his having had no involvement whatso-ever. I couldn't believe it, but thanked him politely by telling him to 'fuck right off'.

At the High Court my arrest pled guilty to several of the robberies and was sentenced to eight years' imprisonment.

My divisional commander at the time put me forward for a Chief Constable's High Commendation for my actions, and once those chain of events were in motion the awarding of the commendation was a given. I've never known anyone nominated for a commendation by their division to have it disputed. In my case, I was awarded nothing.

It was, and is, unheard of, and would need to have been rejected at the very highest level. Why? Who knows? I never played politics and had made a few enemies at a high level so perhaps it was a slap down. They could stick it because what was indisputable was that those robberies had been cleared because I put shoe leather on concrete. Besides, the only recognition that matters is that of peers you rate who you know would do the same (and probably twice as well).

I finished my period as acting inspector very highly appraised and not solely for the ATM result. My shift had performed as well as any other in the division, and better than most, and they'd had been a pleasure to be in charge of. I hoped that, in line with any other officer who successfully completed a period in a higher rank I would be afforded the opportunity to clinch the rank substantively, but that didn't happen. As with the rejection of the commendation I was never given a reason, although an incident a couple of years later provided me with a possible explanation, but I'm running ahead of myself.

I'd thoroughly enjoyed the different role I'd undertaken, but on resuming detective duties realised that solving serious crimes and over-coming the challenges associated with successful crime detection provided so much satisfaction.

Over the next eight months, among other serious crimes and inci-dents I found myself investigating four suspicious deaths. I resolved them and on each occasion libelled a charge of murder against those responsible.

40

PROBABLY ANY ONE OF US

Given my experiences in the police, I was acutely aware of how fragile and tenuous life was, but just in case I required further proof the next enquiry broadcast it in huge neon letters.

Any loss of life brings heartbreak to someone, but when it emanates from a celebratory occasion then it only serves to compound the tragedy.

I've indicated that as an investigating officer I tried to do the best I could for the victims of the crime. That didn't necessarily mean that I formed any great empathy with the victim(s) or even any empathy at all. It simply meant that I was paid a decent wage to carry out my duties in a thorough and professional manner, and my own self-pride and the fact that I didn't like losing ensured they got the best service I could give them. I never wanted someone to come back to me and accuse me of letting them down by not being sufficiently thorough in my investigations.

Sometimes as an investigator, however, you realise that no matter how much you try, or even how much you want things to be different they simply are what they are, and no amount of diligence or hard work can alter the end result, or the outcome of your investigations.

The vast majority of confrontational deaths or murders result from a background history between perpetrator and victim. A man kills his wife in a drunken rage, drug suppliers murder dealers over a failure to discharge their debts, someone is killed in a revenge for a previous act of violence. In other words, there is more often than not a previous history to the final act.

Motives emanate generally from base instincts such as lust, revenge, jealousy, covetousness etc. That makes the crime much easier to resolve which is just as well, because if perpetrators put as much thought into

253

planning and executing their crime as they do in television dramas they would seldom be solved.

There are also rare occasions, however, when you inherit the aftermath of a series of events which have thrown together people with no previous history or interaction with heartbreaking consequences, and you think 'another time and place and that could have been me'.

It began with a family gathering at a public house lounge in Garscube Road, Maryhill in August 1998, celebrating a sixty-fifth birthday. About twenty yards from the pub was a street junction that led to a housing scheme consisting of tenement flats. Youths from the housing scheme would gather near the pub. A set of metal railings separated the pavement and roadway and they'd often sit on those.

The patrol officer would often move on any youths who gathered there due to long-running complaints from the people who lived in and around the gathering point(s), because being young they would, after a while, become bored and mischief would follow. The mischief might take the form of minor acts of vandalism or underage drinking followed by shouting and swearing or annoying passers-by.

At some point during the evening a group of about five boys, who had been at the railings and were aged fourteen, sixteen and seventeen, tried to get into the pub, but they had been stopped by the door steward. Having failed to get into the pub they hung around at the railings just a short distance away, and were still there when the party in the pub broke up, and the guests started making their way home.

One of those guests was the forty-three-year-old son of the woman whose party it was. Together with his wife he began to walk home to their house which was only a short distance from the pub.

As they passed the youths someone from the group would appear to have said something or asked for a cigarette. The man refused the request and possibly words were exchanged, followed by a scuffle. The man fell back, struck his head on the concrete pavement and was knocked unconscious. His brother-in-law, who was nearby, ran over and was involved in an exchange of blows with one of the boys before the group of boys ran off down Trossach Street.

An ambulance was called for the injured man, and they found him breathing and with a strong pulse, but unconscious. He was taken to the Western Infirmary where initial assessment showed he had a wound at the rear or occipital region of the head and had suffered a skull fracture. Patients in Glasgow with head injuries are generally transferred to the specialist neurological unit at the Southern General Hospital.

I caught the enquiry when I came on duty that morning, and the first thing I did was obtain a medical update from the hospital. I was told that he had a severe subdural haematoma and intracranial pressure, and was heavily sedated and unconscious. I knew that was not good news at all.

Since I wouldn't be able to interview the victim, I made arrangements to speak to his wife and brother-in-law later that morning, and then arranged to meet Martin Lupton, who was the on-call Scenes of Crime Officer and Martin Fairley, who was the on-call Forensic Scientist at the location of the incident. I'd worked several crime scenes with both of them and knew them to be conscientious and good at their jobs.

I didn't really hold out much hope of gathering a great deal of forensic evidence from the scene owing to the nature of the incident. It had happened in the street, and so it was unlikely there would be fingerprints, and there was no suggestion that any of the youths had been injured, so I didn't anticipate a great return from that avenue of enquiry.

Martin Lupton photographed the location and surrounding area, fingerprinted the railings and collected various soft drink cans and bottles which were in and around the scene, for subsequent fingerprint examination. Martin Fairley took a blood lift from the scene, but we felt that would be the victim's.

The local housing authority had a CCTV camera covering the area. It was situated quite a distance from the scene, but it may have captured something that would assist in identifying the group involved in the incident and advance the enquiry. I allocated the task of seizing and examining the footage to 'Stevie'. He was then a Detective Constable and part of the team I worked with regularly. Stevie was very tall – about 6'3" – with rather piratical looks, and was a really keen cyclist and skier. He was a first-class detective and very thorough, and although examining the footage would be laborious I knew that if there was something there he'd find it.

I tried umpteen doors in and around the crime scene, but didn't find any worthwhile witnesses. I returned to the office, and was told there was someone waiting for me and was given the name. I recognised it as the pseudonym of an informant I had, and was briefly hopeful that he may have heard about the incident and had come to give me some good news.

It was good news, but not for my enquiry. There had been a break-in and theft of over £40,000 worth of designer clothing from Helensburgh, a small town that sits on the north shore of the Firth of Clyde. It was first-class information and normally, although it hadn't occurred in my area, I would have been all over it, but not that day. I contacted CID officers from the area of the theft, and introduced him to them later that morning, but not before he'd put the touch on me for some money. He got more subsequently (and officially) after it transpired the information was accurate.

Back with my own enquiry I spoke to the witnesses who had been present at the scene, and their assessment of the scene was that the victim had been with his wife and walking home. He'd been asked for a cigarette, and when he refused the request the group of boys attacked him, knocked him to the ground, and began to jump on him and kick him. His brother-in-law went to assist, and was also attacked and sustained a cut to the temple area.

An independent witness, however, a taxi driver, had come forward and claimed that although he hadn't witnessed the incident he had seen the victim walk up to the group of youths. I made a trip over to the Southern General Hospital for a face-to-face with the medical staff regarding the victim's condition, but it was the same stock answer. He was unconscious, sedated and there was no change in his condition, but I think I knew what would eventually happen.

I'd supervised the crime scene examination, knocked on as many doors as I could, interviewed the available witnesses, tried to pry as much as I could from the medical staff, asked the uniform personnel who patrolled that area for the names of the youths who hung around, and Stevie was on top of the CCTV.

Word had been left that the stolen clothing information had resulted in an arrest and recovery, but not surprisingly, I couldn't get enthused about it.

It was 10 p.m. and I'd done as much as I could for the sixteen hours I'd been on duty. I hoped tomorrow would bring something fresh and it did, but not in the way I expected.

41

NON-BROTHERLY LOVE

The following afternoon was Monday, 10 August 1998, and I was in a CID car having just re-canvassed the area around the Star and Garter pub. A call came over the radio that shots had been fired in Finlas Street, which was in our area. A victim was still on scene.

I arrived there to find a man being removed by ambulance and a red Renault Megane abandoned in the middle of the street. I only caught a quick glimpse, but was happy I knew who the victim was. I'd assisted in arresting him for a murder several years previously, where a man had been gunned down outside the Ashfield Social Club. I went to the High Court at Glasgow to give evidence, but our case collapsed when one of main witnesses refused to speak up or identify the man we'd charged.

Given that it was in the middle of the afternoon and had happened near an industrial estate, we had a few witnesses. We spoke to several of them and the story emerged. There had been four men involved. The victim and a 'friend' had a confrontation with the other two, who had been in a green Mondeo motor car. Shots had been exchanged between them before the Mondeo reversed back over the one now en route to hospital. The Mondeo occupants had high-tailed it, as had the injured man's 'pal' when he knew the police were en route.

I had a look at the red Renault Megane which was in the street outside of an ice cream van premises. It had a gouge in the lower section of the rear passenger door. There was also damage to the rubber around the front offside window. Shell casings were lying on the roadway.

I closed the street to traffic, had the scene controlled and arranged for Ballistics and a Scene of Crime photographer to attend. I also arranged for a tow truck to lift the Megane and remove it for a proper and controlled forensic examination once we'd cleared the scene. As I was in the middle of making these arrangements I noticed a Traffic

Officer with yellow chalk making his way towards the shell casings.

I shouted to him and asked what he was doing and he told me that he was going to chalk around the casings. He must have watched too many movies or television in which investigators blithely chalk around bodies and cartridges, but that isn't done. Introducing anything into a crime scene before it has been documented photographically leaves you vulnerable to allegations that you have manipulated the scene.

Then a woman showed up at the scene that confirmed my suspicions as to who the injured male was. The woman was a sister of the McGovern family previously mentioned in chapter 13. By the time of the shooting they'd become one of THE criminal enterprises in Glasgow and the West of Scotland.

I arranged for her to be taken to Maryhill and eventually cleared the scene and returned to the office. I'd arranged for a firearm residue test to be carried out on the injured male at the hospital; a test that involves swabbing the hands and nose to ascertain whether the person has fired a gun recently.

Word was relayed to me that the injured man had given the name Thomas Storrie and discharged himself from hospital. The cops who had gone with the ambulance were bringing him to Maryhill.

I was standing with the McGovern sister at the back yard as the injured male was assisted out of the back of the police van, and knowing there was as much chance of her telling me the truth as a tramp turning down a bowl of broth, decided to have a bit of sport.

'Who's he?' I asked her.

'Haven't a clue,' came the reply.

'Were you given up for adoption when you were born?'

'Naw. Wis ah fuck,' came the indignant reply.

'What about a Swiss finishing school. Did you board there for a long time?'

'Naw. Are you aff yir heid? Whit are you talking aboot?'

'Just that I thought you would know your brother, Thomas, when you're standing nine feet away from him.'

The sly smile and the, 'Aye awright,' followed.

Thomas McGovern was examined by a Police Casualty Surgeon who decided that the leg injury required hospital treatment, and he was taken under police escort to the hospital. It transpired that the leg had been broken. He remained in hospital for several days. When eventually released he was arrested on warrant for numerous offences under the firearms act, and attempting to pervert the course of justice by providing false details.

He pled 'Guilty' at the High Court and was sentenced to eight years' imprisonment. His brother, Tony, was one of the two people who had shot at him and run him over, but there was never a sufficiency of evidence to charge him. James Stevenson, Tony's best friend at the time, was questioned as a suspect but denied any involvement.

Two years later on a Saturday in September 2000, Tony McGovern was shot dead in his car outside The Morvern pub in Balornock.

A couple of days after that murder an informant 'Joe' phoned, and asked me to meet him, as he had background information that might be of relevance to the enquiry team. The story he told me was potentially a scriptwriter's dream, loaded as it was with drug dealing, betrayal of friendship, greed, botched assassination attempts and eventual murder.

Tony was in the drugs distribution business and in partnership with his then best friend James Stevenson. Unfortunately for Tony, it seemed that Stevenson practised that old adage of 'no friends in business'. When the drugs were being passed on to dealers Stevenson was adding a couple of thousand onto the price without Tony's knowledge, and was creaming off the extra.

When Tony eventually discovered what was happening he was incandescent and ordered Stevenson murdered. He enlisted the help of two brothers from the Possilpark area, with fearsome reputations, and another male from the Stepps area of the city, to carry out the 'hit'.

Around mid-June 2000, and believing he was being taken to source a firearm, Stevenson found himself seated in the front passenger seat of a car in the Carbeth area. Carbeth is a rural area outside of Glasgow and is covered by another Police Force, the Central Scotland Constabulary. The area forms part of the route taken by numerous keen hill-walkers attempting the West Highland Way. It is scenic, but densely wooded and has a loch nearby. If you were familiar with the area you could effectively conceal a Panzer Division of tanks, far less a body.

There are some 200 wooden constructed huts in Carbeth which many of the 'hutters', as they're known, use at weekends. It was an area very familiar to the brothers as they'd owned a hut there for decades, and they intended to use their intimate knowledge of the surrounding terrain to dispose of the body. The attempt was to take place near a pub known as the Carbeth Inn, but when the time came to pull the trigger the 'hit man' had taken too much Dutch courage to enable him to complete the task. Incredibly, from behind Stevenson and at point-blank range, he botched the job.

Despite sustaining a head injury of sorts, Stevenson, who at that time ran five miles a day, was out of the car and literally off and running. He located a general practitioner in the area who arranged for an ambulance to take him to hospital. Realising that the hospital would notify the police he jumped from the ambulance when it had stopped and before it reached the hospital. Needless to say, he never made any complaint to the police about the incident.

On 24 June 2000, Tony and Stevenson met at the Mike Tyson/Lou Savarese boxing match at Hampden. In true Mafioso style hugs were exchanged, all hatchets buried, peace pipes smoked and everyone was pals again.

Tony must have made other enemies, however, because six days later, on 30 June 2000, he was in the shower at his home at Kenmure Crescent, Bishopbriggs, when someone fired several shots at him through the glass screen door. He sustained a bullet wound to the torso area, as well as superficial cuts to other parts of his body from the screen door glass. Neither Tony nor his family assisted police enquiries, and no one was ever charged with the shooting.

After that, at the beginning of July, a petrol station in Springburn, which Stevenson allegedly owned, was vandalised. That was followed by a fire-raising to a pub in mid-July, which supposedly had connections to the McGovern family.

On the fatal night in September, having survived the shooting within his home, Tony left the Morven public house alone, and walked the short distance to his Audi motor car which was parked outside the pub. His killer(s) waited until he'd entrapped himself in the car before shooting and killing him. The bullet-proof vest he'd taken to wearing wasn't enough to save him. After some time trying to locate him, James Stevenson was eventually questioned in relation to the murder, but no charges were ever libelled against him.

Given that he'd attempted to shoot his own brother and he'd ordered the assassination of James Stevenson, previously his best friend, I don't think you could have accused Tony McGovern of being excessively sentimental. His murder remains unresolved.

42

PROBABLY ANY ONE OF US (CONCLUSION)

Having become involved in the McGovern's attempts to recreate the Gunfight at the OK Corral in the middle of Finlas Street, I didn't conclude duty until 1 a.m. I obviously had enough on my plate with my own enquiry, so the continuation of the McGovern incident was thankfully allocated to another sergeant, and I had the opportunity to try and progress the incident near the pub.

Over the next couple of days I extended the door-to-door canvassing. Stevie had almost given himself eye twists having viewed the poor quality CCTV and timelined what he could make out. He'd made a copy to preserve the quality of the original tape and was working from that. He eventually took the tape through to a forensic laboratory qualified in tape enhancement, in an attempt to improve the quality. There was still no change in the victim's condition.

Any time I contacted the hospital for a medical update I got the impression that I was being given the stock answer in respect of the victim's chances of survival. A lecture on non-missile head injuries, which had formed part of the forensic medicine course I'd taken at Glasgow University, came to mind. The pathologists had indicated that certain responses had to be present if there was to be hope of possible recovery.

I re-read my notes on that particular subject, and armed with negligible knowledge I managed to reach the neurosurgeon in charge of the care of the victim. I asked if the injured man had any motor response, gag reflex or caloric reflex. These were tests carried out by medical staff on coma victims, and were accurate gauges of potential survival.

Motor response is a reaction to stimuli which would be painful to an alert human being; gag reflex is when the throat contracts when the palate is touched; and caloric reflex is when the body can react to cold water in the outer ear. When I posed that question there was a pause at the other side of the telephone before the neurosurgeon told me that it would be best if I made my way to the hospital for a 'chat'.

At the hospital, I was given the news I didn't want but was expecting. The victim had suffered a period of hypoxia – oxygen starvation to the brain – and allied to the subdural haemorrhage his prognosis was very poor. I knew that technically I would shortly have a murder enquiry on my hands. I had more than enough investigative experience so wasn't fazed by that eventuality.

There is a strange anomaly in police investigations – certainly in Strathclyde. A victim may suffer the most horrendous wounds, but if it appears he will survive then any subsequent enquiry is, by and large, progressed by two detectives, even though the incident requires the same level of investigation as a murder. In fact, detectives had a saying that a murder was simply an attempted murder without the victim. Consequently, many detectives experienced in the investigation of attempted murders could make a reasonable job of a murder.

From interrogating the local intelligence system and speaking to the patrol officers who covered the area, I had managed to obtain a list of suspects, and from that list I'd obtained photographs of potential suspects. When the victim's wife had viewed the photographs she managed to identify two youths who had been part of the group. As a result of that identification I obtained warrants to search two houses for clothing and footwear. I scheduled the search for early on a Friday morning.

I'd briefed colleagues and requested that if the word came from the hospital that the victim had died, to call me at home irrespective of time. On the Thursday night before I was scheduled to execute the search warrants I got the call at about 10.30 p.m. He'd died half an hour previously. I showered, changed and drove into the office. I knew I had a lot of work ahead, not least the alteration of the search warrants. They had been drawn up and signed as warrants relating to the attempted murder of the victim.

In addition to arranging for the transportation of the body, the post-mortem examination and preparing a death report I had to redraft the warrants and contact the Duty Procurator Fiscal and on-call Sheriff to have them re-signed.

I would eventually arrest and charge five males in connection with the death. However having dealt with all aspects of the enquiry I knew in my heart that any judicial proceedings would be distilled down to a single accused person.

Initially, the family members had told me that the victim had been jumped and stamped on, but the post-mortem had failed to find any marks or injuries other than the head wound that led to the skull fracture and subdural haemorrhage. The initial impression had been that the group had initiated the attack, but once the taxi driver, who was an independent witness, had been interviewed and the CCTV viewed it was simple but tragic.

The victim had been asked for a cigarette, and perhaps because he'd celebrated too much at the family function, or disliked the attitude of the kid who'd asked, he didn't just walk on. He turned back towards the group and attempted to push or throw a punch at one of the group. The intended target of the push/punch threw a single punch in response. That knocked the victim down and he struck his head.

That single ten-second act left a man dead, and a woman and young girls without a husband and father. How many of us could say that placed in a similar situation, be it as a result of alcohol, false pride or whatever, we would have failed to continue walking? That's how quickly your life can alter irrevocably.

At the subsequent trial the jury returned a 'Not Guilty' verdict against the one boy in the dock, and given all the facts I couldn't really argue with that verdict. A police officer investigates crimes on behalf of the Procurator Fiscal, and if there is sufficient evidence to substantiate a charge against someone then he reports all the circumstances, both for and against the accused, to the Fiscal.

I couldn't have carried out my enquiries into that case any more diligently than I had done, but the facts were the facts, and the evidence was the evidence. Perhaps it was because he wasn't the usual type of victim, and had been a decent working man who was married with three daughters, but I so wanted them to know that I had done what I could, albeit I knew that, given the eventual result, they would have been left with a feeling of injustice.

43

JUSTICE FOR ALL?

Two months later brought another late shift and another dead body.

I was standing in a top-floor maisonette flat off Bilsland Drive in Ruchill, along with David. David was as good a detective as I ever worked with, or would work with. Then he wore his hair slightly longer than normal among CID officers and that, together with his fashionable spectacles, gave him the look of a trendy secondary-school teacher. He had a degree in social sciences, was well read and street-smart in equal measures: intuitive, observant, and a first-class interrogator.

We'd been called there by uniformed officers who'd attended a report of a domestic disturbance in which a female had stabbed a male in the groin. On arrival they'd found the male and two females within. The females were the victim's partner and a neighbour who lived across the landing. It was the neighbour who'd made the call requesting police attendance. The cops checked the male's neck and wrist for a pulse and also his chest and stomach for a heartbeat, but they couldn't locate any vital signs.

The neighbour who'd made the call said she'd knocked on the door to use the phone in the house, and when the door was opened she was met with the gruesome sight of the now dead male lying partly in the hallway and partly in the bedroom door entrance, with the hallway awash with blood.

She'd actually gone to the door earlier as she had no phone in her own home and intended to ask to use theirs. She'd heard the sound of arguing emanating from within the flat, and had decided to leave the phone request until the arguing subsided.

It never ceased to amaze me throughout my time as a cop how a seemingly insignificant or inconsequential action can impact on a life. On going to a neighbour's house to ask for a favour and hearing a disturbance, the neighbour took the course most of us would wisely adopt.

She decided to leave it until later when things had quietened down, especially when the neighbour knew the arguing to be frequent in nature. Had she knocked on the door on the first occasion would it have altered things, or would it have simply delayed an inevitable tragedy?

Whatever the ifs, buts, or maybes, David and I now found ourselves looking at the remains of a forty-three-year-old man whose blood leakage had been such that it caused you to question whether the body really only held seven or eight pints of that vital life fluid.

As with the previous domestic death at Lyndale Road, the victim was again male, and again death had been the result of a single stab wound. In the first case, the cause of death had been a penetrating wound to the heart, but this time the victim had died with blood spurting from a severed femoral artery.

I'd witnessed that type of wound before, and it must be a quite horrible manner in which to die. The femoral artery runs through the thigh and supplies blood to the legs. It is a very large artery, and if cut or severed you have about five minutes to live, unless you receive aggressive medical intervention.

I'm sure there will be a few people who have survived this injury, but the only one I personally knew of was a detective who was investigating a break-in at the Lea Rig public house in the East End of Glasgow. He thought there may still be thieves on the premises and tried to go through the plate-glass window they'd smashed, and just as with the attempted theft of the ski jackets at Littlewoods in 1998, a shard of glass ripped his thigh.

That he lived was the result of his female partner having a good knowledge of first aid techniques. She utilised a belt as a tourniquet and that, allied to the close proximity of paramedics, undoubtedly saved his life. The man we now found ourselves overlooking hadn't been so lucky.

For the last year and a half of his life he'd been in a relationship with the female householder, who was now the main suspect in his death. Alcohol appeared to have been the tie that bound them, and the catalyst in rendering the relationship a vocal and volatile quality.

There had been previous police involvement in the relationship. Ten months before, his fifty-year-old female partner, heavily influenced by alcohol consumption, had called the police and told them that she'd found him dead.

Because of the alcohol, it had taken her some time before she'd been able to direct the police to his flat in Closeburn Street in Possilpark, where the police found him safe and well. She subsequently became abusive towards the police officers in attendance, and found herself arrested for a breach of the peace.

Four months before his death, it was our soon-to-be-deceased's turn to be arrested for a breach of the peace. He'd gone to her flat, demanded sex (request denied), became vocal and hence the police involvement.

Four weeks before his death, an incident occurred within his flat whereby he sustained a head injury which won him seventeen sutures at Stobhill Hospital. He'd been drinking with his partner when a former girlfriend had appeared at the flat. The appearance of the ex appears to have caused some friction between the soon-to-be-deceased and his partner. At one point, after disappearing into a room out with the view of the former girlfriend, the female partner emerged, claiming she'd 'done him in'.

Following his death, we checked his medical records. The story he gave hospital staff when having the head wound treated had been confused, and it couldn't be established whether he'd sustained the injury as a result of a fall or an assault.

Whatever the previous history, we were now looking at the result of an arterial bleed out from a single penetrating wound to his right upper thigh. When the uniform officers had arrived at the scene and failed to locate signs of life one had remarked to the other that he believed the victim was dead. When she heard that, the female householder had blurted out that it had only been a wee potato knife.

That comment, together with the fact she'd allegedly said to the neighbour who called the police that she thought she'd stabbed the victim, caused us to have her removed to Maryhill Office. That also allowed us to manage the crime scene.

Once we'd had the body photographed in situ and the biologist had obtained various blood lifts we carried out a search of the flat. Between the cooker and refrigerator we found a bloodstained knife, and as with the body, we had it photographed where it lay. After we'd finished with the crime scene and carried out a crime scene canvass for any other potential witnesses, we headed back to the office to question the householder.

I thought that in basketball parlance the interview would be a 'slam dunk' given the circumstances. Firstly, the neighbour had heard sounds of arguing when she gone to the door of the flat earlier.

Secondly, an incriminating remark, claiming that she thought she'd stabbed the victim, had allegedly been made by the suspect to the same neighbour.

Thirdly, that remark had been supplemented by another made by the suspect to the officers initially attending the scene. She allegedly said that it had only been 'a wee potato knife'.

Fourthly, we had found a potato knife in a search of the house. That latter find also leant weight to the remark made to the uniform officers, given that they had left the scene prior to the search, so would have had no way of knowing whether such a knife existed.

Given all that, I was sure the tape-recorded interview would be straightforward, but it proved rather difficult.

We made it clear to the woman that she had been detained and would be questioned as a suspect in connection with the murder of the victim. Whether the gravity of her situation had suddenly dawned on her, or whether she had some other underlying reason I don't know, but the interview was frustrating.

She admitted that as a couple they argued all the time, but claimed he was never violent towards her. She was asked how the victim had come by his injury, but said that she had no idea as she'd found him in bed bleeding badly.

From there, she denied making the alleged comments to the neighbour and officers and accused them of lying. She then claimed she had been trying to peel potatoes, the victim had been bear-hugging her, she had three broken ribs (she hadn't), couldn't breathe, so may have pushed behind her with the knife. She then, however, very quickly reverted to denying any knowledge of how the fatal injury had been sustained.

David and I worked a system whereby whichever of us had caught the enquiry would be the main interrogator. The other would observe body language and make notes of any points not covered or not picked up on. That arrangement though was flexible should it transpire that one of us had a previous history with the suspect and was, therefore, more likely to establish empathy.

Having listened to the questioning and watched the woman David eventually interjected. He made the observation that every time the suspect was mentioning being in a playful bear hug and being squeezed hard she pantomimed holding a knife and making a swinging motion. Her response was the nearest we would come to an acknowledgement of responsibility.

She said that she may have tried to push the victim off and may have caused the injury, but then retreated into not knowing how the injury had occurred, and having no recollection of having had a knife in her hand, or having made the alleged remarks to the neighbour or the police officers.

Having exhausted all lines of questioning we arrested and charged her with murder. I had her examined by a police casualty surgeon who found no indication of any rib injury, tenderness, or any other injuries recent or historical.

I was never cited to attend court, but I believe the woman was placed on probation for the killing. Having never been required to attend the judicial proceedings I don't know what plea in mitigation was offered by her defence counsel, but I would be avoiding the issue if I didn't make a personal observation on the two domestic deaths I've included.

Both male victims, and each dead from a single fatal stab wound. The relationships were volatile, but on the fatal nights neither of the women bore any marks of violence. If arguing or raised voices within a relationship is the charge I would have to plead guilty to that crime every second night.

Hypothetically, if those sets of circumstances had been presented to a court of law, but the accused had been male and the victims had been female, would the male(s) have been afforded the same degree of clemency by the judicial system? Would 'the quality of mercy' have been dispensed with the same equity, or would the penalties imposed have been more swingeing?

I'm neither sexist nor misogynist, and I couldn't be more categorical in my condemnation of violence towards women. It is the retreat of the coward, but I also believe that if the law isn't about justice it isn't about anything.

44

IT'S NOT WHAT YOU SAY

Irrespective of how many grim situations police officers encounter, there is generally some light relief waiting around the corner. There had been an armed robbery in the West End of the city, and they had a possible suspect and wanted to place him in an identification parade for witnesses to view.

I was involved in the running of the parade, and we went through the standard rigmarole required when holding an identification parade. If there was one suspect he would be paraded in the company of a minimum of six 'stand-ins'. The stand-ins would be people gathered from the available general public who were of a similar age, height, size and general appearance to the suspect, to ensure a level of fairness.

The suspect's interests were served by his lawyer, who had a chance to assess the stand-ins before the parade, and if he thought it was an unfair cross-section could object. The lawyer was also present within the identification parade room, again to ensure fairness. All were placed behind numbers with the suspect allowed to choose any place in the line-up.

When a witness entered the room, they were told by the police officer that they would now be asked to view the parade, and while viewing from behind the one-way viewing screen the witness was entitled to make certain requests. They could ask the people on the parade to walk, talk, turn around and/or stand side on. They could ask for them to do all or any of those things.

Such requests may have been necessary to allow the witness to identify the suspect. Much would depend on the manner in which the witness had interacted with the suspect. If the suspect had been masked the witness may wish to hear the suspect speak. Similarly, if they had only seen the suspect in profile they may have requested the people on the parade to turn a certain way.

If a request was made for someone on the parade to stand side on then, in fairness to the suspect (so as not to single them out), all those in the parade were asked to stand side on. Similarly, if the witness wanted someone to speak then all had, in turn, to utter the requested words or phrase. The witness in this case had a request. He had been held up and the perpetrator had demanded, 'Yer moneybags' (basically, demanding the bags of cash being carried).

He relayed this request to me and, in turn, I said to the first person in the line-up.

'Number one say, "Yer moneybags."'

Two of the stand-ins were brothers, and as it happened were standing next to each other in the line-up. When it came to the first brother he said the words, but the brother next to him refused, saying, 'Naw, cos' ah'm no moneybags.'

I couldn't believe it and said, 'Number four, just say, "Yer moneybags."'

'Naw.'

'Number four, I just need you to say, "Yer moneybags."'

'Ah'm no' sayin ah'm moneybags if ah'm no'.'

'Number four, we need to move on. Just say, "Yer moneybags."'

'What and get dubbed up [arrested] for something ah've no done? Naw.'

'Number four, you won't be "dubbed up" for anything. All you have to do is say, "Yer moneybags."'

'But ah'm no moneybags.'

By now I've broken into a cold clammy sweat as I saw the parade descending into Marx Brothers territory. I couldn't say to him that he wasn't the suspect here and risk prejudicing the parade, so almost pleading I said to the brother, who had already said the requested phrase, 'Can you ask the male next to you to say the words asked?'

He turned to his brother and said, 'Bobby gonnae for fuck's sake say "yer moneybags" so we can get tae fuck,' which prompted 'Bobby' to take a step forward and in a loud clear voice declare, 'I AM MONEYBAGS.'

By that time it didn't really matter because both the police colleague assisting me and the lawyer were convulsing with suppressed laughter, while I'd retreated to the corner to commence ritual *seppuku*.

45

CALCULATED RISK

I've previously mentioned hunches, and a sense that although things appear normal on the surface, sometimes there is something wrong with the picture. Police officers should hopefully be attuned to that, and be wary of accepting everything at face value, but often repetition can blunt observational skills.

It was early evening in December 1998, and I was at Maryhill with David, Stevie and Angus Buchanan. Angus had jet-black hair cut in a flat top style. He'd been in the Hong Kong police and while there had married a Chinese girl, and hence had the nickname 'The Chinese Detective'. He was a tough lad but intelligent also. He had a nomadic streak and eventually left Strathclyde to join the police in Australia.

Uniformed officers had been actioned to the report of a death. The deceased was a seventy-six-year-old male who lived alone in Boclair Street, in the Temple area of the city. A friend who had a key to the flat had been unable to contact him by phone so she'd called his daughter. She'd expressed her concerns to the daughter who gave her permission to use the spare key she had and check he was okay.

When she went into the flat she found the occupant sitting in a chair in the living room covered up to the chest by a duvet. Underneath the duvet he was wearing a cardigan, pyjama top and underpants. When she couldn't waken him she contacted a neighbour, and also phoned for an ambulance and the police.

On seeing he was obviously dead, the ambulance crew made no attempt at resuscitation. Two doctors attended separately. One was from Medicall (an out-of-hours GP service) and the second was a Police Casualty Surgeon. The former pronounced life extinct and left, while the Police Casualty Surgeon indicated that he would not issue a death certificate as he had no previous knowledge of the man's medical history, but that there were no suspicious circumstances.

That meant that an ambulance crew, uniformed officers and two doctors – one of whom was a Police Casualty Surgeon – were happy with the situation. Uniformed shift supervisors may also have attended the scene as Force Procedures dictated that they should attend a sudden death, but whether they had I can't recall. Either way, those in attendance were content that the scene was sufficiently straightforward to allow members of the deceased's family access to the house.

That was when alarm bells started to ring. The family couldn't find a pair of trousers, worn habitually by the deceased, anywhere in the house. He'd been found trouser-less with a blanket covering his lower body when discovered. In addition, money appeared missing.

The attending cops began to review the situation and contacted us at the police office, indicating that they were unhappy that the trousers couldn't be accounted for. We decided to make our way down to the scene, although so far there was still nothing suspicious about the death. Nothing that is, until the undertakers arrived to remove the body to the funeral parlour, and noticed two penetrating wounds to his abdomen. We were given the good news en route to the scene.

He lived in a cul-de-sac where the houses consisted of rows of tenement buildings with about sixteen blocks of flats on each side of the road and some eight flats per tenement. When we got to the flat the victim was lying on a stretcher on the floor of the living room. Given the unlimited access that so many had had to the crime scene it was greatly lacking in sterility.

I cleared the house and requested the on-call photographer; scientist and pathologist. I also requested that the availability of the Support Unit be ascertained. The Support Unit umbrellas the dog section, mounted branch, underwater unit and firearms sections. It also has officers specially trained in search and seal, riot control, and the part that was of interest to me at that point – crime scene canvassing.

I arranged for the crime scene and environs to be photographed and videotaped. I also asked the Scene of Crime photographer to do the same with the victim, although the body had been moved from the position it had originally occupied. I had the forensic scientist 'tape' the victim for cross-transference fibres. After that was done I had a closer look at the victim and discovered a third and probably the fatal wound on the body. It was under the sternum and was of the large penetrating variety.

When the Support Unit arrived I found that the Inspector in charge that evening was John Stobo, who I'd worked with years previously when on my initial secondment to the CID. John arrived at the scene with about a dozen officers and after I'd briefed them they set to work to cover as many doors as possible.

John had explained to me that he could only spare them for a couple of hours as they were scheduled to conclude duty at 10 p.m. They were scheduled back on duty very early the next day to fulfil a long-standing assignment. Given the start we'd had and the amount of doors we had to canvass I told him I was grateful for any assistance he could provide.

When they'd finished I began to collect the documentation from them which would tell me at which doors they'd failed to gain a reply, or which occupants had been absent from the house and would require follow-up visits.

As he was handing me his docket one cop mentioned two boys who'd been in a house at the far end of the street. There'd been nothing particular about them that he could put his finger on, but he just felt they would be worth a re-interview. I knew about pit of the stomach hunches so marked them down as requiring a more detailed interview by a detective officer.

We returned to the office, and by this time a senior on-call CID officer had been notified and was at the office. I updated him on what had been done up to that point. It was almost midnight, and I'd tasked a couple of uniformed officers with guarding the crime scene, so he decided that there was nothing more to be achieved at that point, and we would pick things up in the morning.

I looked at him in astonishment and said:

Are you joking? There's a pair of trousers missing. Whoever done the old boy took them, possibly because there was something valuable in them. They wouldn't hold on to trousers so they'll be dumped nearby. We haven't even searched the bins, and they might be emptied by tomorrow. We're going nowhere. I'm sending the guys down to search the bins. They can use the Dragonlights [high-powered portable sources of illumination].

I could hear the voice in my head telling me, 'Another Henry Kissinger moment, Ger.' With my usual lack of diplomacy, I hadn't posed it as a request, or a suggestion. Another boss to piss off, but we had an old man who'd survived to the age of seventy-six before being brutally stabbed to death in his own home. If it had been my grandfather I'd have hated to think the police had downed tools for the night while the enquiry was still in an embryonic stage. I also hoped I could reverse the bad start the enquiry had endured.

I asked David, Stevie and Angus to check the rear waste bins using Dragonlights. Nowadays, that request would probably meet with all sorts of barriers involving risk assessments and Health and Safety, but even though in suits and ties they undertook the task without a murmur of protest.

I'd hadn't long begun the various administrative tasks that follow a murder, such as arranging the post-mortem examination, arranging for witnesses to identify the deceased prior to the autopsy, preparing a sudden-death report and so on when they contacted me. They'd found trousers and a bloodstained knife hidden under rubbish bags, in a bin in the back court of one of the flats, about fifty yards from the murder scene.

I arranged for a uniformed officer to stand by the bin shed, and called the Scene of Crime photographer back out to photograph the trousers and knife in situ. I also called the guys back to the office to regroup because, given where the trousers had been found, I knew what I intended to do. The bin serviced the block of flats that housed the two individuals the cop had been unhappy with.

I had a decision to make although to me it wasn't a decision at all. I could wait and defer to the on-call senior officer, who may well decide to hold off until the morning, or I could take the bull by the horns. Given how the enquiry had endured a shambolic start, I felt that we'd been given a large rub of the green. Lady Luck had turned her kind countenance towards us and I intended to exploit it to the fullest.

I decided that we were going for those two before they became comfortable and entrenched in their alibis. I got the raiding party together, and we hit the house and brought both of the boys to Maryhill.

I arranged for Stevie and Angus to interview one, and David and a lad called Trevor, the other. At Maryhill the interview rooms were separated by a stretch of corridor which took a right-angled turn.

It's strange because I thought that I would be really frustrated and tense given that I wasn't a primary interviewer, but I enjoyed overseeing and directing the enquiry. My sanguinity was aided by the fact that I had total faith in Stevie and David as interrogators. They were perceptive and resolute, and I had no doubt they would get to the truth. They did.

Seventeen-year-old Finlay Grant admitted the stabbing and the other gave him up as the perpetrator. The guys had done a great job.

By the time I'd tidied things up, and prepared and dictated the case for conveyance to the Procurator Fiscal's office later that day, it was after midday before I got home. I'd hoped to get a couple of hours' sleep before I was due back on duty at 4 p.m., but the adrenalin put paid to that.

I've never taken drugs, never had any inclination to, and don't even smoke or drink so perhaps I'm speaking from a position of ignorance, but I would match the natural high gleaned from doing good police work against anything chemically induced.

I was later told by a senior CID officer that Jim Orr, who was the Assistant Chief Constable for Crime within the Force, had sent his congratulations on not only good police work, but in resolving a disturbing situation so quickly. Call me Mr Cynical, but I often wondered if he'd been told exactly how the enquiry had come to be resolved so quickly, and who had been the catalyst?

At Judicial Proceedings the Procurator Fiscal was wary that each cousin would blame the other, confuse a jury, and we may be on the end of a 'Not Proven' verdict. I didn't agree but a plea of 'Guilty' to the lesser charge of culpable homicide was accepted by Crown Office. The sentence was eight years.

46

GOOD NEWS, BAD NEWS

Police officers sometimes have to be slightly devious given some types of people they encounter, and I'm sure that won't come as any great surprise. There are many criminals who are so 'cute' or 'fly' that they could play 'tag' all night in a sack of weasels and never be 'it'. Consequently, police officers have to have their wits about them.

I've also mentioned how if a trick is a good one and works once, then with a slice of good fortune, it will work twice. I managed to resolve a firearm situation by a combination of both.

I first used the lure to resolve a relatively minor incident. I was late turn and Stirling police contacted us with a warrant for the arrest of a male, but they'd had no luck in tracing him. They knew he'd hired a car, and they'd spoken to the car hire company in the hope that they could apprehend him when he returned the car. The car hire company had their own problems however. He'd overshot the period of agreed rental and had basically stolen the vehicle.

I checked our intelligence files to see if we had a current address for him, but since we didn't, I told them the best we could do was make the local cops aware of the registration number of the car should they encounter it. Stirling had already placed a 'marker' against the car on the Police National Computer, requesting that if the vehicle was stopped, the driver was to be detained.

As with much of good police work we got lucky. Lucky that is, because we went to buy food to feed our faces. Along with Stevie and David I'd gone down to buy fish and chips at Jaconelli's, a well-known takeaway on Maryhill Road. After we'd made our purchases we were on the way back to the office when Stevie spotted the car parked up, locked up and unattended on Maryhill Road.

We pulled into a side street and watched the car for a period, but it didn't move and no one went near it. We didn't know who our suspect was living with, and if we knocked on the door and alerted him, through a relative, that we were wise to the car he'd simply disappear out of a back door.

I hated being so near and so far, but in a busy division such as ours we couldn't spare the time to watch it for who knows how long. Before anyone thinks, 'You had time to get fish and chips,' you should know that we ended up eating them while watching the car. It was while eating that an idea formulated in my head, and I decided it may be worth a try.

The 'try' was a 5'10" police woman with Scandinavian-blonde hair, pale blue eyes and a figure that would have caused a Trappist monk to palpitate. She was a nice girl and a decent police officer. She was a cyclist, keen on keeping fit and we'd seen her earlier when she'd cycled in to start her shift, dressed in three-quarter-length Lycra shorts.

I contacted her and arranged to meet her back at the office, and left the guys watching the car. I quickly explained our situation and what I wanted, and she agreed without hesitation. She changed into her three-quarter-length Lycras, took a haversack and cycle helmet, and we each drove a car back down to the side street.

The plan was that she would knock on some doors and explain that she was really sorry, but as she was cycling a car had cut her up, and she'd hit the vehicle parked on the street. She was unsure if she'd damaged the car as it was dark, but wanted to afford the owner the chance to decide.

It only took the second door before our man came out. We wanted to minimise risk, and so were very close in case he came on all aggressive, but the way our girl looked, King Kong could have been dancing on the roof of the car and he'd probably have said, 'That's okay, no harm done.' He looked at the supposedly damaged area, and as he did so we were given the signal that this was our target.

He looked momentarily puzzled when he told her he couldn't see any damage to which our girl responded: 'Well, it's a kind of good news/ bad news situation. The good news is there is no damage to the car. Bad news is that these are detectives and you're arrested.'

He knew he'd been filleted like one of Jaconelli's fish, and took it in good part and, in fact, on the car journey to the police office, he said to me. 'That ploy your idea, big yin?'

'Uh huh.'

'Thought so. No offence, but you look like the type of bastard who's pulled more strokes than the Oxford boat race team.'

There was no offence taken. If truth be told I always enjoyed backhanded compliments from the opposition, and I don't just mean villains.

Just before I left to transfer to the Serious Crime Squad a local solicitor phoned the office looking for me. When I spoke to him on the phone he said that he'd heard I was transferring and wanted to tell me he would be sorry to see me leave. I'd had some furious exchanges with him at judicial proceedings, so I told him he'd forgive me if I thought his tongue was firmly in his cheek.

Typical lawyer though. He said that he was utterly genuine, and explained that because of the volume of criminal arrests I'd made it had put a lot of business in his direction. In turn, he'd made a great deal of money from defending those I'd arrested.

I was to receive a similar backhanded compliment giving evidence in the High Court of Judiciary from the defence Queen's Counsel.

While out nosing around with David, we'd seen and arrested, after a short foot chase, a male wanted for robbery. Come trial day, we were waiting to give evidence when the Court Officer informed us that the Procurator Fiscal Depute was almost apoplectic with the Advocate Depute, who'd been allocated as prosecutor.

In cases heard at Solemn Procedure, the Crown appoints an Advocate Depute to prosecute, and at that time the Advocate would usually have had a Procurator Fiscal Depute to assist and advise. Having generally dealt with the case since initial reporting by the police, the Fiscal would be *au fait* with all the ins and outs. This was the first criminal case this particular Advocate had prosecuted, but she'd stubbornly decided that she didn't require any advice or assistance. Unfortunately, she wasn't making too good a fist of things. It wasn't good news.

I was called to the witness box, and was led through my evidence in chief by the Advocate Depute. She asked all the questions she intended, and concluded with the usual, 'No further questions, My Lord,' and left the lectern to take her seat at the table. I tried frantically to catch her eye as she walked back towards the seat.

She'd made the most basic of errors, and the defence Queen's Counsel, who I'd faced before and was as sharp as they came, knew she had as well. I saw him smile and mouth to his assistant. It was breaking protocol as she'd finished her examination of my evidence, but I spoke out.

'Madame Counsel, I'm identifying the man I've given my evidence in chief against as the man sitting in the dock, between the two police officers.' I pointed to the accused in the dock to remove any dubiety.

She'd forgotten completely to have me identify the male on trial. It is fundamental for any witness, when giving evidence against an accused, to be asked whether they can identify the person in question, and if so to point to the person. Failure to do so would void that witness's evidence.

I was sure I caught the Queen's Counsel mouthing an oath towards his assistant. He then stood up to begin his cross-examination of me. It was the shortest cross-examination I'd experienced in that intimidating court. With a hint of a smile he said, 'Sergeant, would it be fair to say you have given evidence in the High Court previously?'

'Yes sir. Numerous times.'

He inclined his head towards me, and said simply, 'Mmm . . . No further questions,' and took his seat. I interpreted it as a compliment.

Two incidents that occurred on 19 November 1999 were eventually resolved by thinking on the run and a bit of deviousness.

A twenty-three-year-boy and his eighteen-year-old girlfriend were in their car in the Lenzie area when a black Mazda sped up behind them, and then after overtaking the driver began to slow and swerve, and continued driving in that manner until the two cars reached Auchinairn Road in Balornock.

Up until then, the road had been of the single-track country type, but now with the roads widened, and safer to do so, the boy and his girlfriend pulled into the side to allow the Mazda the opportunity to disappear.

After driving a short distance the Mazda U-turned and drove alongside the car, pointed a handgun out of the window, and discharged it at the couple. The driver of the Mazda then drove off but U-turned again, and for a second time discharged the handgun at the couple before driving off in the direction of Glasgow. Naturally terrified, the couple flagged down a police car patrolling the area, which attempted to chase the Mazda but lost it.

I was informed of the incident and headed up to the scene together with David and Stevie. I arranged for Ballistics and Scenes of Crime Officers to attend the scene and carry out a scene examination and photograph it. Ballistics believed the gun to have been a blank firer.

While at the scene the dispatcher informed me that an incident had occurred that may be of relevance to our current investigation. A Mazda, driven by a male fitting the description of our suspect, had threatened to shoot a bus driver at Charing Cross in Glasgow city centre. Our suspect seemed intent on causing someone a degree of harm. A registration number had been noted, and the keeper of the car resided in the Kirkintilloch area.

We headed up to the office at that location to formulate a plan of action, and on reaching the office were told that the Mazda was outside the owner's address. I was very familiar with the area. The housing consisted of rows of four-in-a-block flats, and many of the occupants were elderly.

I had two choices. I could make it an all-singing, all-dancing firearm incident, in which case there would be Uncle Tom Cobley and all. That would, in turn, mean houses evacuated in the middle of the night, elderly residents scared to half death by black-clad Heckler and Koch carrying stormtroopers, a possible siege going on for who knows how long etc. etc.

Or ... as we were talking I saw a motorcycle helmet and gear hanging up on a coat stand, which belonged to Gary Vezza, the Patrol Sergeant, and I asked Gary if he'd let me borrow them. Nowadays, I would have had no choice. I would have had to turn it into the circus show I spoke of. Given, however, that Ballistics had pegged the gun as a blank firer I decided to try and resolve the matter through a little subterfuge.

I donned Gary's motorcycle gear and was dropped off around the corner. David and Stevie positioned themselves either side of the close mouth entrance and out of sight. I went up to the first-floor landing and knocked on the door. I spoke to an elderly resident to ascertain who lived in the house, and whether there was a nasty surprise such as an Akita or pit bull that I hadn't factored into the equation.

I didn't tell her I was a cop, but gave her the cover story that I was looking for the owner of the Mazda car parked outside because I'd seen another car scrape it and drive off, and I wanted to give the Mazda owner the number of the car. She told me that he lived in the ground-floor flat, but warned me to be careful when I broke the news as he wasn't a nice man. Swell!

I knocked on the door, and after a short gap I heard the footsteps coming along the hallway, and the voice from the other side of the door asking who it was. I put on an excited voice, as if slightly out of breath, and asked him if he knew who owned the Mazda parked outside because I'd been on my motorbike and had seen a car in front of me clip the Mazda.

I quickly added that as it was dark I couldn't see how badly scraped the car was, but that I had got the number of the car that smacked it. I heard an audible curse followed by the opening of the door. He barely glanced at me, but more importantly his hands were empty. He went charging along the close mouth and out of the door whereupon he was leaped upon from a great height by the welcoming committee. He almost fainted.

Inside the house we recovered the gun, ammunition and drugs. He faced ten charges and eventually received a three-year prison sentence and a five-year driving ban at the High Court. We didn't even have time to enjoy the moment because as we were finishing the search of the house we got word that a prisoner had died within Low Moss, a prison sited within our policing area.

It was a case of tidying up the situation and making our way to the prison to investigate the sudden death. As it turned out there were no suspicious circumstances, but it was that kind of a Division – something happening every other night.

47

TOO MANY HEAD SHOTS

Information is the lifeblood of police work. If you are in possession of quality information then you have knowledge and knowing who, why, and what sets you on the road towards solving more crimes than not.

Informants provide information and quality information can allow you to cut to the chase, and potentially save thousands of pounds in expenditure, as well as save valuable police resource hours. Consequently, informants can almost literally be worth their weight in gold. Oh and before anyone thinks the mention of gold should be read as thirty pieces of silver let me make something absolutely crystal clear. Everybody in the criminal world will provide information to some law-enforcement faction or other given the right circumstances.

Perhaps they won't speak to a uniform officer, but they'll speak to a CID officer, or they won't speak to a Divisional CID officer, but will speak to a Serious Crime Squad member, or Special Branch, or the Scottish Crime and Drug Enforcement Agency (SCDEA), or they may deal with the security services. But at one point or another they'll provide information, Arthur Thompson and Thomas McGraw being prime examples.

I have to say that I always enjoyed recruiting and dealing with informants, but I adhered to strict self-imposed guidelines. Even so, some of my actions may have rendered me subject to 'corrective advice' from senior officers had they known how some things came about.

In February 1998, I got a call at home from 'Glen' who came from Barmulloch. He was small and slight, and had done some boxing when younger, but hadn't been very good, and his face was testament to that, as it resembled a stuntman's elbow. The only thing he'd have been able to box by then were eggs in a supermarket, but fortunately his brains hadn't addled – well, not entirely.

A known drug dealer from Ruchill was looking to kill Frank Ward with whom he had a developing feud. The drug dealer wanted an automatic handgun that Glen had access to. It had been Glen's intention to get the gun to me in any case but the fact that it may now be used in a murder hastened the timetable somewhat. Ward was a bully and horrible individual who came from the Maryhill area. He was about 6'0" tall, overweight and wore glasses. He'd been convicted and served a prison sentence for attempted rape.

As a result of the feud, which was over drug territory, he would go on to kidnap and horribly torture two nonentities, who were connected in some way to the man he was feuding with. He was given a twelve-year sentence for those crimes.

Given the injuries Ward inflicted on the two men he kidnapped, and the nature of the torture (a red hot iron was among the nicer instruments used) then perhaps, in retrospect, I should have left the gun to be sourced, but police officers can't allow themselves to become judge and jury of that type of situation.

Besides, what if because of my dislike and contempt for Ward I hadn't taken the gun off the streets and the 'hit' had been botched, and some innocent bystander had been injured instead? It wasn't something I wanted on my conscience.

I arranged to meet 'Glen' at 11 p.m. that night at the flagpole at Ruchill Park. I always liked that location because at that time of night it was utterly deserted. The flagpole sat high on a plateau and to reach it you had to traverse a winding path. On a late February night it would also be pitch-black, and on the thousand-to-one chance someone showed up identification would be difficult owing to the poor ambient lighting.

Glen was paranoid about anyone finding out that he was speaking to a police officer so I met him alone, which was against Force protocol, but the people who spoke to me weren't silly wee boys who were providing information on who was shoplifting chocolate bars from Woolworths, and informant handling operated differently then.

Nowadays, there are totally different rules governing the use of informants. Should an officer recruit an informant now, he then has to pass that informant onto a unit known as 'Source Handling', and that officer will have no further contact with the informant.

The specialist unit will then assume the role of handling and tasking. The informant for their part is required to sign a contract which stipulates the parameters under which they are permitted to operate. The handlers use assumed names, and at any meetings with the informant there are always two police officers present.

I met Glen. It was a drizzly night and, after talking for some fifteen minutes or so about various criminals and happenings and getting thoroughly soaked, I asked him where and when he intended to leave the gun and was met by the following.

'Oh I thought you'd want it right away so I brought it with me,' and with that he pulled up his jacket and in the waistband of his trousers was the gun with a full magazine inside; a French-made automatic handgun. I didn't know whether to laugh at the absurdity, or hit him about the head with the gun for his stupidity. It would be fair to assume that the circumstances of how the gun came to be recovered were altered slightly.

Maybe I should scratch that idea that Glen hadn't taken too many punches to the head.

Sometimes though, I wondered if the informants were worth the hassle.

'Joe' wanted to speak to me with information on a robbery, but at that point was, unfortunately, a guest of Her Majesty's Prison Service, and naturally didn't want me to visit him in prison. As he was only awaiting trial I received permission to bring him out of prison, using the ruse that he was required to take part in an identification parade for another crime in which he was the suspect.

'Joe' was a shoplifter and always tried to argue with me that he wasn't hurting anyone but huge corporations by his efforts. It didn't matter how much I disagreed and pointed out how everyone suffered, he wasn't for changing, which was pretty much the reason he was in jail awaiting trial.

Later, to maintain contact while he was in prison, I obtained a Post Office Box Number under an assumed name and drew expenses from the police to service the account. 'Joe' wrote to the Post Office Box slanting his letters as if to a mate, but including some excellent intelligence and information under the guise of prison gossip.

All he looked for in return was that I slipped some money to his family, which I did. I'd wait until I was night shift, and it was about 4 a.m. and no one around, and I'd push an unmarked envelope with small amounts of cash through the letterbox.

I collected 'Joe' and squirrelled him into an interview room in the police office. I got him a cigarette and a coffee at which point a senior officer decided he should be in on the 'discussion'. This person, unfortunately, drank too much, and the smell of alcohol when you entered his room in the morning was palpable. The interview room in which I'd secreted 'Joe' was smallish and three people in it made a crowd.

We'd only been in the interview room for about ten minutes before 'Joe' addressed the officer senior in rank to me and said, 'Pardon me for asking, Mr X, but do you like a drink?'

The officer stuttered and stammered, and his complexion blazed even more florid than normal before he said, 'Why? What are you asking that for?'

Joe, who was no silly wee boy, said, 'Because someone in the room is howling of booze, and I know Mr Gallacher and me are both teetotal.'

Things went downhill rather rapidly following that observation, and I had to enlist another officer to help convey 'Joe' back to Barlinnie. When I resumed physical contact with 'Joe' after prison release I caught a broadside.

I always made it clear with informants that I ran the show not them, but I was mindful that their personal security was at stake. Consequently, on this occasion I let him unload on me. Joe had come from a background where alcohol had wrecked the home and he had an aversion to it.

'Mr Gallacher, you want us to keep on speaking, don't ever bring a boozer to meet me. They can't be trusted.'

By that time I'd already fallen out with this senior officer (another in a long line) over the incident, and when it came to my appraisal I didn't get the grades I felt my work and results evidenced. He tried to disguise it by saying, 'I know that's probably not what you deserve, but if I mark you too highly it won't leave room for improvement the next time around.' I told him that was bollocks and that an appraisal should reflect what you deserve.

I'm sure he knew very well that come my next appraisal he would be elsewhere and that's how it proved.

When the guidelines for the handling of informants altered I spoke to each of those I used individually, and made them aware of the revised systems and procedures. I emphasised to them that these were now official instructions, and that even though it may result in a loss of information I was not prepared to risk disciplinary action by failing to adhere to them, or by deviating from them.

As with most people when faced with a decision they made the choice that best suited their interests and self-preservation.

48

TEA (SET) AND (NO) SYMPATHY

Coincidence plays a greater part in police work than one would expect, and a murder in Gourlay Street in Springburn, in March 1999, bore that out, and also how a random sequence of events and a few words spoken in anger can end in murder.

I'd covered an alleged break-in to a flat in the Springburn area earlier in the afternoon. The flat was a hovel and occupied by a couple who clearly had drug abuse issues. It didn't take long to establish that there hadn't been a break-in. They'd lost the key, forced the door of the council property and had told the uniform officers that someone must have broken in.

No crime report had been filed yet, and it would have been a waste of time and paperwork arresting them. The flat was council property and would be repaired either way. From force of habit I asked them if they had any information that would prevent me from charging them with wasting police time. I don't know yet why I did that because although I used informants extensively I avoided, as a rule, utilising drug addicts or prostitutes as a source of information.

I tended not to use them because they were the subject of regular arrests, and I always believed that they trotted out the same information to any officer who arrested them, which meant it was never current, or was fourth- or fifth-hand information. Additionally, both types were unreliable, as they would say just about anything to try and alleviate their arrest situation.

Consequently when he gave me the nickname 'Gordy' and the mobile phone number of a man he said was involved in drug dealing in our area, I simply scribbled it down and put it in my pocket with the intention of checking out the man later (much later). The type of crime he alleged this male was involved in was so commonplace that I didn't even give it a first thought, far less a second.

Some hours later, along with David, I was called to the scene of a stabbing at Gourlay Street. The male occupant of one of the ground-floor flats had left his house on hearing a disturbance at the close mouth and been confronted with a male he'd previously been feuding with. He'd been stabbed on the steps of the close and then managed to get inside and shut the controlled entry door to the close.

From there he made it to the kitchen of his flat where he told his partner that he'd been stabbed and gave the nickname of his attacker. He was taken by ambulance to the Royal Infirmary but died a short time later. He'd been stabbed on the wrist, but the fatal wound had been to the left side of his chest, and had pierced the right ventricle of the heart.

David and I concerned ourselves initially with the preservation of the crime scene and the interviewing of witnesses, and one thing we did notice were gouge marks on the outside of the controlled entry door. They looked as if they could well have been the result of a knife having been plunged into the frame, and so while I knocked on the doors of the other occupants in the close David supervised the photographing and subsequent removal of the door.

We hoped that should we be lucky and recover the murder weapon, then perhaps a forensic scientist would be able, through measurement and examination, to confirm that the weapon recovered matched the gouge marks in the door.

When interviewing witnesses the nickname 'Gordy' cropped up again and eventually the three cherries fell into place with me, and I dug the piece of paper from my pocket, and there staring me in the face was the same nickname and a means to identify him. I showed David the paper and he responded with, 'What? Have we got a deaf and dumb witness?'

'Well partly. We've got a dummy . . . me!' was the best I could muster.

He hadn't covered the alleged break-in earlier that day with me, so had no idea I'd been carrying the possible solution around in my pocket.

From a check with the phone provider we managed to get a name and address, cross-referenced them with a PNC check on the nickname and found ourselves with a suspect. When we went to the last-known address, however, it was a housing complex for the homeless or the socially excluded, and our suspect was in the wind.

We had a possible suspect but needed more evidence, and the following day brought that. A social worker contacted the office to say that he may have information relevant to the murder. He'd had a case-review meeting with a male, and at the meeting the man had seen an evening newspaper lying on the social worker's desk. The front page carried the murder as the main headline. The man had told the social worker that he had been present at the murder.

Armed with the name and address of our potential witness, David and I set out to grab him up for interview. I have to confess that we were both sceptical en route. It seemed just too good to be true. We reached a set of sandstone flats near Glasgow Cross, and our luck held when our potential witness answered the door.

Neither David nor I actually told him our reason for being there. We used the standard phrases that detectives for decades, and in all cities in the world, use when they're looking to sweet-talk someone to a police office without declaring their hand.

It would have run along the lines of 'You'll know what it's about', or 'There's something we need to speak to you about', but with the addition that, 'We've stupidly left the paperwork at the office and need that, so could we speak to you there?' It would have been something like that, but deliberately leaving the purpose of the visit vague.

Once at the office and in an interview room we declared our hand, and were met initially with blank looks, denials and pleas of ignorance. He had substance-abuse issues, which he was trying hard to address, and came from a decent background. Unwittingly, he'd found himself in a nightmare scenario and was wrestling with his conscience. When we made it clear we weren't going to go away, the pangs of conscience surfaced and in what was tantamount to a plea for assistance asked, 'What do you want me to do?'

'I want you to do the right thing,' was all I said in response. Only eight words, but they were enough to open the tap and prompt him to tell us what had happened.

He knew the suspect Gordon MacLachlan and had been with him during the day. MacLachlan had been arguing with his girlfriend, and had bought a tea set to give her as a peace offering. When he got to her Springburn flat and gave her the present it wasn't the salve he hoped it would be. Instead, his girlfriend began to berate him for wasting money they didn't have on a tea set. The gift rejection so infuriated McLachlan that he stormed from the house motioning our witness to follow him.

Our witness said that McLachlan believed the victim had been saying that he (McLachlan) was using the victim's close mouth to deal drugs, and had made it known that he intended to put a stop to it. From the direction of travel the witness realised that McLachlan was heading for Gourlay Street and tried to pacify him, but McLachlan wouldn't pay heed, and when he arrived at his victim's flat he banged twice on his living-room window.

When the victim appeared at the controlled entry to the flat McLachlan produced what the witness described as an SAS-type dagger of about ten inches in length, which our witness hadn't known he had in his possession, and stabbed the victim.

Our witness had been utterly horrified at what had taken place. It was haunting him and that guilt had manifested itself in the spontaneous outburst in his social worker's office, and ultimately led to him sitting in a room with us. After we'd got his statement down we read it back to him under tape-recorded conditions, and he agreed it was an accurate representation of what he'd told us and signed it.

As with the witnesses to the murder of the Procurator Fiscal Depute he'd had to relive the horrible events and was understandably upset, so I fetched him a cup of hot tea and a chocolate biscuit to take the edge off the trauma. To try and shift his mind from the murder and sitting with a cup of tea, David engaged him in small talk about his background. As I've said murder is utterly grim, but every cop will tell you humorous situations do arise during investigations, and it would be disingenuous to claim otherwise.

In chatting, our witness told us that his father ran a public house near the city centre, and as a means of attracting clientele his father would put on gigs for up-and-coming bands. One evening, he had a gig that had sold particularly well. His father was at the door collecting tickets when a group of people appeared looking to get in to see the gig. When his father asked for their tickets one of the group pointed to a tall, bespectacled, quiff-haired individual and said, 'Don't you know who he is? That's Elvis Costello.'

His father, who was a rough Irishman, responded in his best brogue,

'Elvis Costello? I couldn't give a fuck if he's Elvis fucking Presley. He needs a ticket to get in.'

Exit stage left, the alleged Mr Costello and entourage.

Two days later we 'pinged' MacLachlan's mobile phone and discovered he was only a short distance from Maryhill office. A quick check of his associates on the criminal intelligence system led us to a flat. When we gained entrance to the flat the female occupant tried to deny she knew MacLachlan. We found a male who gave David and me a different name, but a check of his chest area told us we had the right man.

Our suspect had been a member of Combat 18 – a neo-Nazi organisation which originated in Britain and held extremist views, most especially in relation to immigrants and 'non-whites'. The '18' derives from the initials of Adolph Hitler and equates to the first (A) and eighth, (H) letters of the Latin alphabet. MacLachlan had 'C18' tattooed on his chest.

He was twenty-six years old and had been sentenced to three years in 1996 for cutting off someone's nose. He'd been released early under licence in 1998. Under interview, he revealed himself to be every bit as odious as one would expect a member of Combat 18 to be. He certainly didn't do himself any favours, and at the end of the interview we charged him with murder. It was a solid case, but Donald Findlay, QC, who was to represent MacLachlan at the future judicial proceedings, was to prove his usual formidable self.

49

PORTOLOGY FOR BEGINNERS

Until I'd taken a forensic medicine course at Glasgow University, I'd been ignorant of how accused persons prosecuted in the High Court, and who qualified for legal aid, were allocated a Queen's Counsel (QC). On the course there had been an input from an eminent QC who indicated that it operated on a 'taxi for hire' type system.

The QCs had a rota, and whoever was next in line when a case emerged was allocated as defence counsel. That system operated in such a manner to ensure that individual Counsel was not tainted by either the nature of the case or the client(s) they represented.

At trial I presented my evidence and Mr Findlay began his cross-examination. He did not contest my procedures, but he did enquire what condition our eyewitness to the murder was in when David and I had interviewed him. I told him I felt he was lucid and credible.

Mr Findlay persisted, querying whether he had been suffering from withdrawal symptoms, and attempted to have me list the symptoms a drug abuser undergoing withdrawal would display. I countered that I was not medically qualified, and therefore it would be remiss of me to try and list the symptoms of drug withdrawal.

I knew Mr Findlay was looking to cast doubt on our witness by suggesting that, when interviewed, he hadn't been fully *compos mentis*, and therefore his recollection may have been unreliable. When I persisted in my lack of qualifications to list drug withdrawal symptoms, Mr Findlay declared that I had worked Saracen and Possilpark for quite some time, and that every person on a Saracen street corner could list drug withdrawal symptoms. When I told him that I bowed to his better knowledge of that (i.e. what took place at Saracen corners) that pretty much ended my cross-examination.

He is one of the foremost QCs in the country, however, and when he came to the cross-examination of David he also displayed his erudition. David had given his evidence in chief, and part of that evidence had been in relation to the gouge marks on the entrance door of the close mouth. The door had been produced in its entirety in the court-room while David waxed lyrical on how the gouge marks displayed every indication of having been caused by a knife.

I'd watched David give evidence in court several times. He was well-educated, had a degree, was very thorough in his court preparation, and was both a strong and credible witness. However, when Mr Findlay asked him in cross-examination when he'd obtained his qualification in 'portology' his frown of puzzlement was palpable.

I could see he was thinking frantically, and although no dummy he hadn't a clue what Mr Findlay was on about, and when cops under cross-examination can't grasp the line of questioning they immediately begin to feel like the cheese in the mousetrap.

David then did what every cop under cross-examination and stalling for thinking time does: 'I'm sorry, could you repeat the question?' When Mr Findlay did just that, and David still hadn't figured what he meant he was forced to profess his genuine ignorance at the line of questioning.

Hopefully, I'll be forgiven if I paraphrase. In his deep, almost drawling voice Mr Findlay said, 'Portology! You've spent the last several minutes presenting yourself to the court as an expert witness on the subject.'

David had to concede that he had no idea what 'portology' meant and Mr Findlay put him out of his misery by telling him it was the study of doors. He'd kippered David with a wonderful line which may have been one of his best cross-examination put-downs. We were fortunate though that, in the grand scheme of things, it didn't matter. The jury concentrated on the evidence before them and returned a 'Guilty' verdict.

I told David that if he'd had a proper education which had involved Latin he'd have known that *portus* was the Latin for door and worked it out. Truth be told? If I'd worked the crime scene and taken the door, and David had transported the witnesses and Mr Findlay had put the same question to me, I'd have been wriggling like a fish on a hook worse than David had been. Oh, and I'm still not convinced that Mr Findlay didn't invent the phrase.

50

IT'S CALLED A 'THREAT TO LIFE WARNING' FOR A REASON

'Frank McPhie's just been shot dead outside his house.'

I knew the information was 100% accurate, because it was David who was the voice on the other end of the phone. I was at home and it was late evening, and although the news jolted me it didn't come as a complete shock.

About six weeks previously, I'd stood with David in McPhie's ground-floor home in a sandstone tenement block in Guthrie Street which was only about 300 or 400 yards from Maryhill Police Office. I'd been sent to deliver a 'threat to life warning'.

If Vass and Bennett were bastards, McPhie took the phrase to a wholly different dimension. Twice he had faced charges of murder, and twice the jury had returned verdicts unique to Scots Law of 'Not Proven'. He was savage, brutal and utterly callous.

He'd been found guilty of a robbery in 1978, and been given five years. He repeated the crime in 1986, and been given another five-year sentence. In 1990, he'd been charged with, but not convicted of, a further armed robbery, before being involved in a £200,000 drug deal in 1992, which earned him an eight-year sentence.

While serving the latter sentence in Perth Prison he was charged with murdering a fellow inmate, William Toye. Toye, who was far from a saint himself, was in Perth Prison for having murdered a man who was scheduled to give evidence against Toye's brother in an upcoming trial. McPhie was charged with entering Toye's cell and stabbing him to death, but the jury decided that the Crown had failed to establish McPhie's guilt beyond reasonable doubt, and he received the first of his 'Not Proven' verdicts.

While in Perth Prison, McPhie was visited by his friend Colin McKay. McKay was another with a reputation for violence. He was about 6'1" and kept himself in shape through visits to boxing gyms. On a couple of these visits McKay was accompanied by Chris McGrory with whom he was friendly.

McGrory saw himself as an upcoming entrepreneur. He had no ostensible means of income, but was able to afford the upkeep of three horses. He had contacts in Dublin and intelligence suggested he was involved in the drugs trade.

In September 1997, just a couple of months after McPhie had been released from jail, McGrory flew to Dublin to be married. McKay was there as his best man, and McPhie acted as an usher. Following the wedding, McGrory and his bride flew to Paris, before returning to Dublin for a christening and then home. Two days after returning to Glasgow, he was found dead in a transit van near a Milngavie golf club. He'd been strangled to death.

McKay and McPhie were arrested and charged with the murder. At the trial, the jury returned verdicts of 'Not Proven'.

McPhie was now clear of all criminal charges and free to continue activities which befitted his pitiless nature. He arranged dog fights involving pit bull terriers and bastardisations of that breed. He 'coursed' i.e., he went out at night and used lurcher type dogs that he kept in kennels to hunt and kill deer.

He would hunt on golf courses and farmland, and when confronted by a farmer would intimidate them. In doing so, he realised another means of earning money. He extorted money from the farmers, and if they failed to pay, their barns would be the subject of fire-raising.

With his already fearsome reputation growing, owing in no small part to his having twice walked free from charges of taking human lives, it's fair to assume that McPhie regarded himself as a major gangster, with no need to fear, or be wary of offending other villains.

It was no doubt that reckless disregard that saw me standing in his living room along with David. We'd been allowed into the house by his wife, and had been sent to warn him that we were in possession of credible intelligence that his life was in danger.

Anyone who's ever been in McPhie's company, or had any dealings with him, no matter how fleeting, will remember his eyes. He wasn't the tallest – around 5'9" – but was stockily built, and had close-cropped, white, receding hair, and slightly ferrety features. He emanated a constant air of aggression, but it was the eyes that told you everything; two chips of blue flint that held neither warmth nor humour. A killer's eyes.

I gave him the spiel about his life being in danger, and the procedures he should adopt as precautionary measures. For all the attention he paid to my words I would have been just as well reciting a nursery rhyme.

He tended to speak in a rapid fire tone. 'You've no' come over here for that.'

Totally puzzled, I asked him what he was talking about

'Ah know you, and you widnae come over here for just that. You're up tae something.'

'What? You don't think letting you know your life is in danger is reason enough to come over and warn you? Try and not *know me* so well, and try listening to what I'm telling you.'

'You're no' over just for that. You widnae come over without another reason.'

'Yeah. That's right. You're too smart for me, Frank. As I was walking along the hallway I hid a shotgun and a kilo of heroin. Can you try and just focus on the actual reason I came over here, which is to tell you your life may be in danger.'

'Right, you've tellt me.'

'Have a nice evening.'

I logged the fact that I'd delivered the warning.

On 10 May 2000, as McPhie parked his van on Kelvindale Road to walk the twenty yards to his close entrance on Guthrie Street, he was shot once and died at the scene. The gunman had fired from a concealed position in the drying area of a block of flats opposite McPhie's house.

The shooter was so confident and in control that he even left behind the rifle, complete with telescopic sight, at the scene. In addition to the close proximity to the police office, it was an additional 'fuck you' to the police as if saying, 'See what your forensic boys can do with that.'

As it transpired, the forensic scientists did manage to obtain a 'low copy' DNA profile. The only trouble was that it belonged to one of the ballistics examiners.

David, Stevie and I were seconded to the enquiry and as soon as the crime scene was released David and I wanted to familiarise ourselves with the area the shot had been fired from. When we checked the surrounding area and tried to imagine ourselves in the mind of the murderer we walked various routes he may have taken.

When we checked the stairwell we could see the black powder smudges from the fingerprint dust, but there were whole sections of the stairwell that had been overlooked.

If the gunman had fled down the stairwell it is fair to assume that he would have been moving very quickly. Each set of landing stairs sloped downwards and fleeing a scene, a gunman may well have placed his hands on the underside of one, or all, of the stairwells to counter-balance losing his footing. None of these had been fingerprinted. It was a glaring omission in the administration of the crime scene.

The senior management had appointed a Crime Scene Manager, but had I overall responsibility for an investigation I would personally have made sure I was satisfied a scene had been properly administered before I gave permission to open it.

An omission like that stems from the compartmentalising system adopted within this country in respect of major enquiries. Of course you have to have faith in officers allocated certain tasks, but if the buck ultimately stops at you it would be advantageous to maintain a 'weather eye'. David and I made a call to the Identification Bureau to have those areas printed, thankfully before they had been accessed by members of the public.

As is usual with enquiries of that type, all sorts of theories and motives were bandied about, and most of them had neither substance nor were based in fact.

There were stories that McPhie had been chased home following a motorway incident; that the killing was revenge for the murder of Chris McGrory, by Republican contacts McGrory had in Ireland; that an embittered farmer in frustration at the fire-raising and/or extortion threats had been responsible; that he had tried to muscle his way into the drugs and/or dog fighting markets. Those were the less fanciful possibilities.

Early in the enquiry, David and I received information from a source in Cadder that McPhie had been involved in a road rage type incident on Balmore Road, with a younger member of the Daniels family (as I indicated in chapter 38 the Daniels were and are among the richest and most ruthless crime families in Scotland). Knowing that this member of the family often used a Chinese takeaway in the Lambhill area McPhie had allegedly ambushed him one evening, and had stabbed him in revenge for the road incident.

During this alleged attack McPhie had been masked, but so arrogant was he that he decided to pull up his mask during the attack in order to let his victim know exactly who was responsible. I have to say this act of bravado probably hadn't been necessary because one glimpse of those eyes and the victim would have known who had ambushed him.

That enraged some members of that family and supposedly threats were uttered about retaliation. On hearing this, McPhie allegedly presented himself at a scrap yard in Lochburn Road, Maryhill, owned by the Daniels family. He made it known that he was aware of the rumours, and that should anyone have a problem with him then here he stood, highly visible.

I can only wonder whether a combination of his own aggressive nature and having twice been acquitted of taking human lives had imbued McPhie with a sense of power or invulnerability. Perhaps he presumed that given his reputation for ruthlessness he need fear no one or concern himself with the reputation of others, but he seemed intent on disturbing the wasp nest.

I always remember my father telling me, very early on, when playing football that no matter how cute, hard or dirty a player you thought you were, there was always someone cuter, harder and dirtier.

We were part of an enquiry team so had to pursue the allocated lines of enquiry thoroughly, but I was fairly content, and I'm sure Stevie and David were of the same mind, that the answer lay with the information we'd received. Whether through bravado or by underestimating his enemy McPhie had placed himself quite literally in the firing line.

Sun Tzu, the ancient Chinese philosopher and battle strategist, wrote a book entitled *The Art of War*. It is required reading for all military personnel, and his first rule is that, 'There is no greater disaster than underestimating your enemy.' McPhie should have considered that.

Being in possession of very good intelligence as to who was responsible for a crime is all well and good, but intelligence does not translate into solid evidence. Finding a sufficiency of evidence to substantiate a charge against someone in relation to this murder would definitely not be easy.

On one occasion, David and I were tasked with adopting a Uriah Heep 'very 'umble' approach to try and persuade an associate of McPhie's to come into the office for some conversation. He'd visited him in prison, and along with McPhie kept lurcher dogs at a 'kenneled' piece of ground near Maryhill Police Office. When we spoke to him we had to endure some disrespect at the kennels in order to have some sort of conversation.

That we put up with some nonsense on that occasion may have caused him to form the impression that we were a couple of mugs, because the next time we went to speak to him was again at the kennels, and he had an audience. He began speaking to us in the same manner he'd adopted previously, but this time the only thing we needed from him was an attitude adjustment.

He was tall, fit and capable and over time has also walked from two murder charges, but at that meeting he was dragged bodily in front of his onlooking acolytes and dumped in the police car. I think it is fair to say we understood one another after that.

There was a chain of thought from certain sections that the enquiry would, given the reputation of the victim and potential suspects, fall into the 'too difficult to solve' category. Personally, I'm an optimist, and I never approached an enquiry with anything other than a positive attitude, although I was realistic enough to appreciate that this murder enquiry was far more likely to be a distance run rather than a sprint.

We had to try various levels of approach. While some people may have been prepared to provide us with bits and pieces off the record, they would not commit to an official statement, and I had a degree of sympathy and understanding for their stance.

At one point, David and I targeted someone who was a disqualified driver but who had ties to possible suspects. His previous sentence for driving while banned had resulted in a three-year term of imprisonment, and when we caught him driving in Balmore Road in defiance of the ban he knew he was looking at a substantial custodial sentence.

We gave him the pitch, but he wasn't the least interested in the bait. The police had the ability to take away his liberty, but those on the other side of the law had demonstrated graphically how they could impose the ultimate sentence – death.

Stevie had been tasked with trying to source the origin of the weapon and even that was frustrating. The weapon had been manufactured abroad in 1953, in a country which had no recognised method of 'rifling'; a method of ensuring that the barrel will safely accommodate ammunition designed for use with that particular weapon.

Having been imported from a country with no recognised 'proving' it had undergone tests in this country before it was classed as acceptable for sale. Records showed it had been proved in this country in 1956, following which it disappeared.

Stevie's research showed that just about every second farmer had one of those rifles, but of more concern he also found that the Forces down south were rather lax in their yearly checks. They were supposed to actually attend at the licence holder's home and physically see the gun and confirm that the certificate holder still owned the weapon.

However, many of the police firearm licensing departments operated on the principle that the farmer/owner would contact them should he sell the gun on. The gun proved impossible to marry to the last owner.

As early as the second day of the enquiry, information had been input about a named male from the Maryhill area having travelled to Ayrshire to source a rifle. David, Stevie and I knew that the male was an associate of the Daniels family and voiced the opinion that the information was credible.

Senior management, however, didn't class the information as being high priority, and consequently it lay dormant in the system until the enquiry was about to be wound down. Almost in a throwaway, tidy-up, last throw of the dice scenario David and I were sent to a former mining area in Ayrshire to trace and interview a possible witness.

We'd slogged for about nine months and this particular pregnancy didn't look like birthing anytime soon. Although we'd felt at the beginning that the information couldn't be discounted the fact that it had been deemed low priority probably meant we were in a cynical mood. Certainly, I don't recall either of us making the journey with any heightened sense of expectation.

It was perhaps in some way reminiscent of when we had been contacted by the social worker who told us one of his cases had confessed to witnessing a murder in Springburn. It seemed too good to be true.

We knocked on the cottage door and were admitted by a young man in his mid-twenties who told us his 'mother wouldn't be long'.

He must have caught our frowns of puzzlement because he followed up with, 'You're from The Provident, are ye no'?'

'Close enough,' said David. 'We're the polis.'

I'm sure in days gone by, after months or years sifting tons of dirt, grit and iron pyrites, panhandlers knew instinctively when the 'real thing' lay in their pans.

Similarly, any cop who has worked a long and difficult enquiry and encountered their umpteenth cul-de-sac, or bottomed out another false lead, knows when they've hit pay dirt.

The almost palpable look of resignation that crossed his face activated the radar and banished any cynicism we may have had about this task. We'd knocked on a profitable door.

We didn't start right in or even confirm his worst fears. I think we threw him the well-used line, 'You'll know why we're here', and just steered him towards a nearby police office. Almost ten hours later, we sat in the unmarked police car at an Ayrshire harbour, watching the boats, and eating fish and chips with our witness.

In the interim, between knocking on his door and sitting there, we'd managed, eventually, to tease from our reluctant witness the information he had. The ability to persuade people to impart information about distasteful crimes and occurrences is a skill. Interrogation isn't about beating and torturing. Thankfully, that method of gleaning information disappeared from the police around the same time as the endemic drinking culture.

There's no skill involved in that. You could get a baboon to beat on someone. It wouldn't make it a detective. I've never been in the situation thankfully, but from a personal point of view I'm fairly certain, that if you started to beat on me to get information it would just make me thrawn and determined not to tell you.

Alternatively, I would imagine some people will tell you anything to stop the physical abuse, but that then results in false convictions, as borne out by the myriad of acquittals in England emanating from 1970s and early 1980s. Besides, my mother used to maintain 'you catch more flies with honey than vinegar'.

Our interviewee could have walked out of the police office at any time. He hadn't been detained or arrested, but it did take a long time of silence, denials, half-truths, small admissions, patient probing, checking and cross-checking before we got to the truth. There are a few officers, but sadly a declining number, who would spend that length of time and refuse to take 'no' for an answer to get the 'burst'.

As a result of the information gleaned, we eventually, in utter darkness, found ourselves at an area of farmland in Ayrshire where the murder weapon had allegedly been test-fired. Even that didn't go smoothly. Owing to it being so dark and us attempting to be surreptitious we managed to get the car bogged down. Only after we'd ruined our city shoes and suits trying to shift the damn thing did we admit defeat and call Stevie at 1 a.m. in the morning to come and tow us out.

I think he said something along the lines of, 'No problems, chaps. It could have happened to anyone. Glad to be of help'. Yeah, right.

The following morning, together with Scenes of Crime and Ballistics Officers, I rode a helicopter down to the scene, and following the recovery of certain forensic evidence a decision was made that sufficient evidence existed to substantiate a charge against someone.

Our witness was introduced to the Witness Liaison Unit who would assume control and protection of him. Neither David nor I would have any further knowledge of his whereabouts or potential new identity.

Graham Pearson who was the then Assistant Chief Constable in charge of crime for the Force came out to Maryhill to offer David and me his congratulations. I think he may have been one of those who felt the crime would remain unresolved, given the degree of difficulty and passage of time.

As a result of the information gleaned by David and me from the witness interview, and allied to what Ballistics had obtained at the farmland, suspicion fell on a Maryhill man, John McCabe. Consequently arrangements were made to detain McCabe in relation to the murder, with a view to interviewing and subsequently charging him with shooting Frank McPhie. David and I were originally scheduled to detain and attempt to interview McCabe, but at the last minute we were switched to another task. McCabe was a lean, physically fit, capable and volatile individual, and someone at a high level decided he and us would have been potentially combustible.

We were both bitterly disappointed, as we had had invested a lot of time and effort into bringing the enquiry to that point, and I'm certain there wouldn't have been an issue. We dealt with people as we found them, and if we weren't met by confrontation or hostility we didn't introduce it.

McCabe appeared at Glasgow Sheriff Court charged with murdering Frank McPhie and was remanded for seven days, but to date there have been no further judicial proceedings against him for that crime.

51

SHAMELESS

At about 9 a.m. on a Sunday morning, in mid-November 2000, I found myself at home on a day off and about to go out for a run when I took a telephone call from a senior CID officer at Maryhill.

A thirty-year-old foreign national, living and working in Glasgow, had been the victim of rape. He was asking me to investigate. It was Strathclyde policy that owing to the sensitive and political nature of rape cases that a Detective Inspector should be in charge of the enquiry. The officer contacting me qualified, but for whatever reason I was being offered the opportunity to take charge of the enquiry.

Rape is such a detestable crime. It leaves a victim not only with a feeling of defilement, but also of a loss of control and empowerment. I don't think the vast majority of men could begin to appreciate the residual mental scarring and sense of distrust.

There were three types of criminals I particularly loathed and they all related to the preying on the vulnerable, and an exploitation of trust – child molesters, rapists and those bogus workmen who conned old people out of their life savings.

Day off or not, I most definitely wanted the enquiry. I was showered, shaved, changed and in the office within a half hour and I learned that the crime scene was the River Kelvin Walkway, near to the former BBC building in Queen Margaret Drive. There was what they term a Crime Scene Manager down at it, along with Keith Eynon who was the on-call biologist.

Crime Scene Managers attend a specialised course at the Scottish Police College which then supposedly imbues them with the expertise to oversee the preservation, collection and administration of evidence at the scene of a serious crime.

I liked to oversee my own crime scenes, and my expertise didn't emanate from a course but from the practical experience of being at literally hundreds of such scenes. I once attended the scene of a fire-raising which wasn't my enquiry, but I was in the vicinity and was always inquisitive.

The Crime Scene Manager was someone who was supposedly classed as an expert in the field, given that he'd attended the Police College courses and now lectured probationers on the subject. Without even walking his crime scene he declared that there was nothing of an evidential nature as the fire had consumed the cause. I took a walk along the perimeter and located a Zippo lighter which it eventually transpired had been used by the suspect.

My appreciation of expertise in the police always favoured someone who had derived their level of knowledge from a practical apprenticeship.

I always had a fear in the police of screwing up a crime scene, and the source of that fear was probably the biologist attending the scene. While I was a probationer he lectured me and other classmates on evidence preservation. He was so scathing in his assessment of how cops carried out that task that I vowed I would be ultra-vigilant and careful at any scenes I attended. So careful was I that at scenes I always wore two pair of latex gloves in case the sweat caused my fingerprints to 'leak' through the first pair.

I got down to the crime scene to be greeted by Keith Eynon who was head of the Forensic Science Biology Department. He was English, very tall and very thin, with an aquiline nose. He adopted a pseudo-resigned tone of voice.

'When I heard you'd got this I knew you'd be down. I was hoping to get away before you arrived with the pernickety requests.'

'Well, you shouldn't have scared the shit out of me as a probationer with your tales of police incompetence when it came to evidence preservation, should you?'

The scene was an inlet which was bordered by the River Kelvin, which at that time of year was in full spate and very fast-flowing. There was a footpath adjacent to one side of the river banking.

I began to walk the scene and make notes on a clipboard. There were signs of spittle at the inlet, and also there were cigarette stubs which looked comparatively fresh in a puddle on the river-banking footpath.

I pointed them out to Keith, and told him I was looking for him to swab the sputum and collect the cigarette stubs for DNA analysis.

There were two detectives already in attendance, one being the Crime Scene Manager. When he heard my requests to Keith, he may have taken them as a slight because he began to ask why I would wish to collect a cigarette stub that was so far from the scene. His view was that it could have been dropped by a passer-by that morning, well after the crime.

I didn't answer that one, which may have emboldened him because with regard to swabbing the sputum he said that umpteen people may have been spitting and, in fact, he may even have spat. I'd still been writing on my clipboard until that comment which caused my head to snap up as if I'd been hit with an uppercut.

'Are you telling me you spat at a crime scene?'

His colleague sensing a Vesuvius type eruption interjected to say that what he meant was that he'd been spitting into the river. As politely as possible I told him that it was my enquiry, and I'd oversee the gathering of potential evidence, and thanked him for his efforts.

The attack had taken place at around 4.30 a.m. that morning, when the girl had been walking home alone following a social evening. She was in a residential area of well-to-do Kelvinside when she was grabbed from the rear by a man who placed his hand over her mouth. The shock caused her to lose her balance and fall over a small garden wall. The man jumped over after her, seized her by the hair, and said words similar to, 'If you scream, you die,' or, 'Scream and I'll kill you.'

That verbal threat naturally placed the victim in fear of her life, and was sufficient to subdue her and render her compliant. Her attacker then took hold of her arm in a grip that was strong but would have allayed the suspicions of any passers-by, and gave the impression that they were a couple.

The male then directed the girl 500 or 600 yards along Kelvin Walkway to the remote inlet where he subjected her to varying degrees of sexual assault, culminating in her rape.

Her ordeal was ended when two young men who'd been at a party at a nearby flat took a wrong turn off the footpath onto the inlet. The victim knew she had been presented with a window of opportunity and pleaded with the boys for help.

Her assailant tried to pretend that they were a couple and were having sex, but the victim persisted in her pleas. The boys were timid by nature and didn't try and grab the suspect, but to their credit they stood their ground, and helped the victim back to her flat. Throughout the journey to her flat the victim maintained that she'd been an unwilling participant, and reaffirmed that to her flatmate when she arrived home.

A call was made to the police at around 5:30 a.m. and after an initial interview the victim pointed out the crime scene, following which she agreed to be medically examined. Unfortunately, and for whatever reason – perhaps language complications – potentially valuable forensic evidence was lost.

It meant the degree of difficulty in solving the rape had just increased by quite a margin.

I walked the route which included large unpopulated areas, and was joined at one point by a senior officer who began to bemoan the lack of CCTV. He'd come from the city centre area, which enjoyed almost blanket camera coverage, which in turn meant crime solving was a whole lot easier than it was in our division.

From knocking on doors along the route the victim had been forced to take I located a witness. The witness had heard a male voice at the relevant time saying words to the effect of, 'Do as I say,' or, 'You'll do as I tell you.'

Unfortunately, the witness had been in bed and didn't know towards whom the words had been directed.

It only lent credence to the victim whose credibility was never in doubt anyway.

I made sure the Force's media services department kept the enquiry in the public eye, but there weren't any real leads. I had contacted Criminal Intelligence for a list of possible suspects who had previously carried out similar crimes, but that only threw up just about every offender throughout Scotland who'd ever been involved in some kind of sexual crime.

Exactly a week after the attack, I arranged for motorists and passers-by using the route of the abduction and rape to be quizzed to see if that would produce any results. I'd already pulled a ten-hour shift, but I grabbed a couple of hours sleep and was back out for 2 a.m. to brief and assist the cops delegated to the task. The reason I was back out wasn't that I didn't trust the cops to do the job properly or I was unable to delegate, but I subscribed to the 'example by involvement' theory.

If people with no involvement in an enquiry are asked to carry out a thankless task – and stopping people and vehicles at 4.30 a.m. on a November morning falls into that category – and the officer tasking them is tucked up in bed, then just maybe something of value may be missed.

I spoke to a taxi driver who had picked up a fare the previous week at 5 a.m. on Great Western Road at Belmont Street, which was very near to the crime scene area. The man was sweating profusely and, unprompted, passed off his sweaty appearance as being the result of his having been running around trying to find friends he'd been separated from. From the description there was a good possibility it was the suspect, but the taxi driver couldn't recall the drop-off point and hadn't called in the fare.

I really needed a bit of luck, and sometimes you get a prayer answered.

With the advance agreement of the victim I'd gone up to the flat with two of the girls from what was then known as the Female and Child Unit. They were specially trained in the interviewing of victims of sexual and physical abuse.

I had provided the girls with a list of the points I wanted clarified, but I also wanted to gauge whether the victim would be able to identify her assailant, and if she would be strong enough to see things through should I manage to arrest her attacker.

Sadly, although utterly blameless, many victims because of the trauma and a misplaced sense of shame won't even report an attack, far less remain resolute throughout the enquiry and subsequent judicial proceedings. It takes strength of character to be prepared to have to relive the ordeal in a court of law.

In the flat, I made sure that I was within her vision but well outside her personal space and kept my mouth shut. If it isn't deemed racist she seemed typical of her nationality – stoic and strong-willed. I was sure she had grit.

In her initial statement the victim had indicated that her attacker had licked her breast area, but when examined following the attack that area had not been swabbed. She hadn't been wearing a bra. As the girls were talking it struck me that the sweater she'd been wearing would have rested on her chest area. There could have been transference of saliva from breast to jumper.

I called Martin Fairley and Keith who were carrying out the forensic examination of the submitted samples and the clothes the victim had been wearing. I rated Martin highly. He was thorough, but just as importantly he was up for the challenge. He would have got there himself no doubt, but DNA profiles were collected from the inside of the sweater and also from a suede jacket she'd worn.

Whenever I inherited a serious crime to investigate I always liked to have a meeting with the chemist and/or biologist who'd be examining the submitted items. Most officers simply handed over the samples to the receptionist. The submitted items were then passed on for examination. That in my opinion depersonalised them in some way. They simply became another item of clothing or shard of glass or a strand of hair.

I liked to try and be up at FHQ just as the scientists were about to have a coffee so I could bribe them with a coffee and biscuit. I'd have a talk with them and provide them with background information on the enquiry. That way the items being examined were no longer simply disembodied objects. I hoped that feeling part of the enquiry would provide an extra incentive.

I'm told that for a period following this rape enquiry, Keith, in his lectures to probationers and in detective training, cited the liaison as a prime example of good practice between investigating officers and forensic scientists.

Ten days after the rape I got the news that the submitted DNA profiles had been 'matched' to a Michael Hirrell whose profile was held on the national DNA database in Birmingham. When I checked the PNC/SCRO (Scottish Criminal Record Office), Hirrell fitted the suspect's description in height, age and hair colour. A check of Criminal Intelligence indicated he was based in Manchester.

I spoke to Paul Moore, a Manchester detective, who'd had extensive dealings with Hirrell and he provided six possible addresses that Hirrel frequented. Paul also told me Hirrell was currently in or around the Manchester area as he was suspected of vandalising his ex-wife's house a day previously.

I submitted a request to the Procurator Fiscal at Glasgow for warrants to search the six Manchester addresses. I was granted the warrants although they had to be countersigned by a Manchester Magistrate, and following that headed to Manchester where I met with Paul: 5'10" strawberry-coloured hair, appraising blue eyes. Very quickly it was clear he was streetwise to the max.

Straight off he started,

'No fookin' weigh he's pullin' that, Jirry. No fookin' weigh at all man.'

In Manchester parlance he was 'mad fer it'. I knew straight off he'd be a pleasure to work with.

Paul had a plan. He left his mobile number with a relative of Hirrell's, emphasising that he needed to speak to him to sort out the alleged vandalism. Hirrell called and arrangements were made to meet him in the Moston housing area of Manchester a few hours later.

Paul drove me to an estate which I'm certain they now use for the series *Shameless* because it was exactly the same type of housing and eclectic mix of residents. We were looking to access a house that over-looked the meeting point, and Paul was offering £50 to the resident most likely.

The first one in the row we tried was a single mother, who answered the door in a crop top and denim shorts. She was about twenty-two and an attractive looking kid. One of the few items of furniture was the high chair in which the baby was seated. She said she could use the money, but didn't want any dealings with the police.

That, however, didn't prevent her from saying that if either of us (or both) wanted to come back later with the £50 ... We slipped her £10 to get the baby some nappies before, once outside, almost collapsing with laughter at the proposition.

The next house was a non-starter from the moment the door opened. Rastafarian and dreadlocks like a Medusa; we were almost high from the residual fumes. 'I and I no' truck wi' Bulmon.' (I think that's slang for the police). 'Have a nice day, sir.'

The third was a possibility as it was lacking residents and we gained entry through a window. Sadly for us, it also lacked the middle section of the staircase, and we needed height to see the meeting point. We could have cleared the gap provided we'd been Olympic-class long jumpers or Sherpas with ropes and crampons. In retrospect, it was probably no bad thing because it was the type of house where they'd used the toilet only after all available floor space had been taken up and I hadn't kept up with my Ebola fever virus inoculations.

House number four was lucky and I was glad given the occupant. He was an old boy who lived alone and was happy to let us use an upper bedroom. He wasn't looking for payment, but he got it. He didn't look as if he had much so the £50 would be most welcome.

The only downside was that Hirrell smelled a rat and kept delaying the meet. Eventually, during one of his phone calls, while Paul was keeping him occupied I used his police radio to have the control room trace the location of the call. He was at a kiosk in Bower Street. There was another white-knuckle ride as Paul displayed his rally driving skills, but we got Hirrell near there and took him to Longsight Police Office.

In the interview I managed to get Hirrell talking which was half the battle. He had a habit of addressing you as 'fella' which set my teeth on edge. He thought he was clever. He admitted being in Glasgow that weekend for a family function. He claimed that he had met the victim while walking home and within ten minutes of this meeting was having consensual sex. The sex had been interrupted by the arrival of two boys, and that had left the girl embarrassed.

I managed to highlight inconsistencies and challenge his story on various points. He gave me a detailed description of his movements up to and including the interruption by the two Good Samaritans, but when asked about any conversation having taken place between all the parties his mind suddenly went blank 'as he was pissed'.

When I asked whether the two boys would have any reason to tell lies he had to concede that they hadn't.

The interview continued in that vein and I managed to chip away at his credibility bit by bit, until eventually he said, 'Shut the fuck up! You annoy me.' He then slumped back in the chair, fixed his gaze on the ceiling and refused to answer any further questions.

That had been my intention, and by then I was happy enough with how the interview had gone. I felt that if the tape was played at any future judicial proceedings he would have damned himself in the eyes of the jury.

Hirrell was transported back to Glasgow for an appearance on the Monday at the Sheriff Court, and I was determined that he would not be released on bail, especially given that a decade previously he'd been given a three-year sentence in England for attempted rape. Additionally, I hoped it may provide the victim with some degree of relief knowing he was incarcerated pending trial.

During the period Hirrell had control over his victim he'd managed to obtain certain personal information from her, and I felt given his history there existed a possibility that he *may* have presented a danger to the victim. He also had a history of failing to appear for trial when bailed.

I conveyed these misgivings to the Procurator Fiscal Depute who inherited the investigation, and she did a great job. Hirrell was fully committed for trial and while awaiting the commencement of judicial proceedings tendered a plea of 'Guilty' and was sentenced to eight years' imprisonment.

52

CENTURY DEPRIVATION

I had problems at my division, inasmuch as I hadn't made the progress I felt my dedication and results warranted. I had never hidden my desire to progress in the police, and was ambitious, but not in a get-there-at-any-cost, stab-in-the-back, trample-underfoot-to-get-there type of way.

I wanted to progress as a result of having served a solid apprenticeship, and having demonstrated my ability to deal with every type of enquiry one could reasonably expect to encounter. Indeed, I subscribed to the French scholar Chateaubriand's view that, 'Talent has a long apprenticeship'.

That wasn't the traditional manner of progressing in the police. There were several routes that assisted one's progress, and most of them involved non-involvement. Non-involvement: that is, in anything controversial (in relation to police work); making a difficult or unpopular decision (or any decision at all for that matter); undertaking too many demanding enquiries, or, heaven forbid, remaining at the coal-face to actually learn your trade.

Now some of those routes may have been available to me, but I eschewed them. I was very self-confident, and felt that although my progress may have been hindered as a consequence I would eventually progress through the system. I believed that dedication, self-motivation, knowledge of police systems and procedures, a willingness to undertake further education, a desire to serve the public through doing good police work, and ability would be sufficient qualities to reach my goal. Talk about naive! I stood more chance of performing successful neurosurgery using only a blunt spoon.

Now, I am nothing if not brutally excoriating when self-appraising. To my detriment I didn't suffer fools gladly. I never sought popularity, and could be unheeding of other's sensitivities when focused on bringing an enquiry to a successful conclusion. I was also intolerant of shoddy or slipshod work. Some may term that bullying, but if so they work from a different word definition from me.

I always regarded bullying as preying on someone weak and defenceless, but I viewed confronting lazy, 'can't be bothered', 'take the money and run' officers as being part of my remit as a supervisor. I worked extremely hard, and while I didn't expect others to work to the same standard, I did expect them to provide a value for money return. If addressing those types of issues is classed as bullying, then 'Guilty'.

I was blunt and totally honest with people in the police and that included bosses, and the vast majority of both cops and bosses don't want to hear bad news. I refused to compromise when I felt something was wrong and I'd 'closed the door over' and had words with various high-ranking officers. Additionally, if I perceived someone to be a buffoon, irrespective of rank, I found it extremely difficult to disguise, and that had also made me enemies.

I've always admired people who if they had an issue confronted you face to face, and once the issue had been resolved there were no grudges and you moved on. Unfortunately, the police are populated by the insidious types who, through a phone call, discreet memo, or the whisper in the right ear, can stultify career advancement.

Now, had I been the type to go golfing with bosses, or sit beside them at select football grounds, or my father/brother/uncle/cousin etc. held or had previously held a high rank within the police, or I was a member of a Freemasonic Lodge, or had inveigled myself into the Headquarters set, then my (perceived) failings would have been accommodated. If you are in the right circle within the police then you can do little wrong, but if you are a strong-willed individual who does not have a 'wire' looking out for you then the odds are stacked against you.

A 'wire' in police terms is someone of high-ranking influence who will look out for you, or smooth your path to progression. It exists in every police force throughout the world, and each has their own term for it. e.g. a 'rabbi' or 'padrone'. Through choice, I didn't attend police functions or socialise in police circles, so that excluded me from opportunities to secure a 'wire'.

Also, before anyone perceives a rant against Freemasonry then that is not my intention. I have far too little knowledge of the subject to hold any proper discourse. A senior officer once asked me if I would like him to propose me for membership, but I declined the offer graciously because although I know of numerous examples of Catholics becoming Freemasons, and even given that I'm a lousy example of a Catholic, I don't feel they are compatible. That is a personal view and choice.

Besides, to quote Groucho Marx, 'I don't want to belong to any club that will accept people like me as a member'. I worked with and for officers who were members of a Freemasonic Lodge, and more decent human beings or dedicated officers one couldn't wish to meet or work beside.

Freemasons do, however, have the potential to exert power and influence over promotions and advancement within the police service, and to suggest otherwise would be disingenuous. Having sworn an oath to assist fellow Masons then a Freemason would logically breach that oath should they fail to assist the progress of a fellow Freemason when in a position to do so.

Using influence to assist people with whom you have some kind of connection is human nature and as old as time. I'll guarantee that it occurs in every walk of life, be it the entertainment world, the military, teaching, the construction industry etc. If I was in a position to assist a relative or friend I'd probably do it, but I would hope that I wouldn't do it to the detriment of someone more capable, or if the relative or friend wasn't competent enough to assume the role.

I was acutely aware of how the system operated, and also how my own hubris was a contributory factor in my lack of progress. I'm not sure how a dictionary defines hubris. I've always accepted the definition given to me by a Jesuit, who defined hubris as stemming from Ancient Greek and was excessive pride for which the Gods will in turn punish you. If my pride and commitment in doing the best job I could was to count against me then I wasn't prepared to sacrifice principles to progress.

I'd undeniably excelled during my period at a higher rank and results wise I'd far outperformed every other similar ranking officer in my division. I had to watch, however, as others who had never been tested in a higher rank, or taken charge of any type of serious enquiry, were afforded the opportunity to progress.

Owing to that failure to be afforded a similar opportunity, I'd already requested and had a meeting at Personnel, where I'd requested a transfer to uniform duty, but the request had been denied. I'd been assured that I was on the radar for advancement and was asked to be patient a little longer. I returned to my division, but had no faith in the assurance as I'd been hearing the same nonsense for years. They seemed happy to dangle the carrot to ensure the results kept coming, but not the reward.

In May 2001, however, that failure to progress became tinged with something more sinister and left me determined at all costs to transfer.

In truth, I had neither admiration, affection, nor respect for the vast majority of senior management operating within my division at that time, but following the incident you could add equal measures of disgust and pity to that equation.

Every morning at 8.30 a.m. there would be a meeting within the muster room of all on-duty personnel, to review the crimes and items of the preceding twenty-four hours. Superintendents, Chief Inspectors, Detective Chief Inspectors, uniform Shift Inspectors, Detective Inspectors etc.; all attended. The Divisional Commander and Deputy were the only real ranking officers who didn't normally attend. When Detective Sergeants, Shift Sergeants, Community Officers and Detective Constables were factored in it was a fair sized audience.

The Saturday previously Celtic had clinched the 2000/2001 Scottish Football League and, as usual whenever this happened, irrespective of whether the winners were Celtic or Rangers, there followed instances of disorder.

The weekend crimes and offences were usually reviewed by one of the Detective Inspectors, and to assist this he would obtain a printout of the crimes. The printout was a synopsis only, and provided a time, date and location of the crime as well as the MO involved. If an arrest had been made the name, address and date of birth of the person charged were included. That was it.

The Detective Inspector when reviewing these crimes began with the words, 'I see there were a lot of Catholics locked up at the weekend.' I was thunderstruck. I'd known him for about fifteen years and had worked with him on enquiries when we held lesser rank, and had played football with and against him. I had never imagined him to be a bigot, but here he was attributing a religion to someone, based solely on his interpretation of their name. He'd been unable to control his fury and bitterness simply because a team he didn't support had won a league.

I waited and waited in vain for any of the officers, senior or equal in rank, to chastise him over the comment, but they sat in silence and by their silence afforded that comment their tacit approval. To this day, I still don't know why someone who prides themselves on strength of character didn't stand up and confront them all at that meeting, but I think that by that time I'd had a bellyful of their lies, false promises and glad-handing their friends.

A couple of officers indicated to me after the meeting was over that they'd been offended by the remark, and I think they were hoping I'd pursue the matter, but I'd fought enough battles in my career by that point, and all I wanted was to remove myself from their poisonous atmosphere.

Bigotry wasn't practised, nor would it have been tolerated by my parents or the secular and religious teachers who'd been instrumental in my character formation. As a kid, when it came to football, I went to watch the Partick Thistle team of George Niven, Sandy Brown, John Harvey, Hugh Tinney, David McParland, Ian 'Cowboy' Cowan et al.

As a police officer, the only thing that concerned me was that whoever I was working with wasn't corrupt, would put in a decent shift, would go through the doors with me, and would be properly prepared to give evidence at judicial proceedings. Otherwise, I couldn't have cared less had they been a gay, amputee, Taoist. It appeared my equanimity wasn't shared. It was time to leave them breathing their sixteenth-century oxygen.

I applied again for transfer and wasn't prepared to be dissuaded by Personnel a second time. In summer that year I moved to 'N' Division where I would work at Cumbernauld, Coatbridge and Airdrie. These are rural towns situated in Lanarkshire some fifteen to twenty miles from Glasgow.

53

AFTERTHOUGHTS AND FORWARD

Several months after I'd left Maryhill I found myself once more in the role of Acting Inspector and standing in the kitchen of a council house in the Coatbridge area. If things hadn't been so desperate I may well have laughed out loud at the incongruity of the situation. Minus the mask, I was facing Freddy Krueger.

I'd made the choice to leave Maryhill, where I'd loved working, but it had still been a bitter pill to swallow. Over the preceding decades I'd been fortunate to work with some first class officers and found myself involved in numerous high profile enquiries. I'd hoped my time and work there would have led to a career progression, but it hadn't materialised.

Now though, having spent my police career working predominantly in Glasgow, I found myself in a 'foreign' environment, but realising very quickly, that the more things changed the more they stayed the same. In chapter 3 I recounted how I'd stood on the street as a 'fresh out of the box' rookie trying to reason with a father in his home threatening harm to himself and his family. Two decades on and I was again faced with a husband and father within his family home, again intent on self-harm and potentially a risk to the safety of his family. Nothing changed in police work, but at least this time we were indoors, so had (slightly) more control and could converse face to face. Over the years numerous technological and scientific advances have been tested and introduced as a means to assist cops in their job, yet despite these welcome additions the principle hasn't differed radically since 1829, when Sir Robert Peel, the Home Secretary at the time, established the world's first professional police force, The Met. (London's Metropolitan Police).

At the end of the day, policing revolves around an appointed group of human beings tasked with ensuring there is a form of law and order within their society. They do so largely by interacting with other human beings to try and find a resolution to something traumatic, horrific, petty, pathetic, or hilarious and occasionally all those elements manifest themselves in the one situation. I'd worked with or observed at close quarters cops from England, Northern Ireland, Belgium, Sweden, Latvia, Los Angeles and Las Vegas. When it came down to it you could pluck a police officer from anywhere in the world, strip away the basic differences in language, legislation and culture and he/she would in all likelihood be imbued with the same cynicism and dark sense of humour and would have the same gripes about bosses and the lack of overtime as their counterpart two continents away.

Additionally, they would in all probability have a tendency to look for an underlying motive when presented with even the most genuine offer of help from a fellow human. That suspicion emanates from the realisation that almost anyone is capable of almost anything given a floating combination of circumstances. There is no mathematical formula, just people with the faults and failings we all have. The majority of us have certain moral standards and principles, but those standards can be knocked askew when misfortune knocks on the door or even a tempting opportunity presents itself. It is the nature of policing that cops encounter others at their most fallible and later shake their heads and ask themselves: how could anyone be so gullible, weak willed, venal, pathetic or downright dumb?

People are strapped for cash with a family to support so they make a false insurance claim or lie about their property having been stolen – again for insurance money. They catch their partner cheating and commit a violent act. They lose their job so they shoplift a computer game so they can give their child a birthday present. Their house is about to be repossessed so they become involved in a mortgage fraud. They have too much to drink and come to the alcohol-befuddled conclusion that their life sucks. I'm not talking about career criminals just people doing dumb things often out of desperation.

Which brings me back to the kitchen at Coatbridge. I'd hardly taken up night duty before I found myself facing two contemporaneous suicide threats. Both were male. One was threatening to throw himself from an upper bedroom window. The other was intent on a slightly more dramatic exit. A substantial volume of high-rise flats existed in close vicinity to Maryhill Police Office. They rose to about 18–20 storeys high and over a period had been the scene of several suicides, with the victims throwing themselves off these buildings. With typical cop crassness someone labelled the poor unfortunates 'The Maryhill Flying Club'.

What they all had in common, other than their method of choice, was that they hadn't first threatened to jump. In their despair, they'd simply leapt from a sufficient height to ensure they ended their lives.

I viewed threats of suicide in a similar vein to interviewing suspects. I always believed that if you got someone talking you stood a better than even chance of getting a successful result. A threat to self-harm was often a cry for help and if they wanted to speak that was a good start.

Given that the man making the current threat faced a drop of about fifteen feet I decided that unless he intended diving head first there was a strong possibility that he may be an attention seeker and wasn't my main priority. I arranged for a couple of sergeants to attend that scene. They were fortunate as they had assistance. The Force 'out of hours' negotiating team had been contacted and were en route as that suicide threat had been received slightly earlier than the other.

From the information that had been relayed to me it was apparent that the other potential suicide had certainly applied forward planning. That, allied to the fact that there were only two cops in attendance, convinced me that was the scene that required some personal input.

The cops couldn't have been more different in terms of service. One had some twenty-five years on the job and the other was, as I'd been in 1981, fresh out of the box. The older cop was one of those solid types who never presented a problem to a supervisor, had a wealth of experience and could be relied on to work with the minimum of supervision. He was calm, even-tempered and reliable.

When I reached the house I contacted the senior cop by radio. I established that he had his earpiece attached to his radio, which meant the man threatening self-harm couldn't hear the conversation. I asked him if he'd established a dialogue and ascertained that my coming onto the scene wouldn't impact on any dynamic he'd created between himself and the male.

He gave me the ok and on entering I thought I'd stepped into a scene from the film *Nightmare on Elm Street*. A man in his late forties was standing in his kitchen with a selection of carving knives, all of varying lengths, taped together to form a very lethal looking set of fingers. Due to the volume of tape, his hand wasn't visible, just gleaming steel.

As if that wasn't enough, he'd then wound tape around his upper body so that the knives were locked against the carotid artery area of his neck. If we couldn't resolve the situation safely things were going to end (very) messily. I could see that the situation was a shock to the young cop who certainly hadn't witnessed anything like this in her pre-cop life and I have to say it was rather disturbing especially when he exerted pressure and the knives marked the flesh. One solid push and the kitchen would have been covered in arterial spray.

Had that happened we'd have struggled to save him. The knives were taped so tightly against his throat, that had he carried out his threat and cut himself, we'd have been unable to access the wound to apply pressure. Additionally, the time it would have taken to cut the tape away would have been another major obstacle to any prospective first aid.

I ascertained that his family members were upstairs in a bedroom and arranged for the young cop to remain with them. I couldn't evacuate them because from where our potential victim stood he had a view of the staircase down which they'd have to walk to reach the front door. Additionally they would have to see him with the knives at his throat. Any appearance might exacerbate what was already a potentially volatile situation. Given that he'd used more tape to secure the knives against his throat than they used to mummify an Egyptian Pharaoh and that Harry Houdini would have been unable to disentangle himself from the contraption, I decided that there was little danger to their wellbeing and so were safe enough where they were, for the present.

The negotiating team were engaged with the other suicide threat, so that left just me and the cop. The cop had done a first class job initiating the dialogue and I was happy to allow him to continue, but when the male saw the braiding on my hat he switched his focus to me. I had considerably more police experience than my previous attempt at negotiation in 1981, but still hadn't had any formal tuition so, as before, I would have to wing it. He emphasised that I better not make any attempt to rush him and as if to underline his point he pushed the knives against his neck.

Rush him!!! If I'd been Luke Skywalker, armed with a Light Sabre I couldn't have separated him from that hellish contraption.

He demanded that he be allowed to see his family but I told him that given the present circumstances that wasn't going to happen and steered the conversation towards him and his background. After a long dialogue he made a throwaway remark, and with it he also, unwittingly, threw me the key to unlock the situation: 'You know at one time I wanted to be a cop.'

I had to stop myself from blurting out that so had quite a few senior police officers but the remark from him gave me the psychological 'in'. I began to angle the conversation towards responsibilities, difficult decisions and choices and finally persuaded – or perhaps bored – him into letting us begin the unwrapping process with the promise of a cigarette once he was free. I've previously mentioned how cigarettes could be persuasive interview tools and this proved no different. He may have taken the trouble to plan his potential method of self-harm but, thank God, he hadn't factored in how he'd service his nicotine cravings.

It took over twenty minutes before we could pronounce that he and the knives were officially divorced and while performing the ceremony it felt even longer as we tried to ensure we kept him calm and onside. After we'd freed him we secured the knives but before we gave him his cigarette and handcuffed him, the senior cop made sure he conducted a thorough search of our self-harmer which resulted in the seizure of a concealed knife. The cop had done a first class job from start to finish and I made sure a note went into his (and his partner's) personnel file highlighting that.

Just as we'd managed to free him, word was passed that the negotiating team were en route. They'd been successful at the other scene. I let them know that, thankfully, we'd had a similar result and no longer required them.

Throughout my career, mainly as a result of huge slices of luck, I still hadn't lost anyone during my experiences as an amateur negotiator. It was a testing introduction to my new policing area, and time spent there would reaffirm that Glasgow didn't have a unique franchise on streetwise cops, gangsters, killers or me. I was sure I'd enjoy my new policing area. Hell, I might even feel welcome . . .